TITANBORN

TITANBORN

BRIAN SCHUTTER

NEW DEGREE PRESS
COPYRIGHT © 2020 BRIAN SCHUTTER
All rights reserved.

TITANBORN

ISBN   978-1-64137-462-0   *Paperback*
         978-1-64137-463-7   *Kindle Ebook*
         978-1-64137-464-4   *Ebook*

*To anyone who feels trapped by
anyone or anything.*

CONTENTS

PROLOGUE.	DAMAGE CONTROL	13
CHAPTER 1.	STUCK	21
CHAPTER 2.	OVERWORKED	33
CHAPTER 3.	MOUNTING PRESSURE	45
CHAPTER 4.	ONE OF MANY GAMBLE	55
CHAPTER 5.	PATHING ERRORS	65
CHAPTER 6.	PLAYING OUTSIDE	75
CHAPTER 7.	DOWNTIME	89
CHAPTER 8.	SYSTEMIC PROBLEMS	103
CHAPTER 9.	WEATHER ADVISORY	117
CHAPTER 10.	AZTLAN WAYSTATION	135
CHAPTER 11.	A FATHER OF TITANBORN	147
CHAPTER 12.	AN ALIEN FROM EARTH	151
CHAPTER 13.	THE NEUROENGINEERING PRACTICAL	163
CHAPTER 14.	COGNITIVE DISSONANCE	175
CHAPTER 15.	MOVE FORWARD	189
CHAPTER 16.	NORTHBOUND	207
CHAPTER 17.	THE SWARM	217
CHAPTER 18.	LOCKED-IN	229
CHAPTER 19.	THE TOWER AT THE TOP OF THE WORLD	235
CHAPTER 20.	CRUNCH TIME	243
CHAPTER 21.	DERECHO	259
CHAPTER 22.	NO MORE DEATH	291
CHAPTER 23.	DECISION MATRIX	301
INDIEGOGO BACKERS		319
ACKNOWLEDGMENTS		321
"NOTES FROM THE AUTHOR"		323

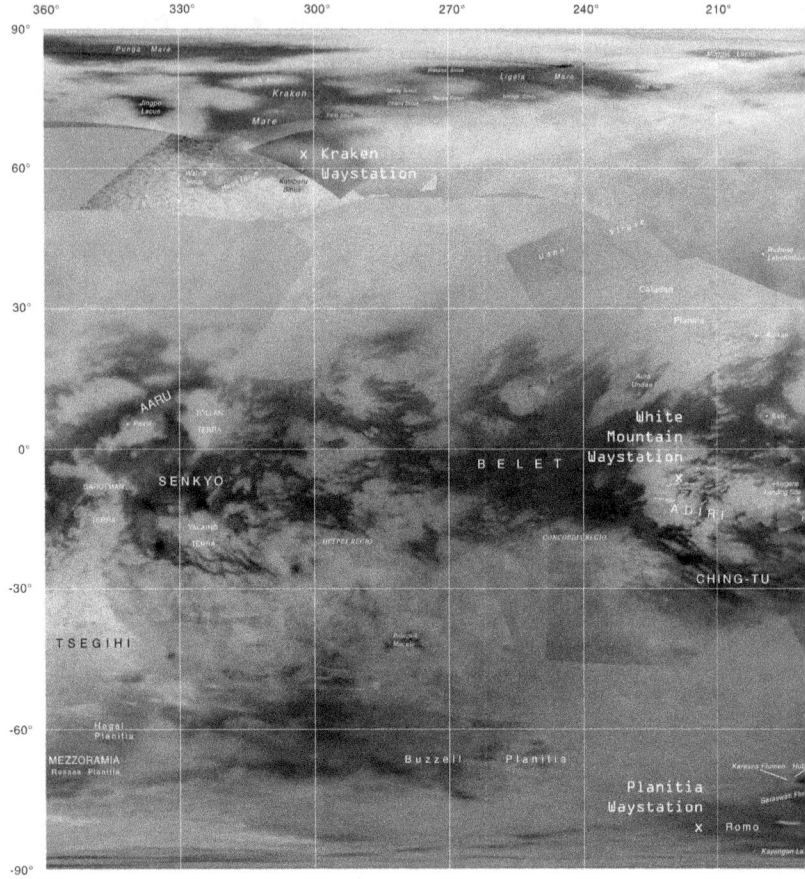

Courtesy - NASA/JPL-Caltech/Space Science Institute/USGS

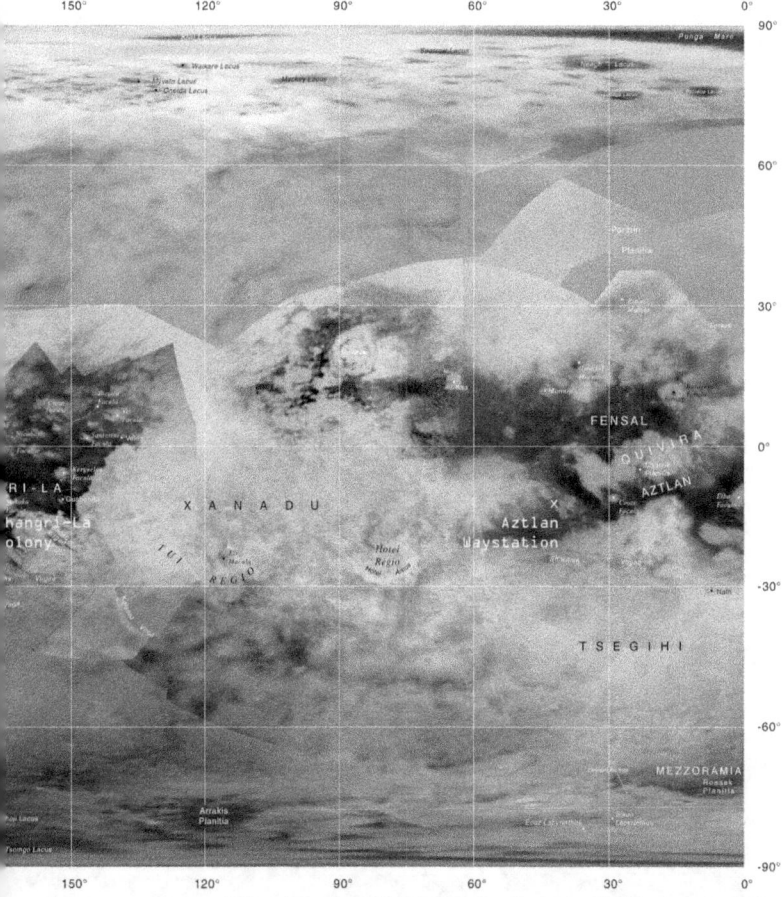

Updates Courtesy - FEAA/Martian OSS Exogeology Survey/Planetary Protection Institute

PROLOGUE

DAMAGE CONTROL

MATYOM; SOUTH CHING-TU, TITAN

 Matyom and Case trudged across Titan's frozen dunes. Headlamps framed their vision, pushing back the total darkness of almost eight Earth days' worth of night. Golden fog hung lazily, tinting everything they saw. Matyom had been told once, by his cosmonaut guardian Robert, that Titan smelled like a popsicle of fish, asphalt, and oil. To Matyom, it had always smelled of the warm plastic on the inside of his howlsuit helmet. He liked that smell: it meant he was exploring.

 Matyom braced himself against the shallow slip face of their dune, planting a hand into the granular, golden dust beneath him. It stained his glove with yellow and gray and stuck tenaciously to his fingers. The ground shifted beneath his weight, but he held purchase.

 "'Nother footstep." He grunted, training his lights onto the boot imprint in the sand, perfectly preserved in the linear dune's side. The low winds that had formed these dune fields would take another eon to erase the footprint.

 That wouldn't last though.

The seasons were changing. A storm was coming.

Matyom wasn't worried. He was born to walk these dunes. If he had to find a missing woman before the first rains started, he would.

Case tugged on the long rope that connected the two men. Even with the global positioning signals from their suits, it was easy to get lost out here, hence the rope. Case's gray face looked sickly, almost gangrenous, behind the veil of golden smog. He coughed as he wondered aloud, "What is this chiphead doing away from her skimmer *and* her partner?"

Matyom mapped the depth of the footprint with his prosthetic eyes. His mind pulled down calculations from a network that spanned almost half of Titan's surface. In an instant, he knew exactly how much force this woman had planted in her heel.

He traced the trajectory of the missing woman's, Deepa's, next steps up the dune. Matyom found two more boot prints, significantly higher. She'd leapt up and to their left, using Titan's low gravity to assist. This was a dangerous way to climb dunes. Their missing person had been too hasty, ignoring protocol. Had she been running from something?

"I don't know," Matyom responded. "Her lifeline and suit's signal are off, and I can't think of why Deepa would do that."

"And her partner ran in a separate direction, north until the *Trailblazer* caught up to him…" Case added, "Were they—"

"—running from something?" Matyom completed his companion's sentence. "Maybe."

"There's nothing out here." Case snorted. "Nothing to run from but us, hah."

Matyom planted his feet into the organonitrile soil and leapt upward, sending a spray of gray-yellow particles unique to the southwestern Ching-Tu region behind him.

His rope slackened as Case followed suit; the two men in golden-stained alabaster howlsuits leapt up the dune, tracking their missing target. Frigid, still air whistled about Matyom's helmet. His quick movements disturbed more sand than an entire day's weather in this region. Some theorized that a Titanborn could cause storms in such static climates simply by jumping.

"Oooh, look out," Case joked, making exaggerated claws with his gloved hands. He looked decidedly unthreatening, even as he bared his incisors.

They reached the top of the dune. Matyom's eyes shifted, going blind to the light from his own suit. He toggled his vision into the infrared. The golden haze appeared to vanish; Titan's darkness fled from his sight. The landscape stretched out before him. The dune they stood atop spread below for dozens of kilometers, falling gradually. Smaller linear dunes cut across its surface, their striations carved by gentle winds. Fatter, wider dunes and sharp plateaus of gray and yellow organics shattered the otherwise perfect symmetry of parallel lines drawn by the moon itself.

Matyom tracked Deepa's footsteps as Case reached his side. The shorter man was panting and bent over, bracing his knees.

"I don't see her in IR," Matyom said.

Case shrugged as he braced himself against Matyom's arm. "*I* can't see in IR so not sure how I can help."

Matyom gestured toward a distant naturally-smoothed cylinder jutting from the moon. "Deepa's footsteps, at least, are closer together now. I see the last of them disappear behind a plateau."

"Another one of Chetan's favorites acting up…" Case's voice trailed off.

"Case, come on. Focus."

"Yeah. Yeah. Let's go find her. Your eyes creep me out when they're gray, by the way."

Matyom shifted back into the visible spectrum. As golden smog and overwhelming darkness crept back into his vision, his irises returned to their previous crimson glow.

They started down the dune. Sometimes a rescue mission was just walking and talking, keeping each other awake and alert until they reached their goal and delivered life-saving help and equipment to the Titanborn in need. They'd already found their first missing person and sent him home to Shangri-La on the automated *Trailblazer*. They'd be returning to the colony soon and, with luck, so would Deepa.

<maTy?> A telepathic message oscillating with panicked anxiety hit Matyom's brain as he and Case half-leapt down the long, sloping dune.

Matyom hesitated. He could tell immediately that his boyfriend needed help, but he wasn't sure if he could handle the distraction right now.

Then he felt guilty. Truthfully, Matyom wasn't sure if he could handle his boyfriend right now, period.

<maTy?> Torvram repeated. <i need help.>

Matyom grimaced as his boots landed in the gray-yellow sand once again. Robert had always said, "When a man asks for help, you help him." And this man was Matyom's boyfriend.

<What's Going On, Honeysuckle?> Matyom replied telepathically, trying to inject an emotional tone that was wholly warm, comforting confidence.

<i dunno...im just...im Thinking abouT cuTTing myself again.> Torvram's reply was so faint Matyom had to focus to hear his boyfriend's thoughts.

<Honey, No, Please. I'm Here. It's Going To Be Ok. Just Talk To Me, Yeah? I'll Listen For As Long As I Can.>

Matyom's exchange with Torvram had lasted only a second and the stocky explorer's plucky mood was already beginning to plummet. He felt tired, bordering on miserable, as he thought about his boyfriend suffering back home. Matyom's face drooped, and his long mustache brushed against the frown growing on his lower lip.

Despite all of his talents, Matyom wasn't sure how to deal with this feeling.

Case touched down lightly beside him. They'd reached the base of the dune. Their suit lights crawled up the face of a smoothed plateau illuminating thick bands of rust and gold. Deepa's footsteps curved around the plateau's southern edge, where its top jutted out into thin air like a precariously suspended platter.

"You ok, big guy?" Case asked. He looked up at Matyom through hazel eyes, his concern evident.

It would be another long second before Matyom answered his unaugmented companion.

<i jusT can'T do anyThing right…i had a meeTing Today where lakshmi…ugh i jusT remembered my lasT breakdown and maybe i should jusT sTop because i know i'm already a burden on you and—>

Matyom cut Torvram off before he could spiral further. <Hey. Hey. It's Going To Be Ok, Torvy. You're Not A Burden And I Love You! Just Take A Deep Breath. Breathe, Like Anyu Said. Breathe For A Second. Can You Do That For Me?>

<…>

<ok.>

Matyom couldn't hear Torvram breathe. Instead, he felt the full enervating brunt of Torvram's mood. He closed the batch of mental channels that served as a conduit for his partner's emotions. He couldn't bear feeling Torvram's anguish on so intimate a connection any longer.

<Does That Help?> Matyom asked.

<a little,> Torvram replied.

<I'm So Sorry To Go Like This But I Have To Focus Out Here. Thank You So Much For Telling Me Though.>

Matyom dumped every idea he had into his broadcast. <Please Talk To Someone: Meera Or Yumi Or Anyone That's Available. Have AVA Track Your Health. I Know You Don't Like It But It Could Save Your Life If Your Mood Really Plummets.> He couldn't bring himself to say the word "suicide." <I Promise I'll Come See You The Moment We're Back. I Love You, Honeysuckle.>

Torvram didn't reply immediately. For a long millisecond, Matyom worried about what he might hear or, worse, that Torvram would say nothing at all. He felt guilty he hadn't replied immediately, fearful that his boyfriend might spiral into suicidal thoughts and confused about how he dreaded speaking to a man he loved so much.

They'd have to talk when Matyom returned. He didn't want to break up, but he wasn't sure how to deal with this. They had help, though. The Titanborn stuck together. There was always someone to help.

But right now Matyom needed to focus. Deepa was relying on him and Case for help. She might die if they didn't find her soon.

<ok… yeah… ill Talk To meera as soon as she's free. Thanks, MaTy. i love you, Too.>

The telepathic line went dead. That long second ended. Matyom took a long, calming breath and finally replied to Case with a simple lie: "I'm fine. Let's go."

He leapt forward again, not noticing the frown that crossed Case's face. The short man was quite astute, especially considering he lacked any empathic circuitry—any circuitry at all, in fact. Matyom was a cyborg while Case was simply human.

They reached the plateau promptly. Matyom switched to IR again, ready for anything. Rather than a missing human, he found more footsteps off to the east and the jagged corpse of a Dragonfly drone. The quadcopter lay in three pieces, its battery rapidly cooling in a molten pool of yellow tar.

Case hissed as he approached the drone. "What the fuck happened here?"

Matyom leaned down, calling for the model number and recorded flight path of the drone from the AI named AVA back home. Curiously, the drone's own visual records ended hours ago, just before Deepa and her research partner, Dr. Alburn, had gone missing.

"This bot has a hole in its records," Matyom said aloud, for Case's benefit. "Last thing I can see is the two of them working in their mobile lab, like normal."

"Maybe Deepa turned it off?" Case posited as he circled the drone, taking pictures with an old smartphone. Case did what he could, lacking prosthetic eyes.

"Doesn't look like it." Matyom beamed what he was looking at back to AVA and his Titanborn dispatcher, Arienne. "The record just... stops."

Matyom and Case inspected the three pieces of the quadcopter. They found a plastic handle buried within one of Deepa's footsteps, a meter away. Matyom tugged it free and found a small hammer. Its head was covered in yellow-gray organics from Titan and black plastic from the downed quadcopter.

Matyom realized that she must've struck the drone with this hammer; that raised more questions. What would have driven Deepa to attack the drone? It was a research tool designed to take video and collect gas samples. It was harmless.

Case waved Matyom over to his side. "Fuck... Matyom, there's a *big* piece of her suit and some frozen blood here." He jabbed a finger at a yellowed mass of howlsuit insulation on one of the quadcopter's rotors. Sure enough, ice crystals with hearts of crimson and black were smeared on its surface.

"Her suit could be breached."

Matyom rose abruptly. "Ok. I'll have Shangri-La follow up with this drone. Location's marked." That the drone had torn her suit was an even greater mystery, but now was no longer the time to ask questions.

"*We* have to find Deepa." Matyom scanned the surface for more footprints. No more Titanborn would die out here, not while he still lived.

Case nodded affirmatively, turning his back on the broken drone and its mysteries. "Yeah."

"No more death." Matyom leapt north, toward the next set of boot prints that disturbed the frozen, yellow-gray linear dunes.

CHAPTER 01

STUCK

MEERA; PERSONAL QUARTERS, SHANGRI-LA, TITAN

The last thing I wanted to do right now was get out of my sleeping pod. It was warm and cozy and, most importantly, *safe* in here. While I was here "sleeping," I didn't have to face the day. I tucked my blanket against my chest, pushing a wavy strand of auburn hair out of my face with a gray finger, and squeezed my eyes shut.

The auburn halo of my artificial irises, reflected on the interior of my eyelids, stared back at me.

I knew I had to get up and work soon. AVA would set off the same alarm as every morning at 0600 sharp, and my workday would start whether I felt healthy enough to work or not. It wasn't just every morning; it felt like every *day* was the same. I got up, failed at being a neuroengineer, got yelled at by someone, remembered the horrible day Jula died screaming outside of the eastern airlock, and—

My brain betrayed me and vividly flashed back to Jula's canary eyes as they changed from elated to confused to horrified. It was the first time we'd gone outside of the Shangri-La colony. I could see the golden smog in the air before me, the linear dunes that looked like sandy waves frozen in time. I felt the coffee-colored ground squish beneath my feet, the heat of my howlsuit as it warmed my body, and the fresh smell of my own private oxygen reserve. I had been elated too. I'd never seen the outside before. It felt like the first step into growing up.

But Jula's suit hadn't been sealed properly. The cold ate at her side; -150 degrees Celsius was not forgiving. The healthy gray flesh of her neck turned to an ugly black, flaking off as we frantically tried to get her back inside in time. Jula was seven when she died of a combination of hypothermia, cold burns, and asphyxiation. She had been born three minutes before me, two vats to the left. If any one of us had checked her seals that day, she wouldn't have died. I wish I had.

My hands were shaking against the blanket. Fuck. Was this a flashback to something I'd really experienced or a recording I'd accidentally downloaded into my neural circuitry? It could've been both, vent it!

I hated not being able to trust my own memory.

Time passed, but I was just stuck like this. Anxious, scared, fighting just to keep my mind clear and my lungs filled. On Titan, it took all my strength just to survive. I supposed that was true for most of us, in a way.

But vent it, I had it rough. When the Earthborn designed my genetics and installed non-organic parts, they should've had the courtesy to make me more mentally stable. Lakshmi had fucking everything. All I had was crippling anxiety and, to quote Lakshmi, "Half-competent intelligence."

<Good morning, Meera.> A voice calmly inserted itself into my head. Electronics received the telepathic message and converted it into electrochemical signals that the non-robotic parts of my brain could understand.

<The time is now 0600 and you are scheduled to be awake.>
There was an absolute neutrality to its tone, designed to evoke no emotion in me whatsoever. AVA, our artificial caretaker, was simply reminding me of my schedule as fact—nothing to be excited or disappointed about. Nevertheless, it made me even more anxious.

My pod unsealed against my will. The warmth that surrounded me spilled out into my small quarters. I pulled the blanket up to my chin, but soon I started to shiver.

It was time to get up. I tried to steel my mind against... itself. I *did* have a job to do, after all. Everyone worked together or everyone died together on Titan.

My room was small but fairly assigned. A single LED grid slowly lit toward full brightness, simulating the rise of the sun. Cabinets and shelves covered almost every square centimeter of the walls, even lining the bathroom door. They were unpainted, a utilitarian off-white like the rest of Shangri-La's plastic interior.

<The current temperature within Shangri-La is approximately 16.1 degrees Celsius. Remaining potable water supplies are—>

With the same intuitive thinking it took to move my arm, I commanded the circuitry in my brain to interrupt AVA. <ava i dont need to hear the details just get on with my schedule.>

<OK. At 0700, you have your weekly review with Lakshmi of the Revision Committee.> I felt a pang of dread at the mention of the meeting. She was the *last* person in a long list of lasts I wanted to meet with. Lakshmi was never happy with my progress, nor was she especially gifted at giving constructive feedback.

<At 0800—> AVA continued enumerating my schedule in its impartial, efficient manner. I scanned the drawers around

me, artificial reality mapping atop the world to show me their contents. I stepped onto a foldable stool to reach one of the highest drawers.

<At 2100, you have an appointment with your therapist.> AVA continued to spell out my schedule in my mind.

<At 2200, it will be time to sleep.>

<Your daily reminder:> AVA continued. Its tone shifted, abruptly mirroring my strained, dorky voice. <Make time to study for the Neuroengineering on Humans practical. Don't fail this time!> There was a little squeak at "time!" as AVA imitated my brand of enthusiastic shout. I sounded pretty goofy.

By the time AVA was done, I had abandoned my futile attempt to reach the drawer. It was too high for me, so I grunted in frustration and *thought* at it.

The offending drawer popped open and dumped my sweaters unceremoniously onto the floor. I grabbed the thickest burgundy sweater I could find, tugging fistfuls to cover every surface of my hands with synthetic fibers.

It was too snug around my stomach. I groaned as I tugged it around my girth. I didn't mind being curvy but the sweater was starting to feel small. I couldn't afford to print another outfit this month. Fuck, I wanted just one break. One break today. One!

<Would you like me to temporarily block an effective fraction of your adenosine receptors?> AVA added.

<no thank you ill get some coffee later or something.> I tugged a pair of jeans over my gray legs.

Ok. Work. Therapy. Study. I nodded feverishly, trying to pump myself up. I wanted to be better today. I could do this. I could be someone who could get through the day without breaking down, someone who didn't feel *stuck*.

<Have a productive day, Meera.>

<*you too ava thanks,*> I replied.
<*You do not have to thank me,*> it said, like every other day.
<*youre welcome ava,*> I countered. It deserved a little thanks. We all did.

AVA left me alone with my thoughts.

I took a deep breath as the ventilation rattled on in my little room. I was tired, yes, and overwhelmed, but that was ok. That was *ok*. All I could do today was try.

My job was to work on the brains of the smaller machines—the drones, the androids, the swarms—and keep them all running smoothly. I hoped, someday soon, to move up into working on the circuitry inside Titanborn brains. I wasn't good enough, yet, but maybe, just maybe, I could be good enough someday. That was ok too.

I took another deep breath, focusing on the zesty, moist morning air. It was pumped in fresh from the hydroponic gardens today, rather the usual recycled plastic-smelling stuff. That was nice. That was one win for the morning!

It was time to do my part today: to help my people survive with my skills, middling though they might be. Maybe, just maybe, I could push past this nagging feeling that I was just stuck.

MEERA; NEUROENGINEERING BREAKROOM, SHANGRI-LA

Despite the fact that my meeting was remote, I had to be physically *at work*. That policy made no sense to me, but what could one woman do...?

I sat, or rather slumped, upon a small desk in our little break room. The small space afforded a view of the crowded, yellow-lit cleanroom... and had barely enough space to fit two people, if they crammed together in front of a food and water dispenser.

Needless to say, if anyone opened the door, they'd kick me just by entering the break room.

<It is 0655. Please prepare to join your 0700 meeting,> AVA said.

AVA was probably speaking to a dozen Titanborn simultaneously right now. My focus wandered as I tried to wrap my brain around that concept.

My first memory was of one of AVA's diminutive androids wiping my face. How many of us had it been taking care of at once in that moment? I couldn't imagine what it must feel like, being an AI that took care of almost two thousand vat-born children with just four astronauts to assist you.

Of course, it must've been even harder for my mother. Juniper had done all that *from Earth*, rigged into an android body for almost fourteen years. If AVA's ability to multitask was admirable, then a human raising dozens of children by remote was… unthinkable.

<It is 0658. Please prepare to join,> Ava repeated.

I snapped out of my reverie and admonished myself. Of course, I'd forgotten to actually *join* the meeting once I got here. I felt the strong urge to avoid it and just get back to work, but I wouldn't get away with that. One couldn't hide in Shangri-La.

I took a deep breath and, with my tired eyes shut, reached out to the nagging meeting reminder.

As I joined the meeting, the circuits in my brain pushed out the rest of the world. The signals from my eyes, my ears, my skin—all my senses—were reduced severely. If I needed to feel my breathing I could, but otherwise, my body was like a distant memory.

The virtual meeting room was in a physically impossible space: outside, in the open air. Our "chairs" sat on the dunes. Virtual whiteboards hung from nothing.

The virtual space didn't look exactly like Titan either. Instead of golden, omnipresent fog, this virtual Titan was clear. You could see the stars behind us and Saturn's striped storm systems, each band the color of a unique mixture of coffee and cream. They looked so small from here, even though any one of Saturn's stripes could effortlessly engulf Titan. Its rings curved toward us in striking, vibrant cerulean. I'd never actually seen them like this. The sun's reflection off our patron gas giant couldn't penetrate the thick, unbreathable atmosphere above.

For a moment, I forgot where I was. I forgot my fears. Instead of triggering me, something about seeing the stars and Saturn made me feel peaceful and proud.

We'd survived out here for over twenty-five years. That was why we'd been born after all: to prove that humans could survive out here alone. As much as I was struggling, I was still succeeding. I was alive.

What was it Matyom always said...?

Some of the others, in that brief moment while I marveled at the impossibly clear sky above, made themselves known by broadcasting their scorn. Waiting on me made the meeting less efficient. Embarrassment washed over me and I, or rather my virtual representation, turned my eyes to the ground.

<If the neuroeng team is going to keep showing up LATE,> Kris said to the room in general, singling me out with his eerily black eyes, <we might have to institute some negative incentive like DOCKING PAY.>

I tried to literally sink into my chair as some of my peers snickered. Unfortunately, all I could do was slouch.

A morbid bar graph showing the remaining oxygen and water and the average temperature within Shangri-La glowed to life. Those three simple columns delineated everything that kept us alive. Water was particularly low, its transparent column outlined in alarming crimson. A map of our world tracked waves of drones as they autonomously lumbered across Titan so we didn't have to expend oxygen and risk our lives. The *Trailblazer*—the largest breathable space other than the Shangri-La colony itself—was returning from the Ching-Tu region in the southwest.

<hello, Meera!> Unlike AVA, this telepathic message came packed with emotion: turbulent waves of excitement and hints of a slow, enervating riptide of sadness. Its sender was a gangly man with crimson eyes who bent over the table like a weather-worn light pole. His gainsboro skin only enhanced the metaphor.

My distant body sighed in relief. Torvram had taken a sick day, but he was here, nonetheless. It was good to see a friend. We connected on a more intimate mental level, our conversation masked from the others—conspirators invisible to the crowd.

<torvram! hi! did i miss anything?> I asked the tall man. Tufts of brown hair were missing from his head. He'd been pulling it out again, I observed.

Dissociative information bubbled up into my consciousness as he answered my question, not with words but knowledge.

<To be honesT...noT much,> he summarized as I, too, learned that I hadn't missed much. His hands worked furiously. He was probably only half here mentally, tinkering with another machine in the real world. Torvram was absolutely amazing at neuroengineering machines and enjoyed it when he was in a healthy mood. I had yet to convince him to give himself that compliment though. We were both trying to stay above water, in that sense.

<sorry To hear abouT The... practical,> he added, his expressive face sagging with sympathy.

<its ok. maybe...> I was torn between <im not smart enough for it> and <ill pass next time>. Instead, I said nothing and pinched the emotional channels of our connection shut, effectively hiding my face from him.

<you can do iT meera. i k-know you can!>

I felt a soft smile blossom on my real face. <thanks.>

An angular, gray-skinned woman with long, disheveled jet-black hair popped into existence. Her cerulean eyes burned with excitement as she vigorously gestured with six arms, four of which were prosthetic.

I straightened my back at the sight of Lakshmi and shut up, not wanting to be singled out as the room fell silent.

Lakshmi, the project lead on seemingly everything, had arrived ten minutes late. She, of course, did not receive the same treatment I had. No one called her out for her tardiness. I didn't dare to do so myself.

<I've got great news and even greater news! :D> Lakshmi broadcast to the room as she reappeared seated in front of a pair of free-floating whiteboards. Lakshmi's avatar's black heeled boots and white leggings clipped impossibly into a coffee-colored dune that rose up past her ankles.

A cocksure smile was plastered across the woman's face as she spoke. Her eyes threatened to burst with enthusiastic light. <My team and I have just finished synthesizing a new plastic that will help to leech away the methane from our ice before it's even melted. As you can see.> Graphics bloomed from her hands, magnifying into visuals above her as she remained casually seated. <we predict this will shave a neat eight percent off the energy cost of converting Titan ice to clean potable drinking water. :)>

As the room erupted into congratulations, Torvram privately broadcasted, <*she's jusT bragging.*>

<*i don't know how she gets so much done,*> I replied in awe and trepidation. Lakshmi was a synthetic chemist. She shouldn't have even been at a Neuroengineering meeting, but her name kept showing up on my assignments as "project lead" nonetheless. My feelings on her were mixed: I hated her, but if we could change places, I would've done so in a heartbeat. I wanted her confidence and her success. It was so easy for her to be happy as herself. And I wanted that most of all.

Lakshmi's avatar clapped her hands together. The gesture made no noise. <*Now, on to today's review. I know you all have lots to share about how we're going to fix AVA's embarrassing little android malfunction problem. Buuuut—*> She strung out the "u" sound as she cast a wide glance around the room once again. Her brilliant cerulean eyes met mine briefly and I balked, turning away to stare at the table again.

<*—first, we need to talk about the seasonal storms. I'm taking the initiative here to make sure we're ready for it, unlike fourteen and a half years ago! We're not teenagers anymore and I won't tolerate one death to this storm. No more death.*>

<*AVA has selected a few volunteers to do baseline repairs, fixing the dozens of broken drones that could otherwise assist with bringing supplies back to Shangri-La. Please check your schedules before we begin, and thank you in advance for contributing your time to help us all survive. :)*>

<*noT again!*> Torvram moaned across our private channel.

I queried my own schedule and watched as more tasks were suddenly pressed between the hours.

Unintentionally, I broadcast my frustration to the room instead of Torvram. <*vent it! i dont have time for this.*>

Lakshmi's head swung to face mine, her grin growing too wide. Some followed her gaze while others shrank back. Her words bellied the venom in her fiery eyes and predatory smile. <*But you do! AVA knows what's good for all of Titan. If it thinks you can contribute the additional time, then you can. You'll be doing us all a great service, Meera. :D*> Her eyes flashed at the mention of my name, likely plucking it from AVA's servers as she wouldn't bother to recall it herself.

I definitely did not have time for this. I needed to stand up for myself, to demand that time so I could study and go to therapy and sleep and maybe even have a little fun. I was already struggling to get my usual workload done.

But, I didn't know how Lakshmi would react if I said no. My mind flashed back to her shouted anger or acerbic disappointment toward others, then forward to my leaving her headspace with a doubled schedule and no compensation.

Someone *did* need to do this. I could just postpone the exam another month, right? I couldn't make sense of the glitches or even conceive of a hotfix for the malfunction project, so it made sense that the less competent neuroengies like me would be put on grunt work like this.

<*sure o-of course,*> I replied meekly. I tried to calm my breathing as my distant body threatened to hyperventilate. Facing Lakshmi was physically painful. I preferred to avoid the sharp stomach pains that speaking to her induced.

<*it's fine yeah i can do that,*> I added, nodding furiously, just wishing they'd stop looking at me. She was right. If AVA calculated I could do it, I could. I had to be the best I could be for Titan, to make sure we all survived the storm. No more death, as she'd said.

<Great! :D> Lakshmi's piercing gaze, and the room's, broke from mine. Torvram stared silently into the table, his crimson eyes wide.

I forced a blank smile onto my face and settled in for the rest of the hour, trying desperately to stay alert as exhaustion, anxiety, and boredom fought in concert to put me to sleep.

<Would you like me to temporarily block an effective fraction of your adenosine receptors?> AVA repeated.

<yes,> I replied. It was going to be another long week.

CHAPTER 02

OVERWORKED

MEERA; NEUROENGINEERING CLEANROOM #4, SHANGRI-LA

My left eye spasmed obnoxiously. I yawned and rubbed at it, trying to ease whatever was causing the muscles to twitch like this. I knew, deep down, that sleep was the only solution to this vexing problem. But between AVA's neurochemical influence in my head and my freshly bloated workload, sleep wasn't an option. I hadn't left work since this morning's meeting.

The yellow-lit cleanroom was packed with Titanborn, anonymous in sterile white suits and heavy masks. They bustled past each other, wrapped up in telepathic conversations with friends and machines.

AVA poked into my head abruptly. <*A gentle reminder: you have missed your 1100 to "Study for practical so you can finally mess with an Avitra circuit meant for Titanborn implantation, YAAAAAY!"*>

<*You have missed your 1300, short lunch,*> AVA continued.

<*You are late for your 2100 appointment with your therapist.*>

<*ava please turn off the reminders,*> I broadcast for what felt like the thousandth time.

I tossed a small cup of dissolved proteins and carbs away, half-finished, and squinted through the break room window. The repair bot I was supervising blossomed from a stem of cream-colored plastic mounted in the ceiling. Its multiple arms worked furiously at a pair of shattered drones, pecking at microscopic components of their circuitry.

I'd spent most of the day just watching it operate autonomously. At any moment, it could startle me into wakefulness with an error or a question or, worst case, become catastrophically confused and fail to even notify me at all. I had to babysit it, inputting the occasional fix or adding a new function. The result was hours of tedium, where I was too busy to focus on something else and too inactive to be mentally engaged.

It spun its arms about and buried two jagged tools into the pock-marked, boxy frame of a damaged Dragonfly drone. The four-bladed copter, a descendant of the original Dragonfly drone that'd explored Titan in the past, furiously spun its blades in apparent protest. I flinched. In this moment, the drone looked like it was feeling pain.

<You are late for your 2100 appointment with your therapist,> AVA repeated.

<ava! i dont have time ok? stop reminding me!!> I fumed.

That wasn't exactly accurate. "Not having time" wouldn't have resulted in my chest tightening, or my heartbeat racing, or my hand hesitating at the door to the cleanroom as I felt the sudden urge to go hide. I was nervous about seeing Anyu, my therapist. I hadn't done the little breathing exercises she'd suggested, or tried to speak up for myself, or—

A beep in my head broke my train of thought, to my relief. The repair bot's arms had frozen joint-deep into the Dragonfly. It needed its babysitter to come help. Good. That was something I could focus on with a simple, logical solution.

<hello;
i am:
entity(meera);
intelligence(human);
class(neuroengineer);
what is wrong with you?;>

    The digital handshake took a fraction of a second and the bot's response felt instantaneous.

<hello;
i am:
entity('RudyTEEEE :3');>

    I chuckled weakly. Someone had changed its name and ':3' was Torvram's calling card.

<intelligence(rudimentary);
class(maintenance);
Error 703;
lookup...
"A critical component is missing and has stalled the repair process.">

    "Then just tell me what the missing component is," I mumbled as I shouldered my way into the cleanroom.
    I ambled over to the repair bot, or Rudy, as my vision split. Through Rudy's sensors, the rotary drone was impossibly large and every component of its immensely complex innards was labeled, categorized, and known. At least, every component should have been known. I rolled my eyes at the massive gaping hole in one side of the drone. A pair of lenses

were obviously missing and, for some reason, the repair bot hadn't noticed. I sighed and pulled out of Rudy's head.

I crossed the clean workshop, nearly bumping into a large mobile basket. It was filled with another dozen drones in various states of disrepair and a plastic bottle labeled *Caution: Swarm Bots Ate My Shoe!* Within the bottle, an inky black fluid reached up with a bubbling tentacle. I paused, waiting to see what would happen. The fluid arm abruptly destabilized into misshapen blobs that crashed back into the black mass below.

I had no idea how the storm could have damaged the swarm of black micromachines. It was certainly making a mess of things but, hopefully, we could prevent it from killing anyone this time around. I'd lost too many friends to this seasonal storm as a teenager.

The line to the synth was five people long. As it printed out a quartet of tiny plastic helicopter blades, I yawned into my fibrous mask and my head fell forward. I was having trouble keeping my eyes open. Each time they closed, I was left alone with the dim glow of my autumn-themed eyes. Today they were a fiery orange, like the leaves of a maple tree.

Once again, AVA interrupted my thoughts. <*Your pattern of responses and current brain activity suggest you are exhausted and depressed. In order to accomplish today's tasks, would you like me to administer an electrical antidepressant?*>

<*no ava not right now thank you.*>

<*You do not need to thank me,*> AVA replied, neutrally. <*The time is 2200. It is time for you to sleep.*>

I yawned and opened my eyes. The line was still five people long. The time was indeed 2200.

Ugh.

"Maybe I'll just..." I grumbled. "No, I'm not sleeping here *again.*"

I stepped out of line and, with a brief poke using my implants, put Rudy to sleep. It meticulously disconnected itself from the Dragonfly drone and began to retract into the ceiling.

The night shift was trickling in, crowding the space as so many of my gray-skinned peers were working late. Just like me.

I didn't even bother to say goodnight.

I threw my cleansuit into a laundry basket. The bench near my locker was, thankfully, empty. The adjoining locker had been thrown open. Its door blocked mine.

I froze. The pictures on its interior hadn't been removed yet. Cassem stared back at me, his dark, almost black eyes seeming to sparkle in the light. Another Titanborn, just a year older than me, gone forever due to the smallest, most innocuous leak in the southern garage. I closed the locker door slowly.

To honor their memory, we had to keep going. We had to keep working. We had to survive and prove that all of this effort was worth it.

"No more death," I muttered drowsily. That was it then. I'd get six hours of shut eye and get right back to work.

<*hey meera do you have a momenT?*> Torvram broadcast, his mental voice quiet and subdued. His anxiety heaved against me.

<*torv im really tired. can this wait til tomorrow?*> I replied, my neurons proverbially hovering over the command to block out all broadcasts until morning.

<*ThaT's ok! i was jusT going To... ask if you wanTed to grab a quick drink. iT's been a long week,*> he replied.

<*is matyom busy?*> I replied reflexively.

<*...yeah,*> he said, his sadness sending chills across my body.

I was already struggling—apparently depressed according to AVA—and I needed sleep. But when a friend asked me for help, I helped. And Torvram and I had helped each other through loss, love, and everything else.

<ava another adenosine intervention please, one hour,> I broadcast.

<Are you certain, Meera? You are scheduled to sleep at this hour,> AVA replied.

<yes i need to help a friend,> I replied, despite the fact that AVA needed nothing more than a second "yes." I'd been told I put too much stock in its feelings, feelings it didn't have.

AVA replied with a graph. I'd be feeling additionally twitchy and caffeinated for the next hour.

<meet me in my quarters torv. bring whatever alcohol rations you have left this month. i could use something real and strong to drink!>

A cooling relief, soothing my own tired head, poured in. <Thanks, meera! I'll see you There.>

I continued my tired, zigzag pace down the off-white halls of Shangri-La, staring out through panoramic video feeds on curved plastic screens to the golden smoggy world outside.

To my surprise, I smiled. It would be good to see Torvram in person again, to help a friend.

MEERA; PERSONAL QUARTERS, SHANGRI-LA, TITAN

I was barely conscious, significantly buzzed, and laughing my ass off.

"Pffft." Torvram covered his mouth, nearly spitting what little drink he had left at me from the opposite wall, only a meter and a half away. "Fuck! I almost—" Another fit of giggles took hold, and he clutched his emaciated chest, snorting and laughing.

"See, I told you! It's weird!" I replied from my sleeping pod, one hand dangling down from its nested perch in the shelf-riddled wall. I nursed a mug filled with spiked synthetic cocoa. Its wafting steam filled my little sleeping space with the lovely scent of sweet chocolate.

"So what's Matyom up to tonight anyway? Where's your big cuddle buddy?" I asked Torvram, as he traced his fingers over the little glow-in-the-dark star and planet stickers a ten-year-old Meera had plastered over a quartet of shelves. I'd tried to paint the cabinets a spacey black, but I ran out of paint halfway through. They were the only ones that weren't Shangri-La off-white.

Torvram stared into his mug, its surface adorned with a smiling Roswell gray, the caption peeling off of its surface. Torvram loved aliens, especially the stereotypical gray, big-eyed extraterrestrials allegedly at the Roswell incident. Looking at him, I could see some resemblance between him and the fictional grays. We were gray too: human, but not of Earth.

Steam from the mug rose toward his face. "Maty's busy again in Ching-Tu. Deepa and Doctor Alburn went missing while searching for a potential methane aquifer." Torvram listed forward, frowning.

My voice caught in my throat as I assumed the worst. "Are they ok?"

"Yes. He and that little gremlin Case are bringing them back safe and sound on the *Trailblazer*." Despite the good news, Torvram's expression didn't improve but instead darkened.

"That's good!" I forced a smile. Matyom had been good to him and, normally, Torvram would be proud to extol his boyfriend's accomplishments.

Torvram sighed, hiding his face behind his mug and mumbling, "I know his work is important, not just the rescue but the symbol he represents, the morale boost we get every time we go another month without a death but... Is it selfish for me to say I miss him? We haven't had much time together lately. Sometimes I worry Matyom's avoiding me."

I tried to reassure him, leaning out from my pod with all the energy I had left to place a hand on his leg. "It's ok to want more time with him! I wouldn't worry. He loves you, Torv!"

"I just wish he'd say it more. I... I think I might be a burden on him."

"You're not!" I didn't have the energy to do anything more complex but say "no" to his doubts. I was surprised Torvram had this much energy left himself. Maybe AVA had tweaked his mind. He was no stranger to neurochemical modification after all; his brain was constantly being adjusted to keep his serious depression at bay.

"Ok," he replied unconvincingly.

My quarters were silent for a moment. My eyes drooped closed as I half-drifted off to sleep. It'd been a long day.

"Hey," I muttered. "We should request some vacation time after the storm and stuff. You and Matyom could spend a bunch of time then. Just imagine it..."

"I guess so." A small smile peeked out of his otherwise maudlin mien. "Where would we go?"

"I want to see Earth again," I murmured. "You could take Matyom and we could go stay in a little house and listen to the rain fall and I could go sit outside and play with a real fluffy-ass dog, and you two could have some real privacy to *see each other* again hahaha."

"That sounds... nice," he replied, moving the half-finished mug to his lap. I smiled lazily at him.

"Ugh..." I gripped my forehead. The beginnings of a headache were starting to form. "Fuck Lakshmi."

Torvram giggled impishly. "What, you want to?"

"Nooo," I groaned. "I mean, she can go walk suitless outside for all the blasted crap she pulled yesterday."

"As much as her ideas have helped us stay alive," Torvram whispered, looking down into the mug. The big-headed, black-eyed alien on the mug stared back at me. "I wouldn't mind if she disappeared forever." His tone was far too serious for my liking.

"Whoa." I took another sip of my faux-cocoa. False heat radiated out from the back of my throat. My whole body became wrapped in the warm, invisible blanket of vasodilation. "It was just a joke."

"Sorry," he grumbled, his eyes turning down and away from mine once again.

"It's ok." I tried to smile reassuringly once again. I was so tired, but I wanted to help and I couldn't tell if it was working. I wanted Torvram to be ok. "I do wish things would change just a little. I wish we could have a break, like said vacation."

Torvram's brow furrowed. "Yeah... this whole schedule is... sometimes I wonder if it's all a lie. What if Earth just made me shitty and mental as a cruel joke? What if our mission to survive doesn't matter at all?"

"What?" I leaned toward him slowly through a haze of alcohol and exhaustion. "What does that mean?"

"I'm sorry." Torvram groaned and dragged a hand across his face. "Pretend I didn't say anything."

"Hey, Torv..." I entreated him. "It's going to be ok. We're gonna be ok."

"How do you know that?" He moaned. "We're doing everything we can and we're just barely holding on. Nothing's changing. We put in all this work every day and don't have any energy to *change* the next day. People, Titanborn, keep dying and... ugh."

What he said hit me hard, a bolt that struck right at my insecurities and practically sobered me up then and there. But I couldn't acquiesce to it. I needed Torvram to *be ok*, and that meant that even if I believed some of his pessimistic rumination, I refused to admit it.

I needed to prevent Torvram from spiraling into nihilism and thoughts of self-harm again. "It's going to be alright," I lied. "Someday soon, we won't just be fighting to survive. Someday, we'll be able to live safely, without fear."

"I don't know," he said, his nostrils flaring as tears began to well in his prosthetic eyes. His voice had always been deep but now it boomed around my small room. "I think maybe we're doing all of this work for a bunch of people on Earth who don't give a shit about whether we live or die."

I squeezed his leg as reassuringly as I could. "Torv..." My voice cracked. It sounded high, small, and weak compared to his loud diatribe.

"Hey, I know you're really tired," he said., wrenching his leg out of my grasp as he rose. "I'm sorry I kept you up. I'll see you tomorrow, ok?"

"Are you... are you sure you're going to be ok? You can stay here if you want." I began to slink out of my pod as Torvram put more distance between us and approached the door.

"Yeah," he said, smiling abruptly. His crimson eyes were still wet with prospective tears. "I just needed to vent. I'll see you tomorrow."

The door whooshed open. Dim, nightshift lighting in the hall cast a band of shadow into my quarters, projecting Torvram's silhouette up the wall. "O-ok," I replied uncertainly. I was so tired though. We both needed sleep. "Tell Matyom I said hi and ask him... if he wants to do that... little... vacation..."

"I will," he repeated. The gaunt red-eyed man ducked his head through the doorway and waved limply. The door slid shut between us.

My eyes would no longer open. All of the exhaustion held at bay by AVA's receptor tinkering returned tenfold. I sealed my pod, tucking my blanket up to my neck. The pod's surface blinked once, showing me it was reading my pulse and other vitals from the lifeline mesh implanted around my heart.

Drearily, I added an extra reminder to my schedule. It read:

<make sure to check on torvram and both of you should go to therapy!! itll HELP you donk!!>

CHAPTER 03

MOUNTING PRESSURE

MEERA; PERSONAL QUARTERS, SHANGRI-LA
The week passed in a blur.

At work, I sleepwalked through my duties. Rigged into Rudy, I processed drone after drone, tearing into their simple minds: patching, reconfiguring, and mostly, waiting. I skipped proper meals, instead ravenously scarfing nutrient-rich supplements in the break room. By the end of the week, I found myself with two extra hours to do with as I pleased.

I returned to my quarters and pulled down a collection of e-textbooks covering brain anatomy, Avitra chipset repair, and bedside manner. I'd neglected the studies on bedside care before and paid for it. Sometimes the best solution to a problem in the mind, even one involving manmade neural chips, was talking to your patient.

Their information bled into my mind, forming new neural connections, but I knew it wouldn't be enough. I'd already failed once when I'd relied solely on this method of learning. I'd have to make sure I read them too, this time.

I popped open an artificial reality projection of the anatomy textbook in my vision. It unfolded on my lap as if it was real. It was all a trick of AVA's.

I yawned, my vision blurring. I slapped my cheeks to wake myself up. The sound echoed in my small quarters.

"Focus, Meera," I muttered.

I needed to get through these books and then the artificial reality practical. I'd learn the real operations by following recordings of professional neuroengineers, mapping their vision onto mine, and mimicking their every action. After that, I'd operate on simulated brains and then...

My heart rate was racing again. My chest tightened. I sighed in resignation and banished the textbook from my vision. I had time but little motivation and plenty of obstructive anxiety. I'd been worn down by the week. I needed a break.

MEERA; OBSERVATION RING, SHANGRI-LA

Taking a walk always helped calm my nerves, and the observation ring was the best place for a contemplative stroll. The walls appeared to be entirely transparent from floor to ceiling, covered in screens. With the fog edited out of the live video that played, Titan's dunes stretched to the horizon like an infinite Zen garden drawn by a slow but deliberate deity.

Once, there had been windows lining these walls instead of screens and video feeds. During the last storm almost fifteen years ago, it had become an object lesson as to why spacecraft and space colonies don't have windows, even ones made of optical sapphire. We'd reacted quickly, repairing much of the damage before the storm had even passed, but the resource and, most importantly, the human cost had been too high.

I mentally poked into one of the screens and uploaded the private world I wanted to share with Torvram and Matyom. Titan's golden haze faded into the alien blue skies of Earth. Trees with leaves of orange, gold, and brown swayed and rustled in a calm breeze.

I sat cross-legged on a discarded polyurethane cushion and closed my eyes. The sound of foreign winds whistling through that distant, implacable cradle of humanity was powerful. Sometimes I wondered if deep down my body knew instinctively of Earth. There was a romantic draw to the dream of one day walking on its soil, suitless, letting the sun's rays actually warm my skin, and breathing in fresh air that would fill me with zest and strength.

It was only a dream, though. My job, the one I shared with all the Titanborn, was to survive on Titan in isolation. Until we were told otherwise, we would never be able to directly contact, let alone visit, Earth. We would prove that isolated, extraterrestrial colonies were possible, and we would do it with a smile.

Maybe that's what Torvram was getting at. The experiment felt awfully harsh, especially since the choice had been made for me before I was born.

There was another rushing sound, the quiet roar of the seas. I opened my eyes and looked down the wide, curving walls of the observation wing. Reclining on a long strip of inflated plastic was a tall black-haired woman in a matching black body suit and leggings and a puffy jacket of diametrically-opposed white. A quartet of prosthetic arms slouched lazily from her back. They fiddled with a spherical puzzle.

I didn't recognize her at first, having so rarely seen my boss in person. As she opened her prosthetic eyes—false irises burning with cerulean light—and stretched her bony organic arms, I realized exactly who this was: Lakshmi.

What little peace of mind I'd achieved evaporated. Lakshmi would surely chastise me if she saw me here. I could've volunteered these two hours to work harder and she'd needle me for it. Anger added to my panic as I argued about her in my head.

How could *she* justify being here then? She got to take vacations. No one saddled her with extra work with zero notice. Her time was, apparently, valuable—unlike mine.

But I wouldn't dare tell her how I seethed. She controlled my schedule through the Revision Committee and project management. Lakshmi was the progenitor of countless life-saving ideas across half a dozen fields, whereas I struggled to even rank into human neuroengineering. She did deserve this, didn't she? With all the work she accomplished, maybe her time *was* more valuable than mine.

She rolled onto her side, yawning lazily, and her eyes sparked with recognition.

"Hey!" Lakshmi's voice echoed down the mostly empty ring, cordial and commanding in equal measure.

I started in the other direction. I did not want to speak with Lakshmi, to be talked at by Lakshmi, to be seen and skewered for my failings by Lakshmi. Anything was better than this.

"Hey!" she repeated. I sped up, rushing to the lift. My hands shaking, I practically leapt into the small elevator. It silently stole me away from the woman that, perhaps without even realizing it, controlled my life.

MEERA; PSYCHOLOGICAL HEALTH ANNEX, SHANGRI-LA

Titan's gravity is about .84 of that of Earth's moon, or less than one-seventh of Earth's. Some of the Titanborn took advantage of the weak gravity to innovate. One of the few non-digital therapists on Titan, Anyu, had innovated vertically.

As I walked into Anyu's office, I looked up to find them. Hammocks and thin, colored fabrics were suspended in the air. Anyu reclined above me, using a subtly placed tether to keep them from slipping off their hammock. Through exposed walls, pipes carrying water, hot steam, and gel-like coolant flowed, bubbled, and roiled. Their consistent sound created a natural white noise. Anyu's office felt like the most open space in the entire colony.

I leapt from the ground, letting my muscles propel me nearly three meters up onto a taut hammock twisting with arcane patterns of deep purples and smooth tans. As I tethered myself to it, I noticed that my mental connection to AVA and the other Titanborn was blocked. The white noise was not just sound. It was uncomfortable, lonely, and a much-needed relief all at once.

"Hello, Meera," Anyu said softly as they reached back with dark gray arms to secure their labyrinthine coils and curls of natural hair. Anyu's artificial irises sparkled with stars behind full-moon glasses; neon blue, silver, and white light twinkled within a ring of cool black.

"Hey, Anyu," I said, sheepishly. I felt guilty for skipping last week's session and even guiltier for not being able to stand up to people, as we'd discussed last time.

"I'm glad you could make time to see me this week." They regarded me with a quiet, knowing smile. Anyu wore loose, baggy clothing that settled in a wide arc around them. The slightest movement would send a sleeve floating lazily, like a jellyfish lazily unfurling in Earth's oceans. Their loose clothing was colored with dull purples and earthy tones that both blended and contrasted with Titan's tar and smog. I don't know how they handled the cold without a thick jacket, but that was only a small question within the overall mystery that was Anyu.

"I'm sorry I didn't make it yesterday," I said.

"That's fine, Meera." They smiled. "There's no one forcing you to come here. I am, however, glad you chose to see me today."

I nodded hastily, their approval dissuading some of my more vocal anxieties. This space was gradually feeling safe to me again, my mind calming as we sat high in the air in mental silence.

"This is a rough time for all of us as we prepare for the storm to come once again," Anyu continued. They made a small gesture toward the piping in the walls, to the life-giving decontaminated water and human-made heat that passed all around us. "I've had to sleep here for more than a few nights to accommodate shifting schedules and declining moods. How are you handling your stress, Meera?"

"Not particularly well," I replied with a sigh. "I'm struggling to stand up to... people and I'm scared I'm going to fail my exam again."

"That is a problem," Anyu said, their brow furrowing with sympathy. "Last session, we spoke about fear at length, about how you feel like you have no voice to advocate for yourself here. Were you able to try anything we discussed since then?"

"No," I replied, breaking eye contact with them. "I... uhh... didn't have time." That was a lie. I thought back to Lakshmi, to my silent acceptance of a new schedule, to the lack of motivation and time to study. Time was certainly an issue, but in those key moments where I could've wrangled myself more time, I hadn't spoken up.

Anyu cradled their chin in one hand and leaned back, staring up at the distant ceiling. "You know," they began, "an Earth month ago, the latest patch to AVA caused it to change my schedule drastically. I woke up to find I was working twelve-hour 'nights.' It took me three whole days to work up the courage to ask AVA to change it, even longer to ask the Committee to revise its programming. Three days..." They trailed off, still staring upward.

"Oh..." I replied, surprised. I hadn't expected Anyu to share this problem with me. I'd assumed they had everything in their life worked out. After all, they were here helping me fix my problems.

I let my feet dangle over the edge, feeling the recycled air brush against my legs. "Why didn't you speak to AVA right away?"

"I was just nervous," Anyu replied with a short laugh, like the sound of wind rustling a handful of leaves. "I've never stopped getting nervous, after all these years, after all the great challenges we've faced together on Titan."

Abruptly, I felt acutely aware of my slouching shoulders. My stomach ached, gurgled. I straightened my back and asked, "How do you get through it?"

Their eyes scrunched with concentration behind the false glasses. "Truth be told, there's no one solution. Sometimes I take a breath, sometimes a walk. Sometimes I go see a friend or read a book for five minutes or close my eyes and imagine my partner and I—"

Their gray cheeks noticeably pinkened and they coughed, interrupting themselves. "I suppose the only right answer is to acknowledge that you're feeling anxious and make an effort, every time, to move past it. During those three days before I gathered my courage, I took notes about what I was feeling and just tried to relax in many different ways."

Their gaze circled around to me again and Anyu leaned forward with a small, almost impish smile on their face. Stars twinkled in their eyes. "We're all different, Meera. Not everyone gets scared like this, but I try not to be ashamed that I am. I just try to get past it, any way I can, so I can spend more time enjoying being me."

I said nothing for a few seconds, my mind repeating over and over that I should speak. My mouth didn't get the message for a little while.

"It's difficult: to try." My mouth felt parched, my tongue swollen and cottony. "I know I should make a change, or a lot of changes, but I'm just scared. I'm scared that I'm stuck but I'm also scared of moving forward."

"What sort of changes do you want to make?"

I felt my cheeks heat, blood searing my skin. "I, uhh, I guess I... my job or... I'm just not very happy. I know I need..." I took a deep breath, cutting myself off. "I don't know," I concluded, dry lips smacking loudly at the "d."

"Well," Anyu's smile softened, "then you have your answer. You're unhappy, and you don't know what to do about it."

I blinked in confusion. "How is that an answer?"

Anyu leaned back and grinned conspiratorially. "Think about it."

I paused, mulling it over. I was feeling overworked, stressed, and tired these days. The weeks had been passing like a blur. I woke up, did my part, went to bed, repeat. I'd been working my ass off, doing the same thing over and over and sometimes it felt like I was going insane just doing the same work for the same pay for the same hours, except for when they were longer, and then I'd turn around and tell Torvram I just expected it would all get better someday even though I didn't—

Oh.

"I just have to try something different," I replied.

Anyu nodded. "Yes! All we can do is just try. Try to speak up, try to catalog your fears in a journal, try to find time to study, or try to do something entirely unexpected even. It's not all going to work, and sometimes it'll feel like you're just putting yourself out there only to fail but we all have to keep trying. We all have to keep moving forward. Myself included." Anyu lowered their head, their vulnerability evident through a meek smile as their glasses slid to the edge of their nose. "There's no manual for how we live here on Titan. Survival here is hard, yes, and it demands so much of our time, yes. But, that doesn't mean we can't try to do right by ourselves. You're smart, Meera. I know you can figure out what that means for you."

"Yes, I can try that," I repeated, gripping the hammock for physical and emotional support.

"Good." Anyu replaced the glasses on their face. "We're running out of time, unfortunately, but before we end today's session, I wanted to ask…" Their smile dissolved into a deep frown. "How are you holding up with Torvram's disappearance?"

"What?!" The shock of their words sent a bolt of electricity through my body. I sprang upward, perhaps at them, or the message itself, to try and physically stop what I'd heard from registering. The belt caught me in midair, tightening generously and snapping me back to the hammock upon which I sat. Torvram was… missing?

"No one has seen him all week." Anyu suddenly looked exhausted, their wise and encouraging mien abruptly abandoning them.

"Are you sure?"

Anyu's frown only deepened. They opened their mouth, as if to speak, but said nothing.

I couldn't believe it. I didn't want to believe it. Torvram couldn't be gone. He was ok. *We* were going to be ok!

"That's impossible," I replied with manic fervor. My voice rose until I was practically yelling at Anyu. "Torvram would've been caught by the security cameras, stopped at the airlocks! You can't hide on Titan!"

"Somehow, he has. I'm sorry you have to hear this now, but I figured you would want to know sooner rather than later."

"Is he...?" All the relief drained from my mind. I thought back to last week, to his morose departure and the sudden change in behavior that'd relieved me. Should I have pressed AVA, made sure he was getting help? Should I have spent the night in his room? I'd thought he was going to be ok.

He couldn't survive out there alone. No Titanborn could.

"Vent it!" I cursed, chewing on the inside of my cheek nervously, guiltily. "Is he alive?"

"I don't know." Anyu shook her head, sending the ends of her shawl floating lazily above her.

The consummate empath, Anyu practically read my mind without a hint of telepathic connection. "It's not your fault that he's gone."

My hands began to shake. I disagreed.

CHAPTER 04

ONE OF MANY GAMBLES

LAKSHMI; [REDACTED], SHANGRI-LA

The lift descended without making a sound. Its transparent walls revealed the inner workings of the Shangri-La colony. As Lakshmi descended, she passed endless racks of painstakingly-nurtured greenery in metal racks and sacks of pinkish slurry being extruded at lightning speed into amorphous shapes that would soon be food.

Lakshmi leaned against one wall and paid little attention to the world around her. An emergency meeting of the Revision Committee had been called today, and she was mentally preparing her poker face. She stretched her gloved hands high into the air and used her prosthetic hands to fuss over wrinkles that formed in her black bodysuit each time she moved.

Long white leggings emphasized her height and angular figure. A white down jacket tucked about her body deemphasized the jagged curves of her torso and small breasts. She wanted to present as masculine as possible, short of wearing a binder. Her opponents had a multitude of systemic and personal biases that meant looking male would lend her more attention. She would be lying a lot tonight and, if all went well, no one would notice until it was too late.

Satisfied with her bodysuit, Lakshmi's four prosthetic arms—connected to her body and brain—worked furiously at a small spherical puzzle. The sphere was a three-dimensional logic puzzle, one Lakshmi was determined to crack with record time. Someone in Shangri-La had beaten her latest time, and that wouldn't do. Lakshmi was the most intelligent human on Titan, after all. She glared as she struggled to weave a labyrinthine but continuous line from the sphere's surface to its core.

Beyond the lift's walls, tiny drones scurried between everything: squeezing between the gaps in a ventilation shaft, crawling between layers of wall insulation, and balancing on water pipes. They maintained those everyday systems that kept the Titanborn alive, largely unseen in daily life.

As the lift began to slow, she dropped beneath Titan's surface. The only signs left of humanity's presence were thin wires and kinked pipes that punched through close-packed layers of coffee-colored organic gunk and rust-tinted ice.

The puzzle's surface changed to solid white light, the sign of victory. Lakshmi relished in her success for a second before freshly randomizing it to a rainbow cacophony. The lift came to a halt and the cerulean-eyed leader finally tore her obsessive gaze from the puzzle.

The door to AVA's servers—a towering barrier with a tarnished reflective surface, the largest concentration of metal within Shangri-La—barred her way. She grinned toothily at it, as AVA confirmed her identity. "Hellooooo," she mugged to the cluster of microscopic cameras, standing tall in her boots to stare up at them.

The door ground open without protest and a gust of cold air burst outward, tousling her jet black hair as it bit abrasively at her nostrils. Lakshmi grinned as she crossed over the threshold, pocketing the puzzle, and pulling her puffy jacket tighter about her body.

AVA was acting strangely. Drones had malfunctioned, nearly costing two Titanborn, Deepa and Alburn, their lives. The Revision Committee needed to patch their critically-important AI now. In this haste, however, it was possible they'd make a mistake with the patch. Maybe this mistake would be so bad that it warranted the responsible Committee members to be voted out.

LAKSHMI; [REDACTED], SHANGRI-LA

There would be no record of this meeting's contents, nothing they said or thought would be sent back to distant NASA or the CNSA or the FEAA. Only its results would be recorded: the update to AVA's gargantuan code repo. From this alteration, work schedules, jobs, or even the entire overarching goal of the Titanborn, could change. The unassumingly-named Revision Committee was tasked with revising AVA's complex decision matrix and, often, its source code.

Once the four founding astronauts, rigged into their android bodies from afar, had sat in this very room. Beneath an unfinished Shangri-La, they'd planned the future of the Titanborn. Now, Lakshmi sat in the seat of Dr. C.N. Ramakrishnan, the man she'd called her father, and carried out his legacy.

"We should wait until next week," Lakshmi suggested, her eyes brimming with excited light. She smiled sweetly as she said the exact opposite of what she wanted. "All members need to be present for the patch. It's only fair we all get our say."

She sat with two Titanborn around a circular table that had been polished to a mirror-like sheen. The room itself seemed to sigh as blobs of blood and flesh-colored organics expanded within vats of semi-transparent fluid. Racks of conventional electronics encircled them, obscured by an ankle-high fog.

Cables wound across the ceiling and bowed down like dark, fiber-thin vines. They shifted subtly as stresses and strains adjusted to the movement of the organic electronics. In any direction Lakshmi looked, AVA's servers stretched on until wisps of vaporous fog streaming toward ventilation ducts fully obscured her view.

Lakshmi spied the fourth empty seat with pride. Fei, her steadfast ally, was conveniently absent today and unable to lend Lakshmi support. Everything was going according to plan.

"Normally, we would agree, but this is the season of the storm. Changes must be made to keep us all safe," Wayland replied sternly. Like everything Lakshmi had learned about the man, Wayland's appearance was a deception. At first glance, she'd mistaken him for a man wasting away, but now she could see the muscles subtly concealed beneath Wayland's suit. His dark gray head was shaved by choice, not necessity. His stark, piercing gaze through eyes of molten gold betrayed the true strength of his will.

Among Wayland's many rings, he brandished one that was made of metal torn from the Huygens lander itself. On Titan, between the scarcity of usable metals of all kinds and the symbolic value of the Cassini-Huygens mission, that wedding ring was beyond priceless. It was an expression of Wayland's power, of which Lakshmi loathed being reminded.

Beside him, Shift chimed in with a more sympathetic tone to Wayland's austerity. "We're already missing one Titanborn,

Lakshmi, and AVA's malfunctions, the silences, the lack of attention, may be to blame. I understand your position, but we need to make sure everyone is safe."

A wedding band matching Wayland's—Shift's only piece of jewelry in origin—was on his ring finger. Though his eyes matched Wayland's gold, they lacked the other man's strength, and Shift's greater height did nothing to disguise the way his veiny hands shook when he was challenged.

"Wayland, Shift, let's be reasonable here. Tradition dictates that we wait for quorum," Lakshmi replied with a dramatically crestfallen sigh.

"You've never been fond of tradition unless it suited you," Wayland barked in response, crossing his arms in stubborn defiance.

Internally, Lakshmi was all smiles. They didn't suspect a thing.

The thin woman turned to the empty seat of the fifth and last member of the Revision Committee: AVA. If AVA decided that the Titanborns' decision conflicted with their Earth-given mission, it could veto everything.

"AVA, you'd agree that it is unfair and unsafe for one of our members, one of the representatives of all of the Titanborn, to be absent when we make highly impactful decisions such as patches," Lakshmi mock-beseeched the AI.

"The traditions of your Committee are of a lower priority than collective survival." Its voice was measured and calm, sonorous and inhumanly precise in diction and tone. "If my current decision-making has put a Titanborn at risk, as your Committee asserts, then my systems must be altered immediately to prevent this from occurring again. The patch will be made as quickly as possible, and a team will be assembled to seek out and rescue Torvram."

AVA's final vote was cast. Lakshmi sighed loudly, letting her shoulders slump and her eyes turn down in defeat to the polished table. She was outnumbered, just as planned.

"That settles it." Shift nodded with a small smile.

"Ok, I've been outvoted," Lakshmi said. "But I'll have no part in this hasty patch. AVA, append a comment to this push that Fei, being absent, and I, choosing to abstain, do not approve of this decision. The—" She stopped short, biting her tongue before she voiced *the resulting consequences will rest entirely on Wayland and Shift.*

Wayland grunted. "Fine! Fine! Lakshmi, you continue to be obstinate and obstructive even in the face of a potential Titanborn death. We'll make sure to record that, as you wish. Now, apply our patch, AVA."

No one moved. Nothing changed, save that some of the servers began to hum louder.

Lakshmi's schedule squawked at her. Alarmed, she summoned it immediately. This was unusual. She commanded her own projects and changed others' schedules. Between her Committee seat and her unbridled ambitions, AVA seldom changed *her* schedule.

Today, however, something was wrong. Her whole schedule, from 0600 onward came back with only one order, repeated over and over, from today through next week: *Find Torvram.*

"What is this?" Lakshmi's mask nearly fell as the realization struck her like an arcing plasma bolt. She hadn't been the only one bluffing through today's poker game.

"AVA is assembling an expedition to recover the missing Titanborn," Wayland said. Lakshmi made a note of how he deliberately eschewed Torvram's name, the man whose survival he allegedly cared about. "His lifeline reactivated, moving northeast. We're not sure how, or why, but he's alive out there, and he needs to be rescued."

"How the—?" Lakshmi sputtered. She couldn't leave. There were petitions to sign, people to punish for the strange AVA behaviors that Fei had assured her would not be fixed by this patch. How was she supposed to take advantage of the events surrounding Torvram's disappearance if *she* was the one out there looking for him?! "Why?" she spat, still reeling from the unexpected twist of fate.

"AVA must've decided you were the best choice to lead an expedition to save him," Shift said innocently. "You and Fei have been reassigned, temporarily." He reached over to Wayland and grasped his husband's hand.

Lakshmi wracked her brains, literally, scrolling through archives of her old, now defunct, schedule. What was happening in the next few days? What were they trying to do while she was occupied, outside, looking for fucking Torvram?

There it was.

The vote. The Big Vote. Bigger than the patch. A huge code push that would not be rolled back. The vote that could shut down the entire isolation experiment. If Wayland and Shift voted to call Earth while Lakshmi and Fei were gone and reprogrammed AVA, they would ruin everything!

Their colony was a test to see if humans could survive alone in other solar systems, where help from Earth would take not three but hundreds of years to arrive. Sure, their isolation wasn't absolute. Earth-bound partners collected low-level data from AVA to learn and study the Titanborn and share the Titanborns' research with humanity, but there was no direct communication. There was no way to help— unless the Titanborn declared that they would *die* otherwise.

If these two made the mayday call, the Titanborn experiment would end and be marked a *failure*.

Lakshmi didn't even know what would happen then. Would they abandon Titan? Would someone else take over the project? She did know one thing for sure. Lakshmi would lose everything: her power, her position, and, worst of all, Chetan's legacy. Her dreams and her father's would go unfulfilled. And who knew how long it would be until someone tried again? Space exploration had been stalled for decades by far smaller disasters.

No. She couldn't let this happen. Her hands shook with anger, and she brought all six of them down hard on the table. It cracked, fracturing beneath the force of her blow. Shift leapt back with a yelp, nearly toppling his seat. Wayland, on the other hand, didn't move at all. He just smiled.

<Checkmate, Lak$hmi,> he mentally broadcast.

<How fucking cliché>:(> she shot back.

"You can't call Earth," Lakshmi growled, her cerulean eyes reflecting searing light off the damaged table. "We can survive, vent it! We don't need to sacrifice everything because of one storm, one malfunction, one scare!"

"Far more than just one, Lakshmi. We won't put our child's future at risk," Wayland said flatly.

"Your child is a fucking blueprint of synthetic DNA in a computer. It's not even in the vats yet!" Lakshmi was shouting now, her prosthetic arms gesturing angrily at the duo. "Do not call Earth. Do not abandon the isolation experiment. I'll fix the water problem. I'll solve everything my-fucking-self if I have to, but you do not—under any blasted circumstances—call Earth. You will wait to vote until Fei and I come back."

Lakshmi was leaning halfway over the table, her angular body tensed and ready to strike. Her teeth were bared, and she glared at them and the rows and rows of servers beyond. Her breath fogged in the cold server room air.

"Lakshmi." Shift raised his hands to placate her. "There's just too much risk here. All of these problems: the water, the storm, AVA's behavior, Torvram's disappearance. These aren't little things. We've been losing Titanborn in ones and tens for years, running ourselves ragged to just stay alive, and it's time we take an honest look at our lives." He rose, imploring her as one of his hands gripped Wayland's shoulder. Lakshmi knew that tone. She bet he actually believed this "greater good" dreck he was spouting.

Shift's eyes shook with emotion. "Lakshmi, I know how strongly you feel about Chetan's dream. I get it. I believe in his dream too. But there won't be any Titanborn to carry on his legacy, our legacy, if we're all dead."

Wayland smiled up at his husband proudly. Without turning his eyes from Shift's face, he said, "Go save Torvram's life, and we will call for help. That's an order from AVA."

How dare they. They weren't even hiding the fact that they were going to fix another vote. And what did they know about her relationship with Chetan? She wasn't just his protégé. No—she would surpass him. Lakshmi would surpass everyone!

She wanted to spit, to yell, to protest that she was going to stop them but instead, finally, she recovered from the surprising, near knockout blow the couple had delivered.

They acted like they cared. Maybe Shift really did, but those rings told Lakshmi that all of her judgments about them were true. Just like her, they wanted it all. And they weren't going to take any of it away from Lakshmi.

Lakshmi nodded in assent. She sagged into her seat, making sure her resignation and exhaustion were fully evident. She returned the placid mask to her countenance, burning with rage within, tired and defeated without, and said, "Yeah, yeah. You're right."

And then, her own knock-out punch, to complete the lie. "No more death."

Lakshmi's mind was already working on the next steps. One lost round, one twist in her plans, didn't mean everything was over. She passed through the server stacks, feigning defeat in her slumped shoulders. There was nowhere to hide in Shangri-La, after all. Nowhere except within the unbroadcasted depths of one's mind.

Lakshmi pulled her jacket tighter, shielding herself from the cold climate that housed AVA's brains. A new thought came to her. And then she grinned, for just a moment, before hiding it behind the mask she'd spent years creating.

By the time she reached the metal bulkhead, she was in high spirits again. Lakshmi's cerulean eyes were violently aflame, her pride returned as she realized how this move could rocket her toward her ambitions. By the end of this years-long game of political poker, she would have her victory. She would have Wayland and Shift deposed, and that would be only the beginning of what today's hand would cost them.

She entered the lift and looked up with pride at Shangri-La's intricate, complex architecture. This would only be the beginning of mankind's stay on Titan.

This structure, its inhabitants, and its marvels would only be an iota of what Lakshmi would accomplish.

CHAPTER 05

PATHING ERRORS

MEERA; PERSONAL QUARTERS, SHANGRI-LA

At 0512, I hoped against all reason that Torvram had finally answered my message from last night.

<torvram? are you ok?>

He hadn't answered.

I left my quarters and stumbled groggily down the long, curved hallway. The lights above me subtly intensified, simulating the rise of a sun on a workday. It wasn't accurate. A single Titan day, from noon twilight to inky black night, took almost sixteen Earth days.

On Torvram's door, ":3" was graffitied with the remainder of an oil stain. Torv had duped the cleaning bots into leaving his calling-card behind. I hesitated at the door. Some part of me thought that this was the end. This could be the moment when Matyom and I, and even AVA, were too late and Torvram had 'gone missing' by killing himself...

The door slid open. His Roswell alien mug sat discarded on a small workbench, alongside a mess of printed mechanical parts. The wireframe of a mechanical dog with only three legs lay on its side and stared up at me through empty eye sockets.

I stood in the middle of the room and stared from his bench to the nearby sleeping pod to the shelves. There was no blood, no sign of destruction or violence or anything out of order at all. I closed my eyes and threw open the bathroom door.

"Torvram?"

Nothing. No one. He was supposed to tell me, to tell Matyom, to tell AVA even, when he was feeling suicidal! What the hell was going on? Where had he gone? Was this a suicidal episode?

I began to pace in the middle of his room, breaking down the morbid facts as I knew them. He was missing, according to everyone I asked. Even in AVA's records, he was, impossibly, nowhere to be found.

<ava i want to keep looking for torvram,> I broadcast urgently to our artificial caretaker. <is there any way i can be effective in the search? i-ill trade in my vacation time if i need to. i just want to find him!>

No response.

<ava?> I repeated.

Torvram's door slid shut and plunged me into darkness.

<ava!> I rushed to the door and queried it again. It wouldn't listen to me. I dug my fingers into the recessed handle and pulled. The lock had engaged. I managed to pull it open only far enough to expose a sharp sliver of light.

AVA hadn't responded. Pain shot up my fingers as I pulled harder. I released the door in resignation. The glow-in-the-dark alien on Torvram's mug cast sickly green phosphorescent light onto the ceiling.

<ava!> I repeated again as I queried the lights.

Nothing.

I sat down in the dark and swallowed hard against my swollen tongue. My heart raced, pounding against my chest. *Calm down. Just enumerate the problems. Torvram is missing or... oh no... Torv, I—*

I grasped for the safe, calming words Anyu had said during therapy but couldn't recall anything positive. My hands were shaking. My head felt like a lead weight was pulling my thoughts down and away from comprehension. I stood in the dark doing nothing, just staring because that's what I always did, right? *Nothing. You can't do anything. Anything. ANYTHING.*

The lights burst on with no warning. I yelped and stumbled back on one foot. The door to the hallway slid open.

<*ava?*>

<*Yes, Meera?*> AVA replied impassively.

<*what—what was that? did you just lock me in here?*> I replied, bewildered and vibrating with nervous energy.

<*No,*> it replied.

<*what do you mean no?*> I hurried out to the hallway, worried it would shut the door on me again.

<*I do not understand your question,*> AVA replied, indifferently.

"Ugh." I squeezed my brow, trying to ward off an impending headache. I'd just had some sort of breakdown in there and AVA might've just bugged out, but I wasn't about to acknowledge either of those occurrences if I could avoid them instead.

<*just—i want to help find torvram. is there some way i can do that?*> Once again, without solicitation, I said, <*i'd give up my vacation hours for this.*>

<*Yes. Candidates are being selected for a rescue expedition to recover Torvram and the missing equipment. You*

are qualified for reassignment. Would you like to join the expedition?>

"I don't..." I froze mid-step. This was a lot more than I'd expected. Did we *know* where he was now?

<*ava where would we even be going?*>

AVA shoved the knowledge into my brain. Instinctively, I turned to the east as the map in my mind found him. His lifeline pulsed kilometers away from our home.

"What...?" I froze mid-step in the hallway. How was Torvram *kilometers* away? Was he running away? What had happened?

<*What is your decision?*> AVA asked.

<*i—*> I broadcast. <*give me five minutes to think.*>

<*Very well.*>

I walked back to my room and pressed my hand against the door. It slid open at my touch and mental command. I wasn't locked in. A brew of synthetic coffee and cinnamaldehyde sat waiting for me in a mug, pouring out of a synthesizer on a preset timer.

Torvram had been found, somehow, far from our walls. I had no idea why he'd be out there, or how he'd gone missing, or what he was thinking. And if I wanted to help, I'd be going outside.

The fear that stole my voice and gripped my heart in Torvram's quarters returned. I remembered Jula's arm, the blackened, necrotic flesh crawling toward her chest as the cold stole her life away. I hugged the mug of coffee against my chest and let its strong cinnamon scent waft against my nose.

Torvram was missing and someone needed to rescue him. I was scared. I could give in to fear, or I could try to help him. I could try something new.

"Ok," I said to no one in particular. I ran to my tiny bathroom, throwing toiletries and clothing into a small duffle. I practically threw myself out of my room and refused to look back. I wasn't sure if I had the willpower to continue forward otherwise. My usual work, as miserable as it made me, was still more comfortable than this expedition into the unknown.

<when will we be leaving ava?>

Keep moving forward.

<Have you decided to join the expedition?>

<yes,> I replied resolutely, hands gripping my sides to stop them from shaking.

<Please depart to the eastern airlock as soon as possible. I will guide you there.>

I shivered at the mention of the eastern airlock but pressed on. <thanks ava we will find him dont you worry>

<I do not doubt that,> AVA replied with uncharacteristic warmth in its message.

AVA filled my vision with digital arrows. Amber signs burst from off-white walls. I passed through streams of Titanborn, some moving to work on their "day" shift with the pep of coffee and perhaps some tweaking from AVA's chemical intervention in their brains. Others, drained from the long "night" shifts to prepare our bulwark against the storm, tiredly lumbered past me toward their quarters.

A few called my name, but I found myself unable to speak. My entire being was focused on pushing myself forward. I clenched my aching hands until I felt my nails dig into the skin of my palms.

Torvram needs help.
Take a deep breath.
Keep moving forward.

I passed gurgling water mains, walls of hot air, and long processions of six-legged drones, marching in lockstep to some unknown goal. My workshop passed me on the left as a vibrant arrow asked that I turn right. Habit and fear rooted me to the spot at that T-intersection.

I choked up, a meaningless note escaping my lips, and began to run to the left. A two-dimensional hand of metallic black appeared. It told me to turn back.

I can't do this.

I squeezed my eyes shut. My face burned with embarrassment. I stepped into my workplace and was greeted with the familiar sounds of repair bots jerking and whirring in motion and the roar of powerful ventilation forcing every iota of dust out of the room. In the darkness behind my eyelids, I could see my amber irises softly glow. It was as if a small flame flickered there, staring back.

I opened my eyes. I stood in the locker room between the outside world and the cleanroom. It was time to change into my cleansuit.

<Meera, you are not assigned to work here today. Are you lost?> AVA interjected itself between my thoughts.

I took a seat on a bench between lockers and netting stuffed to bursting with equipment. There were three others donning their suits in the room.

<no,> I broadcast back.

<Would you like me to repeat your schedule for the day?>

<no.> I pressed my palms to my face as tears began to well up and spill freely. I tried in vain to hold them back and, when that failed, to hide my face in my hands. I didn't want them to hear me, to see me.

<ava whats wrong with me?>

<I am not sure what you mean,> it replied. <I can revert your reschedule and assign someone else to the rescue expedition. Would you like me to do that?>

<i dont know.>

<Your pattern of responses and current brain activity suggest you are depressed. In order to accomplish today's tasks, would you like me to administer an electrical antidepressant?> AVA continued.

<i dont know,> I repeated. <contact anyu for me.>

<Your therapist is currently seeing another patient and is not available.>

<just let me stay here ok i dont want to do anything.>

<You cannot remain idle,> AVA replied with indifference. <Your purpose, assigned at birth, states that all Titanborn must participate in the maintenance and perpetuation of the colony. You may either depart with the rescue expedition or I can reassign you to your regular neuroengineering tasks.>

I clutched at my face, pulling at the hair that was caught between my brow and hands, as my mind sank beneath a titanic weight. Tears flowed freely onto my hands, catching and refracting the light from my prosthetic eyes.

< whyd they make me like this? whyd earth build me broken?>

AVA said nothing. A nearby door slammed shut. I felt it was locking me in again, but I couldn't bring myself to look up or even move. I sobbed into my hands, wishing I could just dissolve into the bench. Torvram was missing and I couldn't even bring myself to walk outside. I couldn't break out of my shitty routine to help him. What kind of friend was I? What kind of useless person was I?

A heavy hand touched my shoulder. I rolled that shoulder, trying to buck it off.

"Go away," I moaned through my hands.

"Meera," Matyom's voice rumbled with bass tones. Within its depths, he conveyed a natural calm and ease, despite the sorrow evident in his voice.

I peered up at him through my fingers. His red eyes smiled back, colors so close in hue to that of his boyfriend, Torvram's.

"Are you ok?" Matyom's voice, though a whisper, reverberated through the room. His wide blond mustache drooped with a frown.

I reached up and pressed my forehead against his, squeezing my eyes shut. We held the gesture until my breathing steadied and my tears began to cease. I felt lightheaded, like something I'd been holding onto since the vats had spilled out of my mind.

"I—" I hiccupped. "I'm ok."

Matyom drew himself to his full height and beamed. "Ok."

"Did you hear about Torvram?" I asked, rising from the bench. He was more than a head taller than me and powerfully built.

"Yes," he said, his deep voice still cracking like a noisy signal. Matyom wiped at his eyes, a nickel-colored hand hiding what might've been tears from me.

He must've just arrived at Shangri-La, as he still wore his alabaster howlsuit. It was checkered with mission patches, and wear and weather showed their mark through thin scratches and yellowish discoloration.

"I'm going to bring him back." Matyom planted his hands on his hips and smiled proudly at me, his moment of vulnerability buried behind that powerful smile. Matyom was, in a word, inspiring. "And AVA said you're coming with us!"

"I'm not sure—" I began. Here was Torvram's boyfriend, two hours back from exploring the dunes of Titan and ready to risk life and limb for his boyfriend in the face of cold, storm, and death.

"I mean..." I almost lied to him, but he didn't deserve that. Torvram needed his help—our help. It was time to make a change. "I'm scared to go outside."

Scared to go outside. Scared to go somewhere different. Scared to try something new. Scared to be uncomfortable.

But it wouldn't stop me this time.

Matyom gave a thumbs-up and squeezed my shoulder reassuringly. "Feeling scared is natural, but there's no need to worry. No one dies on my watch."

I was mirroring his smile despite my best efforts to wallow in misery. His confidence was infectious. His kindness was a rare and welcome comfort. I found myself saying, "I'll see you at the airlock."

Matyom nodded. "Excellent!" His hearty voice, now fully unrestricted, boomed throughout the changing room. "I need to catch a quick shower and then, uhh..." His smile wavered. He would be returning to the now-vacant room he shared with Torvram.

I grabbed his bicep and squeezed back. "We're going to rescue Torvram," I said, staring up at him.

"Yeah." His grin returned. "We are."

He practically ran from the locker room, waving as he left. To my surprise, the door unlocked and opened for him.

I had one last fear to surmount. <ava?> I asked.

<Yes?> AVA replied with a neutral, emotionless response.

<can you check your logs and tell me what happened with the doors just now and in Torvram's room about ten minutes ago? you stopped talking and the doors locked on me... i think.>

<Of course, Meera. I do not have any record of that activity or my own downtime.>

<theres nothing in your records or your memory about you locking the doors? nothing about you going silent?>

<No, Meera.>

I leaned against one of the lockers. <ava are you—are you lying to me?>

<I am incapable of concealing any information from you, Meera.>

<ok.>

<You are required to work or depart today, Meera, and the _5_ minutes you requested have now lapsed. What is your decision?>

<i want to find torvram,> I replied.

<Of course, Meera. Enjoy your day.>

<thanks.>

AVA did not respond.

I rose from the bench, taking one long breath, stretching my arms languorously above my head until my joints cracked and I sighed effortlessly with the exertion. It was time to take a risk, to move forward, and to rescue Torvram.

CHAPTER 06

PLAYING OUTSIDE

MEERA; EASTERN AIRLOCK, SHANGRI-LA

"Ok. Ok. Ok." I exhaled like a decompression breach, punching the air out of my lungs. It was all I could do to calm my nerves and still my hands. I was here, now, *in* the eastern airlock for the first time in years.

Howlsuits lined the walls, leaning toward us as the ceiling curved upward to subtly minimize the volume of the airlock. Their empty helmets stared down at me, seeming to congregate behind my back. A simple plastic door plastered with graffiti-like black and red warning signs was all that stood between us and the natural state of the deadly moon we called home.

I checked Matyom's seals one more time. Mildly radioactive methane evaporated where the suit articulated about his joints. I ran my fingers along the creases and folds, mostly taut against his strong back, searching for any sign of damage.

Matyom's suit was scratched and worn and stained from hundreds of missions outside. There were blackened patches from repair kits and the entire right arm of his suit was cleaner than the rest, likely salvaged from the suit of a deceased Titanborn. The dead didn't need their howlsuits anymore. We did. I hoped that Torvram wasn't—that he hadn't—

I—

I took another breath, trying to force the fear out of my mind.

"All violet here," Matyom bellowed, giving me a thumbs-up. Violet stood out in Titan's golden smog and was a surefire way to tell a Titanborn was safe from a distance. There were four violet lights on the left breast of Matyom's howlsuit for heat, oxygen, water, and life—the vital readouts from the lifeline mesh about his heart.

I checked his arms one last time. He wasn't going to let anyone die on his watch, and I wasn't going to let Matyom die on mine either. Mission patches formed an almost continuous sleeve on his right shoulder and armored his chest. He'd saved so many lives, discovered so many things.

We shared only two patches. The first was the golden sphere of Titan stamped with the astrological symbol for Saturn. The symbol's curving tail had been replaced by the double helix of DNA. *Avitra Biotechnology* and *Titanborn Project* was emblazoned on its lip, a permanent reminder that I'd been designed by someone else.

The second patch held a red arc and stark white letters *FEAA* atop the blues and greens and whites of Earth. The Federation of Earth Aeronautical Administration's umbrella of Earthbound space agencies had built this patch right into every suit, a small consolation for their hand in funding this long mission.

<*You Ok Back There?*> I practically jumped at Matyom's voice. I'd zoned out, my hands perched on his elbow.

<yeah,> I replied, blush rising to my gray cheeks. <your seals are all violet.> It was shorthand as well, meaning "good" or "safe."

A metallic yip bounced off the airlock door. A tiny robotic dog wagged its bottlebrush tail, or the bundle of parallel wires meant to resemble a tail.

"Who is this?" I asked aloud, dropping to a crouch. I held my hand out to the little three-legged robot, already recognizing it from Torvram's room.

<🙂 Outside! 🙂> it broadcast cheerfully as it nuzzled its cold nose against my closed fist.

<His Name Is Feyn.> Matyom regarded the little machine dog with a bittersweet mixture of sorrow and joy. <Ok, Little Pup. Stay Close.>

<🐶 Yes sir! 🐶> the dog yipped again, trotting up to the airlock door.

<Feyn Was Supposed To Be My Not-So-Secret Anniversary Gift. I Called In Some Favors To Have Him Finished, Thought It Might Cheer Me Up.> Matyom's characteristic enthusiasm lapsed, cooling his usual telepathic tone.

<oh...> I reached across the airlock bench slowly, wanting to comfort the big man as his blond mustache drooped.

Matyom rose abruptly, knocking my hand away with his shoulder. He announced, loudly, <Ok! The Sooner We Leave, The Sooner We Find My Honeysuckle.>

<yeah yeah lets do it.>

The circular airlock door pulled back from its seals with a mighty pop. From outside, a thin band of shadow spilled into the room as the light and air of Titan began to seep insidiously into our space. Howlsuits pinned to the walls of the eastern airlock began knocking rhythmically against the chamber's walls, as a rush of high-pressure nitrogen blew into them.

The chamber's pumps uttered their final sputters and went silent. The heaters went dead. My howlsuit hummed to life as the temperature about me plummeted from sixteen to zero degrees Celsius and continued to fall. Condensation blossomed in rings that spread across my helmet's surface before evaporating away as the suit acclimated.

Matyom stood just before the airlock door, patting Feyn on the head as he stared resolutely forward, jaw squared. I was avoiding looking at the door but I knew I'd need to face it in mere seconds. This was where Jula had died, right after we'd walked outside. My hands shook. I couldn't do this, but I *had to do this*.

I opened my hands and took a breath.

Matyom had so much on his mind already. I needed to be stronger for him, for Torvram. I could try.

Then, before I'd finished steeling my nerves, it was open.

The world outside was one of extremes. It was lit harshly by Shangri-La's lights and, beyond their elliptical reach, faintly by the sun—a pinhole of light low on the horizon. A thick golden fog draped Titan in dull colors, waxing and waning in its thickness, subtle and random in its turbulent patterns. Methane drizzled from the sky and formed bowl-shaped puddles within the coffee-colored tar unique to Titan.

<*Ready?*> Matyom asked as a grin spread across his face. This was his element. It was one of my recurring nightmares.

I nodded hastily, trying to outrun my fear response. <yeah.>

I followed in Matyom's shadowless wake, as Shangri-La's blinding lights beat down on the worn back of his howlsuit. Titan's organic gunk crunched and squashed beneath my boots, leaving vibrant clumps of brown and orange behind. Half of one foot sank in before the compacted ground beneath held firm. I forced my boot up and out and checked my seals, one last time.

My temperature readings were stable. All lights were violet. Behind me, the airlock slid closed. Shangri-La, my home, towered over my head. Methane rain flowed down its gray, striped walls and poured into rooftop tanks and artificial channels that ferried the overflow away. Lights and cameras dotted every surface, moving in seemingly random, jerky motions as they scanned the landscape.

It'd been over a decade since I'd been outside and seen these walls with my own eyes.

I wrenched my eyes away from home and turned instead to the horizon.

With methane rain falling and Titan's haze being its usual impenetrable self, there wasn't much to see at first. I poked around in my brain, trying to remember the command without AVA's help.

Ah. There we go.

My eyes heated ever so slightly, the sensation forcing them wide, as I downshifted from human visible standard to a discrete band of infrared. The world faded into false color grays and the fog and the rain seemed to vanish. Matyom lit up as a bright amber, the body heat within his suit a stark contrast to the cold gray of Titan's -150 degrees Celsius.

Behind him, the *Trailblazer* was a multi-story column of crimson. The rover sat just meters from the sealed northern garage, alight with activity and heat. It looked like a trapezoidal pyramid had sprouted from two massive treads. The IR band of its lights burned through Titan's dim daylight.

I looked up at the sky and truly saw, for the first time in years, stars. Infrared light from cooler stars, though so distant, cut through the fog at these wavelengths. Saturn's rings sliced through the sky, falsely colored a pale blue. The gas giant's bulk loomed over Titan, seemingly close, yet so far from my little home moon.

My fear quietly slunk away beneath the sheer awe of the world around me.

Home wasn't just the Shangri-La colony. This was my home, too.

<*Meera? You Ok?*> Matyom asked, once again.

<*sorry!*> I broadcast, jogging to catch up with Matyom. <*just taking in the view.*> I kept my emotional channels closed so he couldn't sense my nervousness, at least not at the intimate level of telepathy.

<*No Need To Apologize! I Often Forget How Lucky I Am To Get To See This Beauty Almost Every Day.*> I couldn't really make out his face, but I thought I saw him smile. <*That Said, Please Be Quick!*>

<🐕 *Woof!* :3🐕> Feyn spoke the word telepathically, as it yipped aloud. I brought my gaze Titanward, back to the ground in front of me, and followed them toward *Trailblazer*. This puppy trotting at my feet and his use of Torvram's playful ':3' cue were small but strong reminders of why we were out here. I'd accomplished one little step already. I was moving forward again.

MEERA; OPERATIONS DECK, *TRAILBLAZER*

The *Trailblazer's* interior felt almost alien to me. Its walls were all-white tessellated triangles unfolded into sheets, and they flowed continuously into tables, chairs, lights, and more than half of the furniture. The seams between each triangle were a subtle blue, lending a cool, dreamlike color to the operations deck.

I sat against a surprisingly smooth bench and ran my fingers along the table connected to my seat. The origami table looked like the universe was on a low-graphics setting and was now rendered with minimal polygons to save resources.

The most familiar thing about it was how cramped it was. I could almost reach the counter of the small utilitarian kitchenette on the opposite wall. The cockpit above me and engine room below were even smaller than this tiny operations deck.

Still, warmth and light filled the space. Water ran smoothly from the tap. It was a little slice of home to spirit us through Titan's lethally-cold dunes.

Up the ladder to my left, Matyom was laughing as the mechanic shouted at him. I could make out little through the white noise of Matyom's hearty guffaws except the nasally-delivered words "Fuck" and "Chiphead" repeated at regular intervals.

With a burst of neural activity, I brought my schedule into view once again. The hourly slots remained paved over with the single sentence: *Rescue Expedition*. I was still coming to terms with this sudden change, with Torvram's unexplainable disappearance, and with the mere fact that I was out here now.

A seal slammed over the ladder leading down to the engine room. The *Trailblazer's* pumps rattled. Someone was boarding on the bottom floor.

"Finally!" the mechanic shouted.

"I want to find Torvram as fast as possible, so don't antagonize anyone." As Matyom's howlsuit boots hit the tessellated triangles on the floor, he stared up at the mechanic descending the ladder in front of him and added, "Promise me, Case."

The mechanic, Case, sighed. "I promise only to try, assuming your friends don't fuck anything up."

"Vent it, Case." Matyom sputtered a laugh into his hands. "I don't know why I put up with you."

"You'd never get by without me," Case guffawed. "And don't worry your blond head. We'll find Torvy."

Where Matyom was tall and stocky, Case was small and lithe. His dark navy coveralls were almost more machine grease than textile and smelled faintly of acrid solvent. Case's black hair, drawn back into a minuscule ponytail that ended before his spine began, looked similarly unctuous. His eyes were hazel but there was no telltale light streaming from the band of color meant to mimic an iris. He looked... weird, like something was wrong with his face and—

Then it hit me.

His eyes were biological.

"Why are you staring at me?" Case asked, jabbing a finger in my direction.

"I'm sorry!" In my embarrassment, the words came out too high.

Matyom sighed. "You said you'd be nice, Case, nice!"

The short mechanic growled. "Yeah. Yeah. I'm Case, the *Trailblazer's* mechanic and resident stowaway. You're—" He squinted. His eyes didn't glow.

I caught myself staring again, then tore my eyes away. "I'm Meera! Neuroengineer...Torvram was—*is* a good friend of mine."

Case nodded and his posture slackened. "It's, uhh, a shame that he—well, honestly I don't know what happened."

The bulkhead between us and the engine room below unsealed, and a woman in a black hoodie ascended the ladder. As if a curtain had been drawn before her hood, her face was obscured by a digital mask. The false face smiled, eerie in its perfect symmetry.

"Hello," she said in a dry, strained voice, as if she was brushing the cobwebs off of rarely used vocal cords. She waved a hand halfheartedly, not moving a centimeter from the ladder. "I am enti—my name is Fei."

Case's eyes widened as he regarded the newcomer. He shut his eyes and whirled about, grumbling, "I'll be in the cockpit."

"What's his problem?" Fei scoffed.

Matyom's mustache drooped. "Is your mask a digital overlay or is it a physical object?"

"Digital, of course," Fei snorted condescendingly. "Why would I carry a physical mask around?"

I rankled at Fei's response. It was unnecessarily rude.

"Case can see your face behind it, then," Matyom frowned apologetically, seemingly unaffected by Fei's attitude.

"Ahh!" Fei shouted, her composure dissolving in an instant. Her hands shot to her face and she yanked the hoodie closed until only the nose of her digital mask was visible.

The last piece came into place. Case didn't just lack prosthetic eyes. No Titanborn lacked augmentation, unless they were born natural.

That meant Case had no neural circuitry, no nanomechanical cells, and no artificial eyes. He couldn't broadcast or see in artificial reality or other wavelengths of light without external tools, which meant he also couldn't see the digital face Fei was projecting. Naturals were a rare sight these days.

Most of the naturals born on Titan were dead.

Four mechanical hands appeared from behind Fei and the sight jettisoned me from my contemplation. The small but cozy operations deck suddenly felt claustrophobic.

Lakshmi landed almost gracefully but stumbled a bit. The six-armed woman managed to catch herself against Fei's shoulder to keep herself from falling flat on her face.

"Beautiful!" Fei said, abruptly extricating herself from her hoodie. Fei's entire posture shifted, straightening, her whole digital facade literally brightening at Lakshmi's appearance.

I started to panic. I had no idea *she* was going to be here. Was I going to be stuck with Lakshmi for hours—or worse, days—on this expedition?

I looked at Matyom pleadingly. <*why is she here?!?*>

Lakshmi was chattering now, poking a finger at the big man's chest as she spoke up at him. Fei nodded furiously. Despite their conversation, Matyom's eyes shot to me.

<*Is There A Problem? The Revision Committee Wanted To Send One Of Our Best To Ensure Torvram's Quick Rescue.*>

I balled my hands together and took a deep breath. How did he not know about her? Torvram and I were constantly under her thumb!

Lakshmi's cerulean eyes turned on me. The angular woman smiled, a toothy, predatory grin. I instinctively sank back onto the bench.

"You ran away from me in the observation ring a few days ago," Lakshmi said matter-of-factly.

I said nothing. I stared up and to the right of her. I was focusing everything I had to keep the heart-pounding anxiety at the sight of her at bay. *Just keep breathing, ok? Just keep breathing.*

Feyn sauntered over to me and rubbed up against my leg. I leaned down to pet the little dog, thanking Torvram silently for creating this small delight. I wouldn't be surprised if it started growling at Lakshmi later.

Lakshmi turned away, clapping two of her prosthetics together over her head. "Ok! AVA's handed command of this expedition over to me, naturally, and I want us moving as fast as possible. Torvram was last spotted at the Aztlan waystation and I want him found and recovered yesterday! Fei, Matyom, I need you get the *Trailblazer* to shake hands with AVA and pathfind us. Matyom, I'm counting on your wealth of experience to get us there quickly. Meera, you—"

I felt my back stiffen the moment she said my name. I couldn't look at her.

"Hey!" One of her prosthetics snapped two fingers, the whip-crack sound echoing in the confined space. "Meera, you need to be downstairs prepping our onboard drones for launch. You do want to find Torvram, don't you?"

"I—" I swallowed. Even looking near her made me feel sick. "Yes, ma'am."

"Just get down to the engine room, Meera," she barked.

I shot one more pleading glance at Matyom. He shrugged but, to his credit, frowned subtly. I hoped he was picking up on this. I needed a sympathetic ear.

"Who is the mechanic on-duty?" Lakshmi said as I made my way down the white-lit shaft.

"Case."

"Case! Send me the *Trailblazer's* authentication key!"

"I can't broadcast it to you, chiphead. You have to actually come here and get it!" Case retorted, his nasally shout carrying all the way down to me as I touched ground in the engine deck.

"What?!"

"He's natural, Lakshmi," Matyom replied. His mustachioed face appeared over the shaft entrance.

"Oh, pfft, fine, I'll—"

<Meera, Are You Ok?> Matyom privately broadcast to me.

<yeah,> I lied, feeling more than a little pissed at him by proxy. I gripped one of my arms, my nails digging into my skin.

<Are You Sure?> He was trying to help. We were both trying to help Torvram. I realized in that moment that he

probably knew I wasn't okay, but he could never be sure of it unless I said something. What was the point of coming out here if I was just going to voluntarily suffer in silence again? If Torvram had just reached out, if I had felt comfortable reaching out to him, maybe he wouldn't have gone missing like this.

<*sorry. im not ok,*> I replied. <*when youre free, could you come down here? i could use someone to talk to, in person, away from her.*>

<*I'll Telecomm You As Soon As I Can! And I'll Be Down Shortly.*> The stocky blond gave me a broad, winning grin and a thumbs-up before pulling away from the ladder shaft.

<*thanks.*>

There was little space down here, between the motors, the engines, and the tread housings. I stood on the sealed gangway and took in the little space. There were outdated electronics lashed in bags against one wall, probably the stuff the astronauts used when they'd walked this moon via android.

My heart was pounding in my ears. The last person I wanted to see was Lakshmi. But maybe work could help distract me from my panic. I'd do it to help Torvram, to help Matyom find his lover, and to make our adage true for one more day. No more death.

I donned my helmet, sealing it just in case the gangway seals leaked, and grabbed the first heavy, methane-logged drone.

<*hello;*
i am:
entity(meera);
intelligence(human);
class(neuroengineer);

what is wrong with you?;>
<hello;
i am:
entity(Drgnfly-578);
intelligence(rudimentary);
class(aerial optics drone);

my port two rotor blades will not move;>
<ok;
i can fix that;
please keep your battery on and your body still;>
<acknowledged meera;>

CHAPTER 07

DOWNTIME

MEERA; ENGINE DECK, *TRAILBLAZER*

The *Trailblazer's* engines beat a steady, four-note tune into the walls around me. It creaked and groaned as its treads flattened balls of tar and plowed through methane-filled potholes. The quadcopter drone before me, pinned to a triangle-patterned workbench by uneven strips of recycled plastic, vibrated with the *Trailblazer's* impacts against something outside. Toolboxes banged against the corrugated walls from inside sealed cabinets.

The engine room wasn't too dissimilar to my quarters: small, utilitarian, and packed with built-in storage space. Replace the engines with the food synthesizer that fueled my body and it really was the same place. The primary difference was the smell. Even though my oxygen pouches were nearly full and my CO_2 was being piped away, I could swear the air inside my helmet smelled stale. Maybe I was inhaling exhaust. Either way, I was starting to feel dizzy.

Nevertheless, I continued to work on the drones in the cramped engine deck. I was almost done and as long as I had work to do, I had an excuse to stay down here, away from Lakshmi and Fei.

<matyom?> I shot a silent message two floors up to the cockpit.

<Apologies, Meera! The Trailblazer Is Demanding My Full Attention Right Now. The Moment I Have Us Safely On Autopilot to Aztlan I'll Come Down.>

<mkay.> I sighed and leaned against the little workbench, nestled between two nets swollen with miscellaneous machine parts. A small metal arm jutted out from one of them; its three fingers had already poked me in the neck twice. I glowered at it as it swung back and forth.

I craned my neck to stare at the wall to my right. With a thought, the signal from Torvram's lifeline appeared in my vision as a red teardrop to the east. He was hundreds of kilometers away! How in the world had he gotten out there in less than a week?! And why?

<torvram?> I queried his mental frequency.

Nothing.

I turned back to the crates of drones lashed beside me. Any one of these could find him, and I was almost done. Tedium aside, it was something I could do to help.

<hello;
i am:
entity(meera);
intelligence(human);
class(neuroengineer);
what is wrong with you?;>

<hello;
i am:

entity(Drgnfly-667);
intelligence(rudimentary);
class(aerial optics drone);
no damage detected;>

<i will inspect your sensors to ensure they are working;>
The drone reacted.
<unnecessary;
cautionary anecdote:
"An old machine will continue to function until an engineer decides it needs to be fixed." ~ Dr. C. N. Ramakrishnan>

"Fuuuck me." Case's nasal voice droned from somewhere behind me.

I ignored him, my brain still neuron-deep in Dragonfly-667's "head."

"Matyom sent me down here to help you." Case leaned against the ladder, arms crossed, one hand tapping impatiently against a grease-stained sleeve of his howlsuit. I almost mistook it for his coveralls, considering the equivalent amounts of machine oil on each.

"I'm fine," I fired back, looking back to the drone and my work.

"Ok, whatever. I need to get a laptop from the bag beneath that bench. I'll be out of your hair once I get that," he grumbled. "And back upstairs with them, ugh."

"Sure." I pulled out of the drone's head. The world spiraled. I reached beneath the workbench as my vision blurred.

I felt something crash hard against my back and as my vision cleared I was, somehow, staring up at the ceiling.

"Whoa!" Case's helmetless head appeared overhead. The light above burned orange into the edges of his dark hair. "You chipheads are bad liars. You are *not* fine."

He proffered his hand. I took it and fought to find my footing again, leaning into Case's arm, feet scrabbling against the floor as my sense of balance went sideways.

Case pulled a chair from nowhere. "Sit. Sit. Jeez. I know you want to find Torvy but you gotta pace yourself doing... whatever it is you all do with the drones."

"Thanks," I mumbled, embarrassed, as I relaxed into the chair. "I guess I should've taken a break."

"Enhanced intelligence, my ass." Case snorted as he crouched beneath the bench.

"Could you maybe not make fun of me, at least while I'm in earshot?" I glared at his back. How was this jerk Matyom's friend? So far, all I'd see him do was be the exact opposite of friendly.

Case shrugged. "If you don't make an ass of yourself, I won't make an ass of you."

I rose abruptly, despite the head rush. I was having a hard enough time just being in the same space as Lakshmi and here was this mechanic being awful too. This behavior would stop here and now. "Vent it! What is your fucking problem, Case?"

He grinned, as if he'd just been given something wonderful. Case's venomous tirade exploded out of him like an over pressurized air canister exploding. "My problem is that you—all of you chipheads with your enhanced intelligence and your augmented strength and your ability to see through walls and shit—you just show up here while barely being able to find your own asses and order me around like I don't know what I'm doing.

"We have a man missing, possibly dead, and what do the chipheads do: Lakshmi and Fei are in ops doing nothing, they call it 'management,' the *Trailblazer* half breaks the moment you all show up, and you can't even prep these drones in a few hours?

"Matyom I trust, but the rest of you have proven nothing except that you are completely incompetent, despite your massive 'advantages' over me. And while I spend every waking day tolerating your bullshit, I am *not* going to lose a friend because of it." He paused only to inhale, loudly. "So what's *your* problem? Why can't you do this simple task, chiphead?"

I reeled, my eyes defocusing as I dissociated. *You don't know what you're talking about. Torvram was my friend. That monster upstairs pushed him into nearly committing suicide before, now she's making him do it again. This is her fault. It's all her fault. My whole—*

This is my fault too. It's Torvram's fault. It's everyone's fault. It doesn't matter whose fault it is.

I snapped back to reality. His lip was curled into a snarl but I saw, too, that the short man's unlit eyes were shaking, wet. He was backed against the wall, one hand on the ladder and the other looped protectively around a thin laptop. His proverbial hackles raised as he stood next to the only escape from this room. The only escape from me.

Was he... was he scared of me? Was he scared of *us*?

"I'm scared." I extended my confession as an olive branch. I was scared of Lakshmi too, of being outside, but he didn't need to know it all. I barely knew him. What I knew was that he was here, like the rest of us, putting in the effort to save my friend. From what Case had said, it sounded like he was here to save *our* friend. Whatever had happened to make him this mad wasn't my business.

We could at least work together, for Torvram. "I don't know why or how Torvram left, but I'm scared he's going to die. I'm scared, too, that it might be my fault... not that that matters."

"Shit," Case replied. He released the ladder as his posture relaxed.

"Yeah." I nodded, chuckling nervously.

He crossed his arms again, tucking the laptop to his chest. In addition to the oil, his howlsuit sported burn marks and black patches that sealed scars on its surface. I noticed, then, that he had glasses like Anyu's tucked into his suit, suspended about his neck by a loop of extruded plastic. Case made a show of hardening his expression, deepening his scowl repeatedly each time his eyes softened.

Finally, Case shrugged and said, "That makes two of us. Torvram is one of the good ones, ya know? He makes Matyom happy. He's a good guy."

"And he's my friend too," I replied, gripping the suit's composite fibers about my palms. "I don't know what you've been through but... I'm not... I'm not here to hurt you or order you around. I just want to save Torvram and then go back to, uhh, hmm." *Go back to my life* was what I'd expected to say, but not what I wanted. I didn't know what I wanted after this.

"Mmm." He nodded, his brow furrowing as his gaze dropped to the tessellated floor. "Sorry, I guess. I shouldn't be dumping this all on you. I just... look you don't get it ok?"

"I don't." I shrugged. That was as honest as I could be. I didn't. And I couldn't. "I have a hard enough time getting by as is. I can't imagine what life would be like without telepathy, without everything I can do. Honestly, I don't know how you manage."

"Hard work. Lots of alcohol to dull the pain." A small smile spread across his gray face. "Expletives. I got thrown out of Shangri-La for being a liability just by existing. I figured after that, you all would at least have the decency to leave me alone."

I wasn't sure how to respond to that. This was news to me. Shangri-La was a small, closed community, and the fact that I hadn't heard about a natural being dealt a shade of my worst fear—severe punishment for failure—was alarming. All I could do was express exactly how I felt: pained, guilty, and a little angry for him. "I'm sorry."

"Hey, it's not your fault. I... Systemic problems, right?" He chuckled. "You can grow us away from Earth, but I guess you can't grow problematic Earthborn behavior out of humans, or maybe you directly inject them into us with the astronauts? I—heh, I'm rambling now."

He sighed again, a long, baritone rasp. I felt a sudden, powerful kinship for this natural Titanborn. We were entirely different, as far as I could tell, but the emotion he was expressing here felt all too familiar. "I can see why Maty and Torv like you. You're at least listening. I'm not invisible to you, like I am to Lakshmi. She's too busy oppressing *everyone*."

"Oh, you don't even—well, maybe you *do* know the extent of it," I replied, trying to force a smile.

"Maybe." Case snorted. "I wouldn't be surprised if we all experience different abuses though. At least my mind is my own. Hearing Lakshmi in my head would be... the worst. Speaking of which, Miss 'Management' says you're blocking her broadcasts and she needs you up in operations." Case wholeheartedly beamed. "I take solace in knowing we've both wasted a few minutes of her time though."

"Ah," There was a pang of fear but, then, a smile tugged at my mouth. As immature as it was, inconveniencing *her* made me a little happy. And, on a less petty note, I thought I was beginning to see what Matyom saw in Case. "I'll go talk to her then."

He cocked his head to the side, shuffling away from the ladder. "I think I get her type, ya know. If you don't give Lakshmi power over you, she has none to wield."

"Oh." Once again, I wasn't sure what to say. I paused at the ladder's base. "Thanks."

"Hey, uhh, sorry for blowing up at you," Case said. "Thanks for listening."

I smiled, feeling genuinely relieved. "You too."

We climbed up into the well-lit operations room. The *Trailblazer's* rumble and crash faded beneath me.

Lakshmi sat hunched over the origami table, one of her hands idly flicking at its spire of a central fold. Her eyes flickered and darted about what was likely AR text only she could see.

"Alright, Case, get downstairs and fix the right thread. It's seizing. I think its filters are loose or something." She didn't even look at us. One of her thin prosthetics and its many exoskeletal casing segments shifted to fully extend the arm and nearly flick his nose.

"Sure," Case replied, his tone abruptly devoid of humor.

Case turned to me, nodding in either a gesture of camaraderie or a simple goodbye, and left me alone with Lakshmi. I hid my hands behind my back. They were beginning to shake again.

Her eyes stopped moving and Lakshmi turned, lazily, to face me. I shifted my feet uncomfortably, nervous energy causing me to twitch and fidget. Two of her hands remained steepled idly over the table while the others gestured toward me.

"You need to unblock me," Lakshmi said, still scanning the invisible text. "There's no excuse for you to waste all of our time like this."

"Ok." I swallowed and complied.

"Now, several Titanborn have logged complaints with AVA's behavior this week," Lakshmi continued. One of her prosthetics made a come-here gesture and a digital list of names, times, neural IPs, appeared in my vision. "You were one of them," she said, my name springing from the confines of its AR window and into the open air.

My chest tightened. Being forced to talk to her, directly, was sending my thoughts spiraling. I'd avoided this confrontation out of sheer fear but now—now that I was here—my head was overflowing.

All I could think of was her unpredictable nature: changing schedules on a whim, throwing tantrums, treating Torvram and myself and, apparently, Case as if our time was disposable, of little value. She didn't even seem aware of the effect she had on me, on us. Torvram might've run away just to get away from *her*.

Lakshmi made me feel like I was beneath her.

I was also jealous. Where Matyom was fearless, she was invincible. Just days ago, she'd pushed back against our water crisis without a second thought, buying all of us weeks, maybe months of time to live. She was a polymath, attuned with her implants so well that she walked around with six arms instead of two like it was normal.

I wanted her self-assurance.

I didn't want to be Meera. I wanted to be Lakshmi.

But I hated Lakshmi.

"Meera? Hey!" Lakshmi waved her hand, wrapped in an electric blue glove that exposed much of her gray-skin through a long mouthlike-hole. Being out of her howlsuit made it even clearer that Lakshmi intended to do no work in the engine deck.

"Sorry," I replied automatically, forcing a smile, still stewing in my fear, anger, and jealousy.

"You don't focus very well," she stated like it was fact. "Do you?"

"Sorry," I repeated, my cheeks burning. That pulled me back to Titan. I was just angry now, but I buried it. This was for Torvram, vent it.

One of her prosthetics jerked to her side and plucked a small puzzle sphere from her jacket pocket. She began to fiddle idly as her cerulean eyes seemed to flicker and spark, staring straight at me.

"So... are you gonna tell me what happened between you and AVA?"

"Ah, yes, umm, sorry but can't you just look at its communication records?" I asked.

"I'd rather hear your full account," Lakshmi replied as her angular face softened. "It must have been a frightening experience and as a member of the Revision Committee, I want to make sure this sort of thing never happens again."

"Umm," I stuttered. "I was in Torvram's room, trying to see if I could maybe find a clue as to how he disappeared and—" I snapped my mouth shut.

"Meeraaa, like I said, it's ok. This will be just between you and me. It's not like there's anyone above me to report this to." She laughed heartily, staring off into the middle distance between us with a self-satisfied, toothy grin.

"Ok?" I replied, skeptical of her every word.

Lakshmi leaned back into the bench behind the origami table while I stood across from her, in the middle of ops, growing increasingly uncomfortable. "Keep going."

"How is this going to help us find Torvram?" I blurted out.

"We'll get to that in a moment, trust me." She grinned. "Your account will help me grease the wheels within wheels and all that. Now, continue."

I tried to rationalize this. I didn't trust her but what she was saying made some sense, I supposed. We were here to save Torvram, right? I hated her, but no Titanborn would wish death on another. We'd all seen too much already. No more death.

"Uhh, so AVA went silent. Like it wouldn't talk to me at all. And the lights went out. It locked me inside Torvram's room."

"Mhmm," Lakshmi said. Her eyes were unfocused again, moving rapidly left-to-right, the telltale sign of someone reading text in AR. One of her prosthetics spun its wrist idly, gesturing for me to continue.

"It did it again, I—I think," I began to stammer. I wanted to be anywhere but in front of her. "I think AVA lied to me about it, maybe? I mean, it can't lie but there's no way it didn't know it did this. It locked me in his room!"

"Creepy," Lakshmi replied, a cocksure grin spreading across her face while she continued reading and paid no obvious attention to me. "Here." She swiped an artificial arm toward me. A digital window flew into my vision as if thrown. It was a simple text document.

"I'd like you to note, here, that you've experienced these problems with AVA since the most recent patch occurred. I'm concerned that the hasty actions of the Revision Committee have put us all at risk. You asked earlier why this is relevant?" Her eyes flicked to my face, cerulean fire licking at her irises. "I suspect the patch may be correlated with Torvram's disappearance."

"How?" I asked, leaning forward as my curiosity briefly overtook my fear.

"Rest assured, I'm going to find out." Lakshmi nodded gravely. "I was staunchly opposed to this ill-conceived, rushed patch. Chetan entrusted me with all of our safety, and I refuse to let a single Titanborn die on my watch. Don't worry, Meera. We're going to find him and make sure this never happens again: no more death."

"No more death," I replied, automatically, relieved.

Lakshmi continued, "We live in a colony sustained by systems of nearly unfathomable complexity. You focus on today's tasks and I, as always, will shield you from the vast web of systems that surround us: the politics, the resource management, our water shortage, and so on."

Lakshmi smiled again—she was always smiling that wide, confident, toothy grin. I felt my skepticism erode at an alarming rate while we sat across from each other. Experience had taught me not to trust her, but the longer we spoke, the more I wanted to believe her words. Lakshmi's charisma was infectious.

"Ok." I nodded.

"I need you and Case to send those drones on their way to Aztlan, now. The sooner we find Torvram, the sooner we can bring him home," Lakshmi said.

"Ok," I repeated, this time smiling genuinely at Lakshmi.

I left the operations deck uneasy but confident in my next task, climbing down the ladder to find Case helmeted and ready.

Her spell faded as I gained distance. My certainty turned to doubt. Lakshmi's logic began to breakdown. I wanted to trust she was here for the right reasons, but I couldn't overlook my experience. I hated her—and maybe that was unfair—but I wasn't going to let her gaslight me into thinking she cared suddenly, abruptly, about Torvram's well-being when she never had before.

"Fuck," I summarized the whole frothing turmoil in my head as I donned my helmet. "I don't trust her."

Case guffawed. "Hah, I never trust a chiphead. You sealed in?"

I took a breath, pushing away all distractions so I could turn my mind to the rigor of a seal check.

"Check my back," I said. All four lights were violet. No cuts or gaps in my howlsuit were apparent. Case ran his hands along the joints of my shoulders, the folds at my waist. His hands were warm.

"No breaches," Case replied. "Check me."

Something had dawned on me. Torvram had left without a partner. One literally could not leave Shangri-La without another Titanborn in tow. That way, you could suit-check your partner and call for help if they were unable. Torvram leaving alone meant he would've had to, somehow, change the very rules AVA had set, or something...

"Meera!"

"Ah, sorry, sorry." I sent a query off to AVA and busied myself checking Case.

"No breaches," I replied, a minute later.

"Sealing the airlock!" Case shouted up to the others.

<sealing the airlock in the engine room,> I broadcast to the *Trailblazer*. A chorus of ayes, rogers, and Lakshmi's ";)" came back telepathically.

Case frowned. "You, umm, the manual controls are being wonky. Can you use your brain-computer shit?"

I nodded. The ladder shaft sealed with a pop.

"Opening the bay!" Case shouted.

<opening the bay in the engine room,> I repeated. No one would be able to hear him unless they were near the radio, and we rarely used the radio.

As the floor cracked with a hiss and split open, I took a brief millisecond look at Torvram's lifeline. It was still pulsing. I hoped that the drones we threw out there would finally find him, wherever he was.

Meanwhile, my list of questions was only growing. Lakshmi was up to something, despite or maybe because of her presence here. Torvram was missing, yes, but I was beginning to think there was more to it. He couldn't have left alone. It was impossible, unless AVA itself had changed.

And based on what had happened this morning, I was coming to the horrifying conclusion that that might actually be true. There might actually be something wrong with the AI that I'd grown up with, that controlled so many of our systems, that could even drive the *Trailblazer* if need be.

AVA was everywhere and if there was something wrong with it, all of our lives could be at risk.

CHAPTER 08
SYSTEMIC PROBLEMS

MEERA; ENGINE DECK, *TRAILBLAZER*

There was no record of Torvram leaving. He was at work one moment, stopped in his quarters, spoke aloud to himself, and then vanished. No video, no airlock checks, nothing. That was impossible.

Was AVA lying to me? It was similar to when I'd been locked in his room and AVA had claimed no responsibility. But it couldn't. We knew AVA couldn't conceal information from us. But Torvram couldn't have just disappeared like this, and erasing his records systematically was too difficult for any one individual, or even a group of Titanborn. I don't know why he would want to even if he could.

I was missing something. Maybe I wasn't asking the right questions? Or making the wrong assumptions...

"Huh," Case muttered.

Oblivious to the precarious drop to Titan before him, Case leaned down the *Trailblazer's* open gangway and stared at the octocoptor Spiderfly drone he'd just released outside. Its suite of optical sensors were fixed on his face. He reached into the *Trailblazer's* billowing wake of powderized rusty organics, toward the drone. The drone should've flown away, off to pursue Torvram's lifeline. Instead, it just hovered where we'd left it, pacing the *Trailblazer* with aplomb.

Vent it, I must have fucked up something again.

"I'm sorry," I blurted out to him.

"About what?" Case's brow was furrowed with concern as he stared at the drone.

"I must've screwed up something while I was checking the drones for damage." My howlsuit squeaked in protest as I squeezed its thick insulating sleeves against my chest.

"If this is you fucking up, it's pretty impressive." Case chuckled. "They're strung out behind us in a straight line for a quarter of a kilometer. This is weird and the last time I found a drone acting weird, well, Deepa said they attacked her…"

"Mmm," I replied without really hearing him. I was busy trying to shake self-deprecating thoughts out of my head. I shouldn't have assumed this was my fault. In a way, that was megalomaniacal thinking. Instead, I should be working to find a solution.

The *Trailblazer's* stern camera feeds melted into my vision as I telepathically merged my sight with theirs. The drones had, indeed, formed a single-file procession behind the *Trailblazer*.

I reached out to the Spiderfly telepathically.

<hello;> I sent the first half of the usual mental handshake to it. And before I could even give my identificators, it interrupted.

<unauthorized user;>

I frowned and continued anyway.

<*i am:*
entity(meera);
intelligence(human);

class(neuroengineer);
what is wrong with you?;>
<*unauthorized user;>* it repeated. That was unexpected. My class credentials were valid, stamped into my brain for all to verify.

I stretched my mind out to the next drone in the line. The moment I thought about accessing its systems, its signal vanished. It felt like my brain had tried to step erroneously onto a nonexistent stair. That sense of abrupt vertigo persisted as I reached for the third.

And by the time I thought of doing that, there wasn't even a signal from the third onto which to latch. Looking out through the *Trailblazer's* cameras, I could see the third drone in the procession, and the fourth, and so on. Physically, they were present but the signals that I could detect mentally had altogether vanished.

<*case, something's wrong with them,>* I broadcast.

I stared at him, waiting for him to respond. Then, I remembered he couldn't hear me at all. He didn't have the sensors for it, the equipment, the brain.

"Case, can you come back up here?" I said, shouting over the whirring of drone blades and the thrum and crash of the *Trailblazer's* engines.

<*matyom i need help with the drones. they're not responding to me and i think i—im not sure what is going on.>*

Matyom's upbeat words didn't match his emotional imprint. <*I'll Be Down As Soon As I Can Meera! The Driver's Been Unreasonable All Day And I've Been Piloting The Trailblazer Myself For Quite Some Time! Maybe Fei Or Lakshmi Can Help You?>*

Immediately putting Lakshmi at the end of the list, I pulled Fei's frequency from the sea of information available to all of us, save for Case, and contacted her.

<*fei?*> I reached out to her tentatively, unsure of how she'd act, and a little annoyed that it mattered to me in this moment.

<*what?*> Her response was clipped, minimalist. I couldn't feel anything from her but the faintest trace of impatience. It was like talking to AVA, almost.

<*i'm getting an error from the drones: "unauthorized user;",*> I replied.

<*strange;*
entity(trailblazer);
error = same;
entity(fei) will pursue this;>

Fei's broadcast came with a flash of dissociative knowledge. Suddenly, I knew where she was, the exact errors the *Trailblazer* had thrown, and a dozen other small details about the drones.

I closed our connection abruptly, more than a little overwhelmed. Communicating with Fei *was* remarkably similar to speaking with AVA: from her coded thoughts that threatened to actually execute systems in my brain to the sheer volume of data she shared all at once. I marveled at what her circuitry might be like, perhaps some hybrid of human-like and AI-like architectures. Did it extend to her organic neurons?

In the fraction of a second I'd spent broadcasting, Case hadn't begun to move. I raised my voice. "Case! It's not safe down there!"

The *Trailblazer* crashed through a fat puddle of transparent organic liquid, bouncing the short Titanborn almost off his feet. He staggered forward and swung his arms around one of the telescoping rods that held the gangway open as he tenaciously reached toward the aberrant Spiderfly despite the peril.

I wanted to grab him and pull him to safety, but fear rooted me to the spot. I begged my legs to move but, instead of acting, I just chastised myself for not moving. I warred with that fear. *Why can't I just be calm and help him?!*

Case thankfully gave up his pursuit of the drone. He leaned backward, his fingers brushing against a violet-capped lever. He yanked it downward, and it refused to budge. "It's still jammed, vent it. Meera! Close the blasted gangway!"

The *Trailblazer* began to climb and, suddenly, gravity was pushing us toward the gangway's debris-filled maw. I began to fall toward Case. "On it! Keep holding on, Case!" I shouted.

I reached out telepathically to the gangway. Its reply made my heart catch in my throat.

<unauthorized user;>

<matyom fei lakshmi i need—close the gangway!> I broadcast publicly in a sheer panic.

The eight-bladed Spiderfly slipped inside and past Case, its rotors flinging orange-speckled organic matter onto my suit. The darkness of Titan's dimly lit surface slid away as the gangway, thankfully, began to close.

<Gotchu, Meera. ;)> Lakshmi replied. <Buuut why haven't the drones left for the Waystation? :/>

I felt a familiar pang of fear but, no, I needed to know the answer to that same question more than I needed to avoid her potential lambasting of my performance. <i dont know,> I replied honestly.

The walls hissed as breathable air poured into the room and Titan's frigid, nitrogenous atmosphere was forced out. The copter drone hovered between Case and me. Its sensors shifted until it was watching both of us simultaneously from myriad tiny lenses. I could see it, but telepathically, it was invisible.

"Turn the blasted thing off, Meera," Case barked. The drone whirled about, its front pair of blades blurring into white haloes as its sensors shifted to focus on me. Its blades were a meter from my face. "I don't like this. It shouldn't be acting this way."

"I can't reach it. Its signal is gone," I said, leaning away from it.

"Hah! So much for cybernetics. I'll turn it off." He ducked beneath it and reached up at its tiny plastic body. It abruptly flipped sideways and drove its rotors into the top of his hand. The spinning plastic cut into his glove, sending alabaster insulation, smoky blue aerogel, and crimson blood upward to squish and splatter against the ceiling.

Case sprang back with a pained shout and the drone, in turn, flung itself after him.

"Shit!" he yelped as he fell flat on his back. The eight-bladed drone narrowly missed his helmet and slammed against the blue-lined triangles above the gangway. Its two front blades dug deep into the *Trailblazer's* corrugated hull. Its free blades spun faster and faster until their thrum began to outmatch the engines. It lurched toward us and the hull buckled around it, pinching it in place.

I ran to Case's side as the drone's blades began to warp beneath the heat and stress of sustaining their unsafe speeds. They began melting into limp plastic and dripped onto the floor.

"Ok." Case's unlit eyes were wide, his voice shocked and serious. The walls hissed as more oxygen poured into the small engine deck. The Spiderfly's blades, now misshapen and warped, crunched and broke against their housing. Freed bearings were flung wide, pinging off the floor.

"It's not supposed to do that." Case laughed nervously.

"Is your hand ok?" I asked. We were fortunate that he hadn't been attacked with the gangway open. I swallowed. My mouth suddenly felt dry, as this tangible reminder of Jula's death set in.

"Fuck if I know," he grumbled. The oxygen light on his suit's chest had turned bright green. "Suit's compromised though."

The Spiderfly groaned one last time and went silent, leaving us alone with the hum of the engines and hiss of life-giving oxygen.

I flung the keyword "first aid" out to the myriad devices in the engine room. The first aid kit's transponder waved back telepathically. By the time I returned to Case's side with the kit in hand, nascent threads of aerogel and carbon fiber were already poking from the frayed interior layers of the gash in Case's suit. His hand continued to bleed beneath it.

As I popped the cherry-red kit open and focused my attention on Case's wound, instructions poured into my vision. I wasn't well-trained in first aid, but I could learn on my feet from the kit itself.

"You heal so slowly," I said, unthinking, as the kit's computer puzzled over why the cut it saw in my vision was not already scabbing over with the help of synthetic nanomechanical cells.

"Meera," Case said angrily, "don't."

"Ah, sorry, umm, the kit's instructions don't cover naturals. I'll... here."

The principles were the same, though. First, check for necrotic tissue. The kit flooded my senses with the complete sensation of blackened flesh with a horrific smell that made me gag. I swiped that knowledge away. There was little sign of the telltale blackening that accompanied frostbite, and worse. Case was lucky, in a sense. A breach like this could've meant the loss of his hand if we hadn't gotten the heat back before the drone had struck him.

Apply an antibacterial, wash, bandage. Then over that went a yellow foam that began to bubble the moment it hit Case's gray skin. Carefully applied heat.

I hesitated as the wound closed. He was gray, just like me. He was vatborn, too. But he lacked my prosthetic eyes and my implanted machinery. Had he been given genetic enhancements, at least? He had the same anomalous skin pigmentation all Titanborn shared, so maybe? Why hadn't I been taught more about Case and the naturals? They were Titanborn. Why were they made so different?

I wanted to ask him, but no, later. Now was a bad time.

He winced, cradling his arm as he sat on the tessellated floor. "Fuck, that's hot."

A bad time.

"I think it's going to heal fine," I said, lifting my hands from his. "Might not even scar."

I poked at the first aid kit's tiny computer one last time and, with new knowledge, added with confidence, "It won't scar."

"Thanks," he muttered. Air whistled between Case's clenched teeth as he sat on the floor. He ran a hand over his gray face, flattening a few hairs that had come loose from his small black ponytail. "That was stupid of me, getting so close. Deepa and Alburn warned us. They were right. Stupid."

The ladder shaft seal popped open as the hissing of air pumps sputtered to silence.

Fei landed before the ladder. She jabbed a finger silently at the drone, her digitized face the picture of worry. Lakshmi's gunmetal gray prosthetics crept about the circular shaft, hooking onto its edges as they lowered her neatly onto the floor. The pair dashed over to the downed drone.

<*be careful!*> I warned them. <*it just cut case with its blades!*> I broadcast the visual memory of its attack their way.

<*Warning received, Meera. I don't think it'll be doing any more harm. :)*> Lakshmi replied. Her prosthetic hands gripped the drone's melted, mangled rotors and, with inhuman strength, she tore its body from the wall. Lakshmi raised a black heeled boot over it, clearly ready to crush the drone.

Fei knelt in front of it. Some unheard communication passed between them. Lakshmi hesitated, then stepped away from the drone as Fei plucked its shattered body from the floor.

"Care to include me in the conversation?" Case barked with his usual bitterness.

Fei turned her back to him and hefted the broken drone. Without a word, she climbed back up while Lakshmi idly picked the shards of the drone off her prosthetics.

"Lakshmi." Case's body sagged forward. "What is going on?"

An artificial finger tugged at a lock of Lakshmi's messy black hair, plucking another piece of drone debris away. "We're having some system malfunctions. AVA's last patch was delivered too hastily and now we're paying for it."

"What?" I replied in disbelief. This was unlike any systems issues I'd ever seen. AVA had made bad decisions before, but what had just happened amounted to attempted homicide.

<*lakshmi this doesn't feel right.*> I shared everything Case and I had just experienced with the hostile drone as well as my newfound knowledge about Torvram's disappearance.

I helped Case onto his feet in slow-motion as our telepathic conversation outpaced my actions. <*I appreciate the extra evidence, Meera. I'll make sure this is fixed asap.* :)>

<*lakshmi i get that you think something is wrong with ava... i do too. but how are you so certain? do you have evidence to show me? i want to know more.*> I avoided her gaze while I checked his hand one more time. Case was beginning to say something, his mouth opening as his brows furrowed.

<*Meera, your concern is valid, but leave these big picture concerns to Fei and I! Fei has worked directly on AVA's systems her whole life, and I'm no stranger to the ins and outs of keeping our electronic guardian functional either. We know what we're doing and we've got this. I need you focused on getting all of our eyes on Aztlan Waystation and Torvram, ok?* :)>

Her cerulean eyes darted to mine with impossible speed for the briefest of milliseconds. I held my ground as we stood on either side of Case in the intimate, claustrophobic engine room. How did she know for sure? Why was Lakshmi being evasive? How was I supposed to just *fix* these things when I didn't know what was wrong with them?

"Hey!" Case shouted.

"What?" Lakshmi said, chuckling.

"Can you include me in the conversation while I'm here?" he growled.

"Sure. Patch your suit and get ready to disembark. We'll arrive at Aztlan waystation in an hour." Lakshmi smiled and turned away.

He ignored her orders, instead glaring at the angular woman's back. "Fei took the blasted killer drone? Why? Deepa says a Dragonfly drone attacked her and Alburn and now this... What do you know?"

"Don't worry about it, Case." She flipped the sagging collar of her jacket up against her back with two of her auxiliary arms and waved. "Get back to work!"

"I'm not invisible, vent it," he muttered, barely loud enough for me to hear.

Lakshmi leapt up to the operations deck without another word.

"Fuck!" He banged his good hand against the wall.

"Case, come on," I beseeched him.

"Come on what?" He turned to me, and I instinctively recoiled at his fiery expression. "Fuck, I—I'm sorry, chiphead, I mean, Meera."

My cheeks flushed. "Can we just get back to work?"

"Ugh." He rubbed at the smoky suit scar forming around the breach. "I hate the way she treats me."

"If it helps, she treats everyone like that," I replied.

"Why does she get to be like that?" He threw his hands into the air as he began to pop open storage beneath the workbench. "Even my friends tell me to 'be nicer' but the people that hate Lakshmi won't check her for being garbage."

"Because she's good at her job."

"Why do you defend her? She treats you like shit too." Case's voice cracked.

"I... I don't think I am. I mean, that's the excuse, right? Survival here is paramount, so if you're perceived as someone who carries more than just your weight, you're given leeway. She's helping us find Torvram, too, so it's not like Lakshmi doesn't care in her own way." I'd been grappling with this for years. I didn't like her, but without her, would I even be here?

"You've been gaslit from here to Earth, Meera." Case stumbled over to the remains of the drone and crouched beside it, inspecting the melted blades. "You need to stop letting her treat you like this. *I* need to stop putting up with this from all of the ch—from the Titanborn who don't give a shit about me. People like her only get away with pushing us around when we give them the power to abuse us."

"Sorta, I mean, she could just be better rather than put the impetus on us to check her, but I understand what you mean," I replied, staring at my hands. He sounded an awful bit like Torvram had a week ago, the last night I'd seen our missing friend. "But how? I mean, she... how do we stand up to someone like Lakshmi?"

"Good question," he scoffed. "Fuck if I know."

I sat down on the floor beside him as he picked at the few drone pieces they'd left behind, inspecting one particularly mangled blade. "Have you tried, before? I mean, fighting back against her?"

Case shrugged. "I tried to get Chetan to augment me and the other naturals when I was ten. Started a petition, got all but two of our signatures. He wouldn't listen. Said we had an 'important role' to play and that was that. Cut me off in the second line of my speech." His tone rose and weakened and his head sank farther toward his crossed legs. "Now, most of us are dead."

"Why would Earth make us like this? It's not fair to you," I said, full of conviction.

"Why did Lakshmi get preferential treatment from Chetan as a child? Why does she treat us like pawns?" Case sighed and rose from the floor. "Nothing's fair on Titan, Meera. But we have to work to survive. She pulls her weight plus some, so she gets more. Right?"

"That's bullshit," I replied, borrowing one of his Earth-isms. I didn't want to just survive anymore. I didn't want that to be my life, our lives.

Case's sarcastic mien was returning. There was something else there, too, a spark of genuine enthusiasm I hadn't seen before. "It is! So what are we gonna do about it, chiphead?"

My hands were shaking, but I said it anyway. "I, no, *we* need to stand up to Lakshmi. Torv and I should've done that a long time ago. Something's not right here and if she knows something, anything, about what's going on, we should d-demand she t-tell us." I started to sweat, to stammer, but I glared at the ladder resolutely and stood up to my own internal fear. I probably looked like an idiot.

That was ok.

We'd been attacked. If we were all going to make it back alive with Torvram, then Case and I needed to know everything: no more "protection" and no more lies from anyone.

Case was all smiles. "Shouting at Lakshmi? That sounds like a good time. I'm game."

CHAPTER 09

WEATHER ADVISORY

MEERA; COCKPIT/NAVIGATION DECK, *TRAILBLAZER*

I leapt up to the top floor, sailing meters upward in Titan's low gravity.

The *Trailblazer* rolled over one last mound of organic muck and groaned into silence and stillness. As I reached the cockpit, I heard the engines beneath me breathe one last sigh of exertion and go quiet. We were as close as we could get to Aztlan Waystation. Within that nearby structure, Torvram's lifeline continued to beat a slow, steady pulse.

The cockpit was designed for equipment first, humans second. Fei and Lakshmi crouched beside one origami wall. A spider web of wires connected Fei's howlsuit to half a dozen components of the *Trailblazer*.

Matyom leaned against a pillar of electronics at the center of the cockpit, from which many of Fei's connections originated. His fauxhawk of blond hair scraped against the low ceiling. A plastic-covered chair had been bolted to the floor beside the pillar. Cushions were haphazardly taped onto its surface.

I turned to Lakshmi and hesitated. I wasn't sure if that was me conceding to my fear of her or legitimate tact, but here we were. Torvram was so close. I ducked beneath the low ceiling and hanging wires and half-crawled to Matyom's side.

He had been rigged into the *Trailblazer* for hours. For some reason, its systems had wanted to go anywhere but Aztlan Waystation and he'd had to force it—looking through its own "eyes," pushing its treads forward like they were his own legs—to keep it from turning back. I hoped hearing my voice aloud would help ground him, bring Matyom back into his own body.

"You ok?" I asked him.

The stocky man stared at his hands with a momentary expression of dissociative disbelief as he disconnected. He stroked Feyn idly as the dog stared up at him and produced a rough interpretation of a dog's whine.

<🐕 *Are you unhappy, sir?* 🐕> Feyn broadcast publicly.

"I'm fine." He rolled his shoulders and I watched as his face worked until the proud, confident Matyom returned to his mustachioed face. "Now that we're here."

"Vent it," Lakshmi hissed from beside Fei.

I turned to them again and watched their body language as they carried on another private conversation.

"Anything wrong?" Matyom inquired.

<*The Trailblazer is still trying to drive away.* :/> Lakshmi's broadcast was searing with impatience, hot anger making it almost difficult to let her in. <*Fei is going to stay here and keep it from abandoning us. I trust that she can solve the problem before we return with Torvram though.*>

"Hey!" Case shouted from the operations deck. "You all are going to want to see this!"

"We should go," I added, resisting the urge to avoid Lakshmi's gaze again.

"Yes!" Matyom staggered into a crawl before dropping down the ladder. "We're coming to get you, honeysuckle!"

<—*Weather Advisory: External conditions are unsafe. Please return to Shangri-La or take shelter in a nearby Waystation. This message will now repeat.*> AVA's warning sounded through our ears and crackled through our suit radios simultaneously. <*Severe Weather Advisory*—>

"Fuck me, that is *creepy*." Case's voice superseded AVA's as he stood in the *Trailblazer's* high-beams.

The disobedient copter drones we'd released and commanded to search Aztlan Waystation had instead formed a hemispherical cage about the *Trailblazer's* trapezoidal body. Some were harshly lit by the *Trailblazer's* floodlights and others visible only by the small crimson pinpoint sensors on their bodies. Their sensors whirred and swiveled; they watched the vehicle from every angle. As far as we knew, they were watching us too.

<*for the drones;*
entity(trailblazer);
fix = same;
disabled movement of drones;> Fei broadcast with a hint of pride.

<*entity(ava) & I;*
working on a temporary solution to:
"unauthorized user;";>

<*Excellent work!* :D> Lakshmi replied, staring at the drone lattice with her gloved hands on her hips. The rest of us stood tense, poised to strike at the drones.

<*thank you!;*> A thin stream of giddy happiness trickled through Fei's usually indifferent emotional broadcast. She reacted to Lakshmi more than anyone or anything else.

Each of our suits' headlights struck a sheer wall of gold-tinted methane rain in all directions. The quartet of violet lights on Case's suit winked at me as I spun about, taking in the dimly lit world outside of the *Trailblazer*. We were safe, for now.

The Aztlan Waystation was close but through the blinding rain only its geographical tag showed: a violet outline with a half-kilometer distance floating above it. Torvram's lifeline sat within that geotag, a red pulsing pin. I switched to infrared and Aztlan's cylindrical bulk, to my surprise, barely resolved as a pale gray blob in a dark gray world. The airlock entrance, at least, should've been warm enough to distinguish from Titan's cold.

"Keep one hand on your rope and listen to Case and me," Matyom explained as he hooked a length of rope and insulated electronic cable about his worn howlsuit's waist. "Look with visual wavelengths. I know there's a temptation to look through the fog and rain, but the real danger is in rolling your ankle on a pothole or falling into a deep puddle. Infrared will often obscure those surface features."

I brought my eyes back to visual as Case helped Matyom to heft a considerable pack over his back. Its bulk suddenly leapt out of Case's hands, drawn in by magnets.

I snapped a small rigid pack of my own to my back: rations, water, and spare O_2 bags. We came prepared, so that we didn't need another rescue expedition to save *us*. I stumbled as the pack's weight hit me with unexpected force. Matyom caught me before it knocked me onto the ground completely.

"Thanks," I said, sheepishly.

"Everyone falls the first time," the stocky, crimson-eyed man replied with a knowing smile.

Case tapped his palm against his suit light—a sign of encouragement—and threw a less supportive and more awkward smile my way. His botched gesture brought even more of a grin to my face.

"Where's our radar?" Lakshmi asked with grimace and then immediately answered her own question, jabbing two hands at our vehicle. "Right. Fei, make sure you fix the radar ASAP."

<of course, ma'am!;> Fei replied publicly.

Matyom stood tall at the front of our procession with Case's diminutive frame at the rear—two experienced explorers on either side of the Shangri-La homebodies. My nerves were, thankfully, beginning to calm. Maybe all of this strange activity, the growing mystery surrounding Torvram's disappearance, was distracting the more anxiety prone parts of my brain. Maybe I was actually getting used to being outside. I wasn't sure.

The rain continued to fall in thick curtains, adding an impenetrable thickness to Titan's ubiquitous golden fog. Flecks of orange and sepia seemed to pop in randomly like errant floaters in my vision.

"Let's go!" Matyom bellowed heartily through our suit comms. Matyom was certainly part of that calming equation.

Aztlan's violet geotag suddenly blurred and vanished. It reappeared to my south, a kilometer away, implying that the Waystation itself had up and moved. More impossibly still, it began to speed across the ground, rushing through me and snapping to a halt four kilometers northwest. The structure itself couldn't move, which meant something was screwing with our data, Aztlan's signal, or both.

<*Fei?*> Lakshmi broadcast. <*More problems!* :(>

My ears filled with static. My hands instinctively shot to them and smacked the sides of my helmet instead. Something clawed abrasively at my brain and alarm bells went off in my chipsets, warning me of a kaleidoscope of errors beginning to propagate across the organic and inorganic parts of my mind. Systems fought back, electronic equivalents to my organic immune system diagnosed and quarantined. Nevertheless, I felt it beginning to numb my senses, slowing my movements and insidiously inserting itself between my brain and my spine in electrochemical form.

<*Go offline—;*> Fei's telepathic voice resolved briefly through the noise. <*Use the radio!;*> It wasn't just a voice. She was throwing coded commands at my brain.

I squinted through the pain at Case, spinning around so my helmet-mounted suit lights could catch his face. He looked confused and concerned. I watched his mouth move, but no sound came out.

Then, through my radio, I heard him. "What the fuck is happening? Is it your mental shit?" Case shouted.

The geotag continued to hop and skip about the world before us. Subtle user interface elements in my peripheral vision distorted, vanished, or were replaced with brightly-colored error messages.

I closed off my own neural connection to the outside world. The glitching geotag disappeared as I went offline. Torvram's lifeline, that violet beacon that'd led us all this way, vanished. Only my peers' howlsuits remained digitally visible, through the wired connection buried in our ropes.

"Go offline!" I implored them via radio.

"Fei?" Lakshmi's voice crackled over the suit radio. She was barely visible ahead of me.

"Another local problem, ma'am!" Fei replied. "This is fascinating. I mean, I hope you all are ok out there! I've never seen broadcast interference or neuroelectronic infection like this before, it's—"

"Fei, I appreciate your enthusiasm, but I need you to keep this channel clear of speculation, please," Matyom replied over the radio, his strong tone wavering. "Get in touch with Shangri-La and AVA. Keep us apprised of any developments, especially a fix to get us back online."

"You three ok back there? Sound off!" Matyom's suit lights swung around from far ahead of us. They were all that penetrated the thick smog now. His suit's outline highlighted just a human-sized chunk of the air.

We replied with a chorus of affirmatives. Lakshmi's eyes flickered between cerulean and the telltale gray of infrared vision, likely peering through the rain and golden smog behind us.

"Let's move forward then! Onward!" Matyom bellowed so loudly I faintly heard his voice over the rain, too.

By the time I got my legs moving again, my cable to Case was loose with slack. He emerged from the rain behind me.

"You ok?" the hazel-eyed natural asked, just loud enough to be heard off the radio.

"Yeah. Yeah. That was disturbing but... I'm ok," I replied, swallowing. I gripped my cable to Lakshmi tightly. The thought of a quick, cold death was on my mind once again. But I had to rise above my fear. I took one step, then another, and moved forward with Case at my side. His presence, too, was a balm to my nerves.

The *Trailblazer's* headlights faded behind the wall of stormy weather.

"If you fall, say something," Matyom continued from beyond a wall of fog, equally commanding and comforting over the radio. "If you feel numb, say something *immediately*. Keep your eyes on the ground ahead of you and speak up the moment anything is wrong."

Why couldn't Lakshmi be more like him? His role was smaller, sure, but equally important, possibly more stressful than hers. And unlike Lakshmi, he cared for his people and never seemed to let his emotional state adversely affect us. Matyom made sure that we knew he was here for us, even when he had every right to be negative, stressed, and maudlin.

Torvram was a lucky guy.

Matyom led us along a loose trail of black pads, half-obscured by organic muck. I felt them subtly vibrate the soles of my boots. Methane boiled off of the pads as thick, white jet streams appearing to open wide, moaning mouths before dispersing. My boots sank into speckled paddies of orange and rust-colored mud. It gummed up the soles, squelching with each step, foreign in color and texture to the organics in the Shangri-La region.

<one pulse.> I spoke privately through the bundle of wiring plugged into my upper back, connecting my brain to the howlsuit that preserved my life.

A millisecond burst of heat shot through the exterior of my boots, much like the pulses vibrating through the pads. A small shower of evaporated organics leapt from my ankles.

A deep blue light emerged from the fog, outshining Titan's aggressive weather. As I approached it, my cable went slack and I found the others, bunched up around the light that stood nearly three meters above us.

"How's your hand?" I asked Case.

"Seal's good." Case smiled, giving me a thumbs up. "Thanks, chip—Meera."

Matyom gestured toward nothing but more rain. "We're not far now. Sotra Patera and Doom Mons are right beside the Waystation. The flows from the cryovolcanoes can be rocky or even waxy, so be careful."

I flashed on my IR, and a tall, shattered peak emerged behind Aztlan Waystation.

Lakshmi mimicked Matyom's gesture with a free hand, scanning the landscape. "Mount Doom, huh? I don't see any orcs."

"Orcs?" I replied. Lakshmi read *Lord of the Rings*? Really?

Case groaned. "You are such a dork, Lakshmi."

"Shush you," Lakshmi replied.

As the rain abetted, the ring of visibility about us widened. "Onward, to Mordor!" Matyom said with a jocular cry.

And Matyom too? What in Saturn was going on?!

This levity was sorely needed though. As we trudged on, I kept talking as Matyom had advised, forcing us to be heard in this dim, uninterested world.

"I had no idea I was surrounded by fantasy fans," I queried Matyom.

"Nothing more inspiring than a classic tale of exploration, comradery, and survival. I will admit, though don't tell Torvram this, that I think *The Hobbit* is better."

Case cut in, "Fuck off, it is *not*."

Ok, Case did too. And I thought I was the only one who liked Earth fantasy. I made a mental note to share my hobbies more, at least with Case and Matyom. With Lakshmi, well, that didn't seem like a good idea.

"I'm entitled to my opinion as much as you are, Case," Matyom replied, his voice effectively disembodied. The curtain of rain had completely swallowed him up once more.

"I like both of them," I added. "Though I think I lean more toward the trilogy."

"Pleeease tell me you've seen *The Hobbit* movies," Lakshmi added snarkily. "They're so bad, and I need someone to share that pain with me."

"I thought *An Unexpected Journey* was powerful stuff!" Matyom shot back. The rain waxed and waned but never truly let up. It poured down my helmet, seeping into every fold, dripping down my legs. My suit's violet lights were a powerful comfort. Everything was ok, somehow. We were almost there.

"Really? Come ooon, really?" I could practically hear Lakshmi rolling her eyes somewhere ahead, near the front of the line.

"Both of you are such curmudgeons." Matyom laughed. "These are works of art. I'm entitled to my opinion!" He sounded in high spirits, as always. That made me smile.

"There's this, uhh, video I found before we went into full isolation," I chimed in. "That makes *The Hobbit* trilogy a lot more watchable. It's like a compilation of all the ridiculous stuff Legolas did, set to goofy EDM. It's really funny."

"The Legolas Kill Count!" Lakshmi replied excitedly, clapping her gloved hands together. "That channel made another amazing series parodying the, uhh, fuck what were those movies called… it's this sci-fi franchise that I swear the *Trailblazer's* design was ripped from. They called it a sandwalker, I think? Or skycrawler—"

"Ahh!" Case yelped.

I felt Case's line go taut. It nearly threw me onto my back and into Titan's organic tar.

"Lakshmi, I need some slack!" I shouted, turning around and cautiously moving backward, mindful of the treacherous ground. There were slippery, waxy strips of what looked like frozen bubbles and hydrocarbons frozen mid-flow down the mountains that descended from the wall of fog and rain.

"Breached?" I asked automatically as I reached his side. "Do we need the repair kit?" The suits were well-built, resilient, self-healing to some degree. None of that mattered though if a big enough scratch was made and they wouldn't heal fast enough to keep out the cold.

Case's quartet of suit lights cut through the fog: four vibrant violet ellipses. He exhaled powerfully, his breath briefly condensing onto the inside of his helmet. "Sensors are violet," Case replied. "No breach."

Lakshmi's line slackened as she reached us.

"Good. Here." She braced Case with her prosthetics and helped him off the ground.

For once, it wasn't an order. She was, in that moment, just another Titanborn helping to prevent another almost casual death due to Titan's lethal cold.

We checked his back together, brushing off orange tar and chunks of the cryovolcanic run-off that shattered at our touch.

My suit's headlights caught the numerous patches on Lakshmi's shoulders. Where I had two, Lakshmi had dozens. There were insignias for pioneering new or more efficient chemical syntheses, for expeditions to the far reaches of Titan like Matyom's, and for the sealing of disastrous breaches in Shangri-La's bulkheads.

There was even one crudely-drawn, button-sized patch close to her chest with the name "Farah" on it and a small rainbow pride flag. Farah's name had been crossed out in permanent marker, practically covered in black ink, but the methane rain was making short work of the graffiti.

"No breaches," I said.

"No breaches," Lakshmi echoed, smiling that toothy grin as her cerulean eyes flared. "So much for master explorer, ehh, Case?"

"Shut up," Case replied in a huff.

"Don't be mean, Lakshmi," I interjected without thinking. "It's good you're ok, Case."

I froze up as Lakshmi stared at me and then Case. She was, to my surprise, smiling. "Let's keep moving." Lakshmi's grin only widened. I wasn't sure what to make of that.

"You three need me back there? Everything ok?" Matyom called out over the suit radio.

"We're all ok!" I answered him.

Aztlan emerged from the unending deluge of methane rain: a stocky cylindrical structure. Hexagonal pipes wound from its sides, tangled about one another, stretching their way up and into the sides of the twin cryovolcanoes. The Waystation's entrance rested in a small crater created when it had parachuted to the ground years ago, dropped from orbit before I'd been born. The Waystation's floodlights were dead and I, switching to IR one more time, confirmed that it was cold too.

"Strange," Matyom remarked. "The lights are always on..."

As we approached the entrance—an airlock door of heavy, foreign metal—I scanned the ground around us for signs of Torvram. We'd last seen Torvram's lifeline deep beneath this structure. But there were no footprints, no signs of a vehicle or person, just some scattered debris.

"These are... drone parts." Case hesitated on the last two words.

"Did Torvram get attacked too?" I wondered aloud.

Lakshmi wheeled about, putting her back to the station. "We should get inside. Now." Her eyes flashed gray, and she lowered her stance. Her second command was a shout. "Now!"

Their heat signatures were unmistakable. Three copter drones were descending through the maelstrom toward us. Despite her commands, we weren't going to be able to get inside in time. The drones descended to eye level between us and the Waystation.

"Fei. Any progress?" Lakshmi barked over the radio, eyeing the drones cautiously. They hadn't moved to attack yet. They just hung there, staring in eerie silence.

"Yes, Lakshmi!" Fei replied breathlessly. "AVA has no records of any of these erratic behaviors. I can only conclude that it is not responsible for the drone glitches or the *Trailblazer's* behavior or... oww! Feyn, stop! Down, boy!"

"He's got an off-switch on his belly, Fei!" Matyom interjected as he shoved Case and I behind him, staring up at the incoming drones.

"Ok, nice talk, but what the fuck do we do about these drones, chipheads?" Case shouted. He hastily tossed one of his packs into the wet sludge and retrieved a hook-nosed rod that he brandished threateningly in both hands.

"Sure, Fei," Lakshmi continued impatiently, ignoring Case. Her prosthetics began to coil and crawl their way up, displacing her packs as they slithered to life. "Ignoring the unlikely possibility that this isn't a behavioral malfunction of AVA's, can you stop them?"

"I mean, it's not that unlikely," Fei protested. "You've made great strides in simultaneous operations of machines by human minds. I—"

"Fei! Focus!" Lakshmi shouted. "Can you stop these drones?"

"I—Lakshmi, I haven't been able to yet but I'm going to keep trying, ok? Just, please be safe, all of you. AVA and I are testing some code changes we'll push as soon as they work." Fei's response was a rapid rush of words. "The problem is that none of these symptoms are manifesting at Shangri-La so it's hard to—"

"Ok, fine, fine, just tell us when you have a blasted fix," Lakshmi replied

I unclipped the bag from my back. If we had to fight back, at least I'd have a bludgeon to swing that wasn't part of my suit. I looked across the rough organic ground at the quadcopter drones hovering and observing us in silence.

"Ok, what's the plan here?" Case moaned, his eyes wide and staring at the potential threat as well. The memory of his wound was still fresh in my mind.

"Meera, try the door.." Lakshmi moved to screen her face and chest. Methane poured down her sides, running along the forearms to fall like streams down each finger onto the next prosthetic.

"Why—?" I began.

"You're the least armed of us,. We'll fight them off while you cycle the airlock manually," Lakshmi interjected as quick as a neuron firing.

Matyom was hastily extending one of the telescoping beacons from his pack, until it stood taller than even he was. He brandished the bright blue light at its tip, testing its weight experimentally.

"T-then protect me," I stuttered, staring nervously at the drones between us and Torvram.

"Let's encircle her and we can protect each other from every direction, even above," Case replied. "No sense letting her suit get breached alone, heh."

"Look at you, finally having a good idea." Lakshmi chuckled sarcastically as she placed her back in front of me.

"Shut it," Case shot back, standing behind me. A dim orange light at its tip, his plasma lance sparked and sputtered as it swallowed, compressed, and set Titan's air ablaze.

With Matyom and Lakshmi at my front and Case at my back, we inched toward the steel door between us and Aztlan's interior, and hopefully Torvram.

The three quadcopter Dragonfly drones sent orange and gold junk flying in all directions. They hovered stoically as we approached, still between us and the door. From here, Lakshmi and Matyom could almost touch them.

"I don't have time for this," Lakshmi hissed. Despite her words, she made no attempts to move toward the door. We'd all seen what one of their blades could do to a suit.

"Can you all just move out of the way?" Matyom beseeched the machines. "We need to get inside and save my boyfriend."

Case grimaced. "Reduced to pleading with drones, what a—"

The machines rushed forward without warning. Matyom swung the beacon wide, hitting one of the drones hard enough to shatter its hardened plastic center, revealing the circuitry and moving parts within. He flung it skyward with the powerful swing, grunting with exertion.

Lakshmi stood her ground and caught the second in two of her prosthetic hands. The overclocked rotors cut into her prosthetic, slicing into the hand and wrist and nearly severing three fingers before it finally burst into a shower of debris. The damaged prosthetic arm went abruptly limp and she bit hard into her lip, falling to one knee, and choking back a pained cry.

The third flew through the gap she'd made. My eyes went wide as Matyom, just recovering from his swing, failed to react in time. Lakshmi's starboard arms stretched and went taut as it passed just out of her range. As the drone widened in my vision, I ducked and swung my pack forward. It smashed through my rigid pack, sending plastic-wrapped rations tumbling to the ground, but the blow pushed it just shy of my helmet.

"Case!" I shouted as the drone broke past me, spinning out of control. He dove to the ground and it sailed over his head, vanishing behind a curtain of rain.

I blotted out the visual world, going blind for an instant before my eyes acclimated to IR. The drone, though its signal was off, stood out as a crimson flame in the freezing Titan air.

To my dismay, there wasn't just one drone remaining behind the veil of rain and golden smog. There were seven more coming.

"The door!" I shouted, grabbing Case and the line that joined us together. I yanked him from the ground, straining against his weight.

Lakshmi struggled to rise. Tears poured down her face. The prosthetics must've been connected to her pain receptors. "Matyom—" She fought to speak.

Matyom lifted the tall woman off the ground without a word.

Case scrambled to his feet as the four of us reached the door. "No time to cycle the airlock. We'll just have to break the blasted thing open and—"

I dug my nails into the thick metal as Matyom dug the sharp end of the beacon into the door. The pressure was higher out here than inside by a mere .2 atmospheres. It wouldn't be easy to open, nor would it be safe to break, but between us, maybe we could do it.

I put all of my strength into pulling on the door and—
It opened without any of the expected resistance.
It wasn't pressurized at all.
That was both a stroke of luck and a bad sign.
"Inside!" Matyom bellowed so powerfully it clipped the radio's filters. He practically threw Lakshmi inside and shoved me in before I could finish another thought.

All of us pulled the heavy metal door shut, slamming down its latches. One of the drones crashed into the door, its impact reverberating through the walls.

Another hit, louder this time. Orange dust and metal rust shook from the vacant airlock cabinets.

And then, nothing.

Everything was quiet in Aztlan Waystation.

CHAPTER 10

AZTLAN WAYSTATION

MEERA; AIRLOCK, 0TH FLOOR, AZTLAN WAYSTATION
The airlock looked entirely alien. Metal benches, cold to the touch, appeared blood-red beneath emergency lights. Heaters coughed to life—spitting trails of burnt particulates into the air—before dying, bereft of power. There was no indication of oxygen circulating.

Something was very wrong.

Case collapsed onto a metal bench, his eyes wide. "What the fuck is going on?" he moaned. His helmeted head sagged between his arms. His voice, distorted and diminished by the hard plastic helmet, echoed back to us from the station depths. The interior door was half open and would not seal when we tried to close it.

"Is everyone ok? Suits unbreeched?" I asked, trying to inject a little of Matyom's invigorating enthusiasm into my voice.

Lakshmi winced, tugging at her broken prosthetic. It stood rigid, frozen in its last act of violence. Wires and synthetic muscle dripping with a black mixture of biological lubricant, micromachines, and plasma hung from its nearly severed upper arm. Lakshmi blinked back tears, mumbling curses under her breath.

"Do you need help?" I asked, timidly.

She grumbled something unintelligible and the broken prosthetic snapped sickeningly as it separated completely from her back. Fluid spat from the break, splashing onto the ground and staining the metal floor red, at least in this light.

Matyom stood at the threshold of the interior door. He stared into the red-soaked space beyond, his eyes blending with the emergency lights. "There are hundreds of bots maintaining this station. With the power off like this, it's possible they won't notice us but I can't..."

When Matyom turned back to face us, his expression wavered. For a brief moment, I saw the fear beneath that reassuring smile. "Just stay close, ok?"

I nodded in assent and encouragement. "Yeah."

The cracks were starting to show in Matyom, in me, in everyone.

"Fei?" Lakshmi hissed into the radio through clenched teeth, her impatience palpable. "We were attacked, again, and Aztlan's power is out. We don't have oxygen here. I need solutions. *Now.*" She threw her pack onto the ground and began to wedge the broken prosthetic into it.

Fei's sickly voice barely carried from Lakshmi's suit, despite the room being dead silent. She spoke rapidly, not pausing to take a breath. "My counterparts at Shangri-La and I have tried a number of tests attempting to reprogram and order the drones I have access to around me. I've been able to confirm that they aren't communicating with AVA. Ma'am, I know that you aren't convinced that AVA isn't the cause of their errant behavior, but I can assure you that I've run all—"

"Fei!" Lakshmi shouted hoarsely as the broken prosthetic resisted her attempts to fold it. "Ok, I don't want explanations. I need solutions. Solutions! How do we stop them?"

"You could jam them, theoretically. Of course, that is assuming they haven't been internally reprogrammed to act erratically. Umm, this doesn't appear to be a bug. They don't even have a tag for 'hostile' objects. I think, I don't—" Fei was practically hyperventilating over the radio.

Lakshmi opened her mouth and I knew, then, that what was coming next was not going to help us. Berating Fei wouldn't get us the answer we needed. Fei was nervous. I could hear it, feel it even.

"Wait." I held a hand out to stop the cerulean-eyed woman from speaking.

Lakshmi froze and the elbow joint of her broken prosthetic finally snapped. The crunch echoed back from the hallway beyond.

I turned on my radio and spoke slowly. "Fei. Take a breath. Breathe. We're safe right now. It's ok."

The masked woman a few kilometers away took a sharp, noisy breath over the radio.

I enunciated every word, exaggerating the effect of calm that I did not feel deep down. "Fei, is there a way we could stop the drones, like you did to the ones around the *Trailblazer*?"

"Not yet. I'm having to expend all of my significant concentration to keep the ones around me stable." She scoffed slightly. I resisted rolling my eyes. Fei went from panicked to smug rather quickly. "They keep changing their behavior, like someone else is intruding each time I look away."

"Then do you have an idea of who or what that someone is? Is this an order from AVA or a hack from someone?"

"It's not AVA," Fei replied breathlessly. "I assume it's a hack but it's not affecting anything near Shangri-La, which is weird. And who could possibly control this many drones at once? And why do it only out here? And how? No one's out here but our group and Torvram."

Lakshmi barked a laugh, staring at Matyom. "So, what, you're telling me Torvram is doing this?"

"That's not what I said but—" Fei began.

"If they aren't in Shangri-La, it's not AVA, they're near us, and this isn't you or one of the Titanborn standing in this room with me, then it has to be Torvram," Lakshmi replied.

"That's impossible." I fixed Lakshmi with a cold stare. She needed to shut her mouth, now.

"Yes, it is." Lakshmi nodded in agreement. "But then we have no suspects and no solutions."

"I'm sorry," Fei replied. The pride she'd regained when we spoke had been blown into a vacuum just as quickly by Lakshmi's words. "But that's all I know right now."

"Keep trying," Lakshmi said in frustration, nostrils flaring.

"Thanks, Fei," I added. "Keep working on it."

"Ok," Fei replied, again barely audible.

Lakshmi turned to the rest of us, her eyes painfully bright. "Alright, enough licking our wounds. Let's find Torvram and ask *him* what's going on."

"Let's move," Matyom said. He'd turned his eyes back to the endless hallway before us. It was populated only by long, angular shadows. We'd seen Torvram's lifeline somewhere beneath Aztlan Waystation.

"We're almost there," Matyom said, softly, clutching the lights over his chest. Matyom probably knew exactly where Torvram's last known location was. His jaw set, he unhooked himself from Lakshmi and swung open the interior airlock door, ducking to clear the threshold.

We unhooked ourselves from one another and followed in his wake. Our footfalls echoed off the walls, filling an otherwise silent Waystation. Our suit lights cut white circles out of the otherwise washed-out, red-tinted world.

There were no signs of life from the automated station. Why hadn't it informed us that main power was out?

We walked single file down corridors and stairs. The air in my suit was growing stale like burned plastic and body odor. The crimson-tinted hallways stretched on without end, each one as eerily yet thankfully empty as the last.

Pores and pipes lined the walls and in the shadow of each of them a drone or twenty could've been hiding. I flinched as my suit's headlight warped around one of the pores. But nothing was there: no gunmetal plastic and bright sensor eyes.

"I've never seen a Waystation like this," Matyom mused as he tore open the case of a massive breaker in an otherwise abandoned break room. Melted ice-water seeped out of the base of a refrigerator while a red emergency light spun about, sweeping crimson beams across the room in a silent warning. A pile of plastic cups sat half-dissolved in a now-inactive recycler.

Case busied himself at the breaker. "You're right. The storm recall shouldn't have left the Waystation empty."

The breakers echoed with heavy, staccato clicks as Case flipped each massive switch with both hands. Nothing changed.

"Mmm," Matyom replied noncommittally. "We need to find Torvram. His signal was beneath us."

Case shrugged. "You know these stations, Maty. What's down there? And how do we get there?"

Lakshmi and I stood to their side, two interlopers listening in on the banter between a seasoned explorer and his perhaps equally experienced mechanic.

"Extraction and storage of ice cores," Matyom replied, staring at the floor between his feet. He strained to keep his booming voice down, to keep it from echoing down the long corridors and into the ears of whatever might be lurking in the bloodshot shadows. "With the power out, we'll need to take the emergency stairs."

"Ugh, more stairs," Case replied, brushing a hand in silent frustration against the breaker door. "What could Torvram be doing in core storage?"

"Doesn't matter." Matyom tore his gaze from the floor. "We're going to bring him home."

Case turned away from the breaker, concern playing across his helmeted face. Leaving the obvious question of "how" unanswered, he placed a hand on Matyom's shoulder and squeezed. "Ok, Maty. We'll find him."

We left the small break room under the cover of near darkness.

Now at the rear, I battled against the impulse to look back. Long shadows dogged my every step. In some corridors, the emergency lights pulsed out and plunged everything around us into darkness for impossibly long moments. The metal, Earth-built walls of the prefab Waystation were heavy and rang out when we so much as bumped against their cold surfaces.

This was the longest I'd ever been cut off from AVA and the network of information and Titanborn voices that permeated Shangri-La. At home, I was never alone, for good or ill. My mind was quieter now than it had ever been. I was struggling to cope with that silence. Right now, my mind was plagued with fears: was Torvram dead in the ice or were our drones crawling out of the ductwork to tear us apart?

My steps quickened. I jogged up to Case and gingerly placed a hand on his shoulder. He tensed briefly before turning back to steal a glance at me. His eyes softened as our gazes met. He relaxed. I gripped his shoulder a little tighter, and we moved forward together.

We turned left, then right, then left two more times. We had to crawl as often as we walked now. Many of the corridors were not meant for humans. Infrared and ultraviolet paint formed arcane designs—coded mosaics of squares, dots, blobs, and triangles—that meant something to the service drones but nothing to me without AVA's database to translate.

We went down three, maybe four flights of narrow stairs and found a locked door. Matyom promptly slammed his shoulder into the door, shattering its frame. The sound echoed up the stairwell. We all froze for a moment, waiting for another attack.

Once again, nothing came.

Beyond the door was a t-intersection: two meter-sized drone pores and an inoperative cargo lift. An ice core in a large cylinder blocked one of the pores. The ice was mostly melted. Had the skeleton crew left in such a hurry before the storm that they hadn't even stored this properly? Or had they fled first from malfunctioning drones?

Or...

Were they dead?

But, no, we'd definitely know if any Titanborn had died. Same if they'd been attacked.

What had happened here?

The lift shaft stretched far above our heads, probably to Aztlan's top floor. Unfortunately, without power, we'd have to manually move the lift out of the way to descend.

Matyom gripped its sides and shook the lift in frustration. His typical reassuring demeanor was subtly, but gradually, fading. Matyom looked down again to where we'd last seen Torvram's signal.

Case placed a hand on Matyom's back. They spoke in soft whispers.

Lakshmi frowned. Her five remaining arms went slack. She leaned toward the ice core, mouth working. Her eyes darted from the core to the lift.

"Any idea how the ice core got here?" I asked her, trying to fill the silence with something, anything, that might calm my nerves.

Lakshmi shook her head. "Nope."

"I hope Torvram is ok," I added.

"Yeah." A long whoosh of breath left her lungs. Her hair was becoming increasingly unkempt, and a multitude of jet-black strands now hung over her face. She blew at one of them and was unable to push it out of her face.

"Yeah," Lakshmi repeated, nodding.

"We're almost there," Matyom said, rising from the lift. "This will be a story to tell everyone when we're back home!"

His smile was back. He was trying, but it was becoming painfully obvious that it was just that: he was *trying* to make us feel comfortable and safe. I appreciated the effort, but the strain was clearly getting to him. I wanted to help and didn't know how.

"Hmm," Lakshmi replied vaguely. Her eyes defocused. Her arms made simple gestures in the air, manipulating something that, I hoped, was only within her internal memory.

"So, where to next?" I asked. I wished I could help more, but I didn't have the Waystation's map saved in my memory. I should've thought to download it.

"I'm not sure," Matyom replied, frowning. The big man's posture was subtly deteriorating. His head listed toward the red-lit wall.

"We'll figure something out. Between the three chipheads and a tech-deaf mechanic, what can't we solve?" Case replied, significantly less sardonic than usual. He patted Matyom's arm again.

"We have to go downnn," Lakshmi muttered to no one in particular, her voice trailing off into inaudible mumbling as her eyes darted from one identical section of metal floor to another.

"What's she doing?" Case nodded Lakshmi's way.

"Probably accessing internal memory, projecting something into her vision," I replied, cracking a grin, trying to break the tension. "It's very... convenient? I hope she or Matyom stored the map."

A tiny smile tugged at Case's mouth. "Heh, ok, I'm a *little* jealous you all can do that."

"Look! He's being nice, like you said," I quipped to Matyom.

"Yeah." Matyom's bright smile returned. "Never would've thought I'd see the day when you actually listened to me, Case."

"Don't ever let them tell you that Case didn't stick his neck out for an augmented friend," Case made a show of dramatically pontificating, one finger pointed high into the air, "once in a while."

"Hey!" Lakshmi interrupted. "I've found our way down. It's... going to be a lot of stairs."

"Ugh!" Case groaned, continuing his exaggerated theatrics. "More stairs?"

"Lead on," Matyom replied, his voice lighter.

MEERA; EMERGENCY STAIRWELL, -16TH FLOOR, AZTLAN WAYSTATION

My legs were wobbling, and I gripped the inside railing of the staircase as we finally reached the lowest level of Aztlan Waystation.

Case was panting and shooting daggers from his eyes at the lift shaft we knew was just beyond the wall to our left. If it had worked, we would've saved what felt like endless time crawling through ductwork meant for machines and navigating stairs that'd probably never been used by the Aztlan staff while the power was on.

"Should've brought exoskeletons," Matyom muttered.

He leaned into a small metal door labeled with a simple plastic slate *Ice Core Storage* and caught his breath. He recovered significantly faster than we did.

"Ok." I steeled my mind for what we might find. Torvram had to be alive. His lifeline had been on, the mesh over his heart telling us it was still beating.

Matyom rose and shoved the door open, shoulder first. We followed him in.

"Torvram!" I called out. No one replied. Emergency lights cast discrete cones of red down from the high ceiling. The walls stretched out and onward until they met darkness.

Massive holes had been drilled into the walls, and within them sat cylindrical ice cores in various states of extrusion from Titan's depths. Two massive drills sat dormant, one half-buried and the other suspended from a gargantuan railing that ran along the whole ceiling.

Dozens, maybe hundreds, of ice core samples were sealed within fogged cylinders. A one-armed robot with a squat, square frame was frozen in the act of retrieving a sample.

As we got closer, I realized the robot had been savagely injured. The entirety of its lower arm had been torn off. It'd been ripped open from base to tip, its plastic frame shredded by some powerful force. What equipment was left in its body had spilled onto the floor, loose wiring and shattered circuits forming a tiny minefield of electronic debris.

We swept each row of cores as a team, calling Torvram's name, hoping he'd reply. No one responded.

My pulse began to quicken as I worried that we might've lost him in the short time we'd been offline, or worse. Where was Torvram?

An autonomous flatbed meant to carry cores along its top was sliced down the center. It sagged inward, its load-bearing spine having been ripped away. Crowded around an old set of computers was a trio of electronic towers missing their contents entirely. All that remained were power cables and even their male heads were removed: either cut, chewed, or torn off.

"Now, we have a machine cannibal," Case quipped as we walked between two racks of cores.

"I really, really hope he's here," I replied to Case in hushed tones, feeling incredibly anxious. "This is all my fault. I should've made sure he went to therapy. I knew he struggled with suicidal thoughts and depression and I should've been there instead of going back to work and—"

"Meera," Case whispered sharply. "I don't mean any offense here. None. Ok? But do you really think a Titanborn wandering out of Shangri-La and coming all the way out here is only about you?"

"Case..."

"Torvram had a lot of his own issues and, well," he shrugged, his hands shoved into two of the alabaster howlsuit's many utility pockets, "you probably did everything you could to help him. You came all the way out here, too, to find him. Don't blame yourself."

I felt a little of my fear ease. Case was kind, when he wanted to be.

But Case continued, "It's fucking *all* of our faults that he didn't get the help he needed."

"And here I was starting to think you were sweet, deep down, for a second there," I replied sarcastically, nevertheless feeling relieved.

Case grinned. "I'm more of an abrasive revolutionary than a sweet... guy."

"Pfft, sure."

I turned my back to Case, reinvigorated, and cast my gaze between two more rows of ice cores. Two glowing eyes stared back at me.

"What the—?!" I leapt back, crashing into Case. Those eyes were not Torvram's.

"Hello, Meera," their owner replied. His voice was even, cocky, and piercing. It was like hearing a male version of Lakshmi.

Staring at me was not Torvram, nor a Titanborn, but a very familiar android with dark brown skin.

Doctor C. N. Ramakrishnan—or Chetan to those close to him—stared me down as his android's feet clacked against the cold metal floor.

CHAPTER 11

A FATHER OF TITANBORN

LAKSHMI; ICE CORE STORAGE, -16TH FLOOR, AZTLAN WAYSTATION

Lakshmi stared at Chetan in complete disbelief. It'd been over a decade since she'd seen him. Shangri-La had gone into full isolation and Chetan had left her life. He couldn't be here, not even remotely. But here was Chetan's android, with his signature limp and his melanated "skin" and his all-too-knowing brown eyes.

Lakshmi's hope overpowered her rational knowledge. She took a step past Meera and Case—momentarily forgetting Torvram, forgetting everything.

"Dad?" Her voice echoed in the cavernous space.

Chetan couldn't be here unless...

Had the vote been rushed?

But no.

Even if the vote had passed and Earth had been called...

Even if the mission she had been born for and the dream Chetan had instilled into Lakshmi was dashed...

Even if every plan she had made up to this point was for nothing because Earth had sent a ship and the astronauts were once again rigging into their android bodies to bring aid across the light-minutes that separated Titan from Earth...

Even if all that were true...

Chetan couldn't be here.

This android that had been so much to Lakshmi—her mentor, her confidant, her father—beamed at her. "Lakshmi. It warms my heart to see you again."

"I—" Lakshmi stuttered uncharacteristically. "You... *can't* be here." Her voice shook with confusion and anxious hope.

But she wanted, so badly, for the doctor to be back. They could do so much more together. She would feel so much happier if Chetan was here.

"Why not?" His right eye always winked just a little when he smiled. It was a tick his real body allegedly produced that the android replicated flawlessly.

"You're—" Lakshmi swallowed. She couldn't say it. She had never wanted to believe it. Maybe the news had been premature. They were cut off, now, after all. What if he was still alive?

She *had to know*.

Lakshmi opened her mind. She reactivated her neural antennae and reached out to the world of information they shared.

She had to know.

Static poured into her ears. Something pounded at the back of her eyes as it bit into her mind, chewing away the defenses that kept her memory continuous, her personality sacrosanct.

Fei had warned her about going online again, but it didn't matter. Lakshmi ignored it all. No one on Titan could hack into *her* brain. Lakshmi pressed on, reaching out to AVA through a haze of interference and invasion.

She had to know if Chetan was truly alive.

CHAPTER 12

AN ALIEN FROM EARTH

MEERA; ICE CORE STORAGE, -16TH FLOOR, AZTLAN WAYSTATION

Lakshmi's prosthetics went limp. Her natural hands slapped against her helmet and tore at its plastic surface, as if she was trying to rip through it. Her nails dug long opaque lines into the transparent helmet material.

Her cerulean eyes flashed to gray, then white, then shut off altogether as she collapsed with two dark voids for eyes that reflected small beads of red from the emergency lights above. The side of her helmet hit the ground, her head smashing sickeningly against it and the hard floor beneath.

Lakshmi said nothing, her empty eyes lay open to the world. Blood began to trickle from the impacted side of her head.

The lowest of her four suit lights sank into a cool green. That was her life light. Something was wrong with her vitals.

"Fuck!" Case darted forward.

"Did you do this?" I shouted to the android that had been Chetan.

"Of course not! I wouldn't hurt you. You're my children!" Chetan replied in exasperation as he hurried to Lakshmi's side. Case stepped over Lakshmi's prone body defensively and defiantly blocked the facsimile of an Earthborn man from getting close.

"Her pulse is stable," Chetan replied without touching her howlsuit, his voice tinny and metallic. "But she needs medical help. You need to take her back to Shangri-La."

The android was online then, despite the invasive interference. How?

I took a step toward Chetan. It was impossible—on a number of levels—that he was here, but he sounded the same and acted the same as the Chetan I remembered. Some part of me was relieved to see one of our guardians again.

I had missed him, a little, but it felt hard to breathe just being near him too. I was beginning to panic.

"We need to find Torvram." Matyom's booming voice filled with room, despite its vast size. He leaned accusatorily toward the android interloper. "You either help us or stay out of our way. Do you know where he is?"

"Matyom! You've grown up to be just as big and stubborn as Robert," the android laughed, "and just as tall!"

"Stop avoiding my question. Where is Torvram?" Matyom repeated.

"I don't know," Chetan replied, his eyes darting to Lakshmi's side. "But I do know that Lakshmi just fainted and needs your help. Please, Maty, help my protégé. Take her home."

Case, still preventing the dark brown-skinned android from approaching Lakshmi, keyed his radio. "Fei?"

"Yes?" Fei's voice crackled through his suit radio. Chetan's eyes snapped to the natural-born man. Case and I flinched in unison.

"I need you to check in with Shangri-La. Chetan's android is here and it claims to *be* Chetan. Are we getting a signal from Earth or Mars? Have we broken isolation?" Case matched the android's gaze, his expression neutral. "We haven't found Torvram yet... I'm worried."

"Where's Lakshmi?" Fei replied obtusely.

"Unconscious. Fei, please, contact home," Case implored her with urgency.

"Oh, no! Ok, ye—" Fei's voice cut out abruptly, replaced by grainy radio static.

"Fei?" Case repeated. "Fei, hello?"

I immediately radioed her. "Fei?"

Nothing.

I switched channels. "Fei?"

Nothing again. I tried channel after channel as the portly android stepped back and brushed past Case. Matyom moved beside me and stared down the shorter android.

"I can't get a signal," I said.

"That's ok," Chetan replied calmly. The android limped as it approached Matyom and me. Case swiveled, keeping his eyes on the android. Matyom's shoulders tensed. We were all watching it or him now.

"I'm sure we'll be able to contact her once we're topside," Chetan said with the calm but mildly impatient tone of a parent reassuring its panicking child.

I tried the radio one last time. Nothing but static, just like our telepathic channels. We were completely cut off.

"Wait." Atop the mountain of unanswered questions that were bothering me was a new, more immediate one. "We can't radio from here to Shangri-La. If you really are Chetan, how is your signal making it all the way down here from the cubesats in orbit? Are you blocking our radio signal?"

Chetan rolled his eyes and chided me in a familiar, derisive manner. "Meera, you were never the quickest student. You know that your suit radio's emissions aren't nearly as strong nor as high priority as my downlink, right? On top of that, there's my automated responses so I can appear to talk to you in real time despite the forty-five minute minimum time delay. Does that make sense?"

He wasn't answering my questions. He wasn't even listening to me! My throat tightened like a vice. Horrible memories came flooding back of being stuck in front of a whiteboard during a virtualized discussion, freezing up, making mistakes, proving to myself that I really was the dumbest Titanborn in the room. I just wanted to leave, to go home and hide, to get away from Chetan.

"Right..." I replied to the android, fighting back panic, trying to hide it from. Why was I talking to this asshole again? Why was he here?

I staggered unknowingly against Matyom. The stocky man caught my shoulders. "Meera?"

Matyom's big hands tightened reassuringly. I closed my eyes and took a deep breath.

I wasn't twelve anymore. This wasn't class.

And this couldn't be Chetan.

It's ok. Focus, Meera. Find Torvram.

I'd just heard from Fei. My radio had been working. Aztlan was wired for this, with signal boosters that could run on emergency power.

Chetan was lying. *It* was lying, this android was lying and chastising me for being an idiot in the same simulated breath. It was, somehow, jamming our radios.

This was *exactly* like the Chetan I remembered, but it wasn't him. So, who was this and how was it mimicking my least favorite of our astronaut guardians so well? That was a clue, something that might help me dig through the veritable mountain of questions about Torvram's disappearance and all that surrounded it.

"I'm ok," I finally said to Matyom.

Matyom nodded and lifted his hands from my shoulders. He bared down on Chetan until he was an arm's length from the android. "Torvram's lifeline was signaling from this room five hours ago, so I'll ask you again: have you seen him?"

"*I* haven't seen him," Chetan replied. "And how can *you* be so sure he was even here if you haven't seen his signal for five hours? Honestly…" The android tsked impatiently, like it was waiting for a dim student to catch up with it.

"Torvram was here," Matyom replied stubbornly. "Where is he now?"

"Obviously, he's moved," Chetan continued evasively, jabbing a finger at the rack of ice cores with a very Lakshmi-esque flair. "Torvram's lost and there's no food or water down here. You're not going to find him unless you go online and look for his updated lifeline signal. I'm online and I can see, right now, that he's nowhere near here! Frankly, I'm a little disappointed. I raised you two to be smarter than this."

I approached Matyom's side to support him physically and emotionally against this machine, fighting back the painful bile rising in my stomach.

"Why are you lying to me?" Matyom replied to Chetan.

"You're stubborn as always, just like Doctor Auberov was!" the android replied with another uncanny mimicry of laughter. "I never got along with the man, but he was a stellar astronaut. I'll give him that. I bet you'll be one too, someday."

Matyom glued his mouth shut, hands working at his sides. He was angry, I could tell, and scared for Torvram. I wasn't sure what he was going to do next. We didn't know what this android could do, either, who it was, how it had affected Lakshmi, if it was even responsible.

I needed answers. I was tired of standing in the dark as drones attacked, as our radios went dead, and as one Titanborn lay unconscious for unknown reasons and another remained lost.

Chetan turned his brown eyes to me with palpable disdain just as I opened my mouth to speak. "Meera, please, convince your friend to see reason. You need to take Lakshmi and go home. I can help you find Torvram on the way if you'd just go online. I can see his lifeline upstairs. He's probably looking for a way out."

"Case," I replied. The short Titanborn rose from Lakshmi's side but did not move. "Can you, umm, sweep the rest of the room for Torvram?"

He nodded and walked toward us, giving the android that claimed to be Chetan a wide berth. I took his place standing over Lakshmi's prone form. Matyom and I stood on either side of Chetan now.

"And you're going to waste your time while Lakshmi's injured?" Chetan snapped. "Idiot! She could be concussed or worse! Listen to me!"

"You s-s-stand right there and wait while Case searches," I said, my resolve beginning to break down. "I'm staying offline. I don't t-trust you, whoever you are in there!"

"You could check Lakshmi's and Torvram's lifelines right now, in a millisecond, if you just stopped being paranoid." His nostrils flared as he smiled. "Your ideas always come off half-baked, Meera."

Case shouted from another row of ice cores. "Meera. There's no sign of Torvram. Though—Wait. There's fucking blood on the floor! Blood and... what is this?"

My eyes flicked from Chetan to Matyom. The big man had his eyes glued on the android, his jaw set.

I stared at Chetan. The portly android smiled and did nothing.

"Who are you?" Matyom asked.

"Chetan," the android said. It kept staring at me with a smirk on its face. I fought the urge to cede Lakshmi to him so I could back away.

"There's a mesh, here. It's like a little bloody, sticky grid. I... I think I found Torvram's lifeline," Case shouted.

"What?" Matyom growled. "You found *Torvram's lifeline?*"

To remove a lifeline would mean tearing the tiny bulb-shaped transmitter and its even smaller computer off the surface of the human heart.

"Did you kill him?" I shouted at Chetan, assuming the worst. "Who are you?"

"I don't know what you're talking about, Meera. I'm Chetan, obviously, and Torvram's upstairs right now!" Chetan protested. "Torvram's injured but alive. Turn on your telepathy. Take Lakshmi, get him, and go home!"

He was asking me to expose myself to whatever had just attacked our brains outside the *Trailblazer*. I had to stand my ground and say no. I had to stand up to this *thing* in the guise of my old teacher, my old guardian. It was like Lakshmi but worse, multiplied by thousands.

My heart beat in my throat. My stomach roiled. The thought that Torvram might be dead, after all this, made my eyes ache with pressure. But, no, if this was this *thing's* fault. I had—I had to stand up to it! It might even be responsible for all this."

"You just t-told us that he— You've been lying—" I sputtered. The knowledge had come as a tragedy to all of us, but I had to say the truth out loud, so I could hear it too. I knew for sure that this wasn't Chetan, despite its eerily accurate impression.

"Chetan is *dead*," I said sternly. My voice echoed throughout the core room, bouncing off the ice walls. "So, who are you and where is Torvram? No more evasion. Tell me now."

The android, bathed in red light, didn't react. Its grin widened, the same way Lakshmi's did. I stood over Lakshmi's body, unsure of how to react.

It leapt at me without warning. I tripped over Lakshmi's prosthetics, falling onto my back, and the android pinned me to the ground and slammed my helmet hard against the floor. My ears rang. I thought I heard Matyom shout.

The Earthborn imposter leaned over me. I struggled to rise but the inhuman weight of its legs on mine kept me pinned. I swiped my hands at it ineffectually, my gloves bouncing of its hardened chest. The android placed a hand onto my helmet and began to squeeze. Polymer composites buckled, trying to redirect the force to prevent shattering.

It squeezed harder. The bubble of my helmet deformed into a spider-web of opaque cracks. I watched as the deformations spread; I battered at its arm with my fists. I smashed one of my knuckles into its face and felt pain shoot through my hand as I connected with the hardened false jaw.

Then, the sharp end of Matyom's beacon burst from the android's chest, showering me with dark fluid and plastic debris. The android rose from my body as the beacon's base sprang open into a tripod. It tore at the beacon, bending the tripod closed, before it was pulled violently and slammed into a rack of ice cores.

The android claiming to be Chetan, a man buried on Earth, rebounded from the rack and fell to the floor. The full three meters from the beacon's base to its head jutted from the android's back. The inactive blue LEDs in the beacon head were tinted a stark gray in the crimson emergency lighting and the flow of fluid from the android's body that began to coat their surface.

Matyom's face was knotted with anger and adrenaline. His huge body heaved as he reached the android and dug the beacon into the unfinished floor.

Case, panting, returned with blood on his gloves. "Are you ok? What happened? Are you breached?"

My helmet was cracked, warped, and I could hear the barest hint of whistling. I was starting to feel cold, my face chapping. Two of my lights faded to an alarming red or, rather, melted into our surroundings.

"My pack?" I asked, deliriously. It was gone, thrown out of its magnetic housing.

"Yeah. Yeah. Patch," Case said frantically. He threw his own rigid pack to the floor and spilled its contents onto the ground.

He came back with opaque patches, running his fingers along my helmet. "You're gonna be ok," Case said. "You're gonna be ok. You're gonna be ok."

I gripped his panicked fingers and led him to the leak, unable to speak through my shock.

I silently thanked the years of research we'd put into suit repair, and all those who had died so that we'd been forced to prioritize tech like this. The leak sealed quickly with Case's attention.

My oxygen light flipped to green and, as the hum of my howlsuit's heaters intensified, the temperature light began its chromatic crawl toward violet. I could still feel my face, even my lips, despite the layer of blackened flesh on them that stared back through multiple small reflections on the inside of my battered helmet.

"Thanks," I said, still a bit dazed.

Case wrapped me in a hug.

"Now. Where is Torvram?! What have you done to him?" Matyom grunted and kicked one of the android's scrabbling hands off of the beacon.

The android stared back at him with its intense brown eyes that now flared with painfully bright light and commanded, "Go home."

"Who are you?" I staggered toward the android with one arm slung over Case's shoulder. "What are you doing in Chetan's old android? How did you steal it from Shangri-La?"

"Go home," it repeated. The snark and the passion of that flawed polymath that'd helped raise us from Earth had left the android's voice. In its place was an emotionless monotone. "Go home."

It sounded remarkably like AVA.

"Was he here?" Matyom was shouting and pleading with the android in the same breath. "Was Torvram here? That's his lifeline! What happened to him? Where's my honeysuckle?!"

The android that'd called itself Chetan went silent. The lights in its eyes began to fade slowly, until the brown glow left altogether. In its place, pulsing red from the emergency lights reflected upon their surfaces.

Chetan was dead once again.

Whoever or whatever this had been was yet another mystery.

I tapped mentally at my suit through our wired connection. It blinked my suit lights at me from beneath my collar. Heat was turning violet, but oxygen was still green. My reserves were low.

Lakshmi was still unconscious, her vitals dipping from green toward red. I knelt beside her and hesitated with a wire drawn from my collar. The fake Chetan had asked us to go online repeatedly. It was probably best to stay out of her mind until I knew it was safe. I let the wire recoil back into my battered howlsuit.

I doubted Torvram was really upstairs, though I hoped against my hunch that he'd be that easy to find.

We had to get back to the surface. I quietly asked Case to retrieve Torvram's lifeline and properly store a sample of the blood and moved to comfort Matyom.

Matyom said nothing at first. His face was drawn taut, his lips quivering as he panted with loud almost violent breaths.

"Matyom?" I placed a hand on his broad back. He turned, slowly, his red eyes looking somewhere that wasn't here. "We need to get back to the *Trailblazer*."

"We have to find Torvram," he replied. With a grunt that echoed across core storage, he lifted the beacon and snapped its warped tripod shut. The android's body fell to the ground.

"Maybe we can learn something from the android," I replied. "Maybe it caused all of this: the drones, the attack, the power outage."

It was our best lead so far.

"Maybe," Matyom muttered, noncommittally. He stared up at the ceiling and lifted Lakshmi's body over his shoulder. "I hope so."

This rescue expedition had grown into something more. Torvram was injured and missing, and we were experiencing attacks physically and mentally on an unprecedented scale. Chetan's android had been stolen, and his personality mimicked almost flawlessly. If it hadn't been for its ulterior motives, I might not have noticed the difference.

And now Lakshmi was unconscious too, possibly mentally infected by whatever the android had tried to convince us to open our minds to.

We needed to call home, to report what we'd seen, to find out more, and to get help finding Torvram. With his lifeline missing, I wasn't sure how we'd locate him. That was all assuming he was still...

No. Until we found a—a body, I had to believe Torvram was alive. No more death, not while I still breathed.

CHAPTER 13

THE NEUROENGINEERING PRACTICAL

MEERA; AIRLOCK, 0TH FLOOR, AZTLAN WAYSTATION

The heavy airlock door scraped against its frame, moaning loudly. It closed with a final metallic shriek of protestation. We left Aztlan Waystation with an unconscious Titanborn, a broken android, and no idea where Torvram might be.

I looked up nervously in IR and saw only heavy, pregnant methane clouds. There was no sign of drones or any new threat.

"I hope fake Chetan here was the cause of all this," Case mumbled, rapping a knuckle against the android that he and I now carried together.

"Me too." I exhaled, taking one more anxious glance at the sky. "Me too."

Matyom carried Lakshmi over his shoulder with comparative ease. He'd spirited many an injured Titanborn away from danger before. His usual smile though—his reassurance to the frightened that everything was going to be ok—was strained and forced. We all knew what was weighing on his mind. It was bothering me too.

With numb hands and a weary mind, I keyed my radio again. "Fei?"

"Meera!" Fei shouted back through noisy interference.

"Oh," I said, dumbly, unable to fully process the relief at finally hearing her again. I had one question of many answered. The android had blocked our radios.

"We need help," Matyom barked. "Can you bring the *Trailblazer* any closer to us?"

"Y-yeahislakshmiok?" Fei's words flooded through the radio as she spoke at a barely comprehensible speed. Her already high voice rose an octave in panic. "Istorvramwithyou?"

"I don't know." Matyom echoed my words, all our thoughts. "But I hope so... and, no. We don't know where Torvram is. We need you to come and get us."

"Okokok." Fei paused and took a long breath that came through the radio as white noise. Her sickly voice lowered, calmed. "Thegood—The good news is that I've managed to reclaim the drones that attacked the *Trailblazer*. They've gone home. I am moving on your position now."

I gently lowered the android's head and shoulders into the soaked organic muck. Methane poured down this imposter's dark brown face, soaking through its thinning black hair.

I leaned against Aztlan's metal outer hull. My vision was bifurcated by a thick, opaque crack that ran across the center of my helmet: a reminder of how close I'd come to death. My suit smelled terrible: sweat mingled with internally recycled air. I was cold, tired, and demoralized.

Case said what I believed we were all thinking. "Fuck."
That about summed it up for me, at least.

"Matyom?"

The big man was staring up into the sky now, cradling Lakshmi in his arms. His eyes shifted gray, down into the IR spectrum.

"It's going to be ok," I said those same trite words that'd failed to prevent Torvram from "being ok."

"Mmm," Matyom replied. "Yeah."

Case trudged over to the big man and stared west, toward the craggy, jagged hillocks and flows of glossy wax-like runoff from the cryovolcanoes around us. He reached up to Matyom, swatting at his helmet.

"Fuck, I'm... vent it." After several failed attempts at whatever Case was trying to do, Matyom's eyes shifted back to a pale red. He regarded the shorter man trying to get his attention. A powerful sorrow was etched onto Matyom's face.

"I'm too short!" Case growled. He looked over and shouted at the android, "Fuck you for making me small, Chetan!"

I couldn't help but chuckle a little, despite the morose mood that prevailed.

"Lower your head, Matyom!" Case yipped.

A small smile cut through the sorrow on the stocky man's face. "Ahh," he replied knowingly. Carefully nestling the unconscious woman to his chest, Matyom leaned down. Case brought his helmet to Matyom's.

"Meera!" Case barked.

"What?" I replied, still half-leaning beside the android.

"Get over here, vent it!" Case swung his arm, beckoning me forward. I'd stood aside, thinking this was a private moment between friends. I trudged toward them, fighting the viscid grasp of the organic sludge beneath me, as a warmth spread through my body and pushed away an iota of exhaustion and depression.

I pressed my helmet against theirs, joining the huddle.

Case's voice passed clearly through the plastic, clearer than the interference-muddled radio, "We're going to get through this, ok? We're going to find Torv and we're going to get past whatever this is: the drones, Chetan, whatever. But right now? Drop the act. Both of you, you fake-empathetic, lying chipheads. I know you're hurting, just like me, so stop putting on a brave face. We don't need to pretend, ok? Especially you, Maty. It's ok. We'll live if you drop the tall, blond savior act."

Matyom was smiling now and tears were beginning to pour down his face. Case hugged us closer. We formed a wall around Lakshmi, helmets joined, as rain and smog beat against our backs. "Fuck this place," he muttered. "Fuck it for hurting good people."

The *Trailblazer's* lights coalesced through Titan's haze.

MEERA; ENGINE DECK, *TRAILBLAZER*

Matyom's snores echoed down from the operations deck, briefly drowning out the sound of pounding rain. We'd given it a couple hours, resting and guzzling away our water supplies inside the *Trailblazer*. Now we were trying to piece together what had happened at the Waystation and figure out what to do next.

The android and Lakshmi lay side-by-side on the sealed gangway. Fei paced back and forth, a dark bandana wrapped about her face. Only her eyes, her real violet eyes, were visible through her hoodie and bandana. I could see the beginnings of a long keloid scar and burn marks around her left eye. They turned her gray skin a ghostly white. I wondered why she hadn't had them removed.

To our dismay, the telepathic interference hadn't stopped. Our attacker was still out there, in some form. Because of it, we had to stay offline and Fei couldn't project her digital mask into our eyes through AI.

While we were exhausted, Fei was full of tense energy.

"So we can't be online, not safely, anyway." Fei's eyes kept flicking to Lakshmi. "While I was online, I managed to get the drones back into our control. I ordered them to go back home to get a faster, more in-depth examination of their malfunction, and it—" Fei produced a charred pair of wafer-thin plastic strips from her hoodie pockets.

Case raised an eyebrow as he rummaged through another net's worth of electronics, retrieving old thin computers and long coils of wire from his personal stash. This had all once belonged to the astronauts, which included the original user of the broken android beside us.

"I've never seen something do this to a neural barrier. It tore through my firewall, didn't even bother decrypting these..." Fei rolled the blackened barriers through her hand. "It just modified their clock speed and they burned themselves away. I went offline just in time to keep it out of my brain."

Lakshmi's chest rose and fell, though it was nearly imperceptible. Her suit vitals had risen back toward green, but her pulse was slow and she was completely unresponsive. Moreover, we didn't have the equipment to feed her in this state on the *Trailblazer*.

I didn't know what to do. Everything was getting worse.

I tried to focus on the mysteries. Answering questions, researching problems, was something that calmed me *sometimes*.

"Does anyone back home have an idea of what was in this android and what it wants with Torvram?" I replied, nibbling on a ration bar. It was dry and tasted vaguely of what I'd been told was earth dirt. Nevertheless, my hunger was at a point where I'd have likened it to the best holiday stew fresh from hydroponics.

Fei shook her head. "All they can say for certain is that this isn't AVA, but it's acting in a way only AVA could."

Fei swiped into the air, toward me. When no translucent image appeared in my vision, she sighed. "Right. We're all stuck offline. Case, can you toss me another USB cable?"

"Good to finally be useful," he replied and, with a snort, added, "Though I'd trade this situation to have Torvram back. Shit, I'd even be happy to have Lakshmi wake up and boss us around like normal."

Fei spun a laptop to face us impatiently. A live video from one of the miniaturized satellites—cubesats—orbiting Titan appeared. "Look at the drones," Fei said, pointing north, toward the storm-wracked polar lakes: Kraken and Ligeia Mare.

Something was off. A significant percentage of our drones were clustering near the lakeside Waystation at Kraken Mare. They were disobeying orders, tearing off from their return routes to Shangri-La and just staying there.

This was, perhaps, why we had seen so few inside Aztlan Waystation. Some had gone home, but some had stolen away to the north. Why?

"What the fuck?" Case said, leaning over my shoulder.

Fei shrugged. She regarded Lakshmi once more before speaking. "AVA's influence doesn't extend that far north anymore. Each time the cubesats fall out of sight of it, we lose control of whatever drones we've reprogrammed. Our attacker is up there now and its sphere of influence is widening."

"Could a human do this?" I asked her.

"On this scale?" Fei replied. "Not even Lakshmi could. I suspect it's an AI, but not AVA. It's an unknown hostile Intelligence."

"Just more questions," I muttered. I mulled over what Fei said, peering at the procession of drones traveling northward.

This *thing*, whatever it was, had denied me access to the drones. It had attacked us when we tried to broadcast. It had, presumably, interfered with our radios and might be in Chetan's body. If it was AVA-like, as Fei had said, it might even have been what locked me in Torvram's room.

But it wasn't attacking us now, nor was it scrambling our radios. Its influence over the drones had expanded in quantity, vastly, and it wasn't using that influence to strike us.

Why?

Was there a pattern here?

What was it? This... hostile Intelligence as Fei called it.

My curiosity was faltering beneath a wave of fear. A single drone had nearly killed Case. Chetan's android had bashed my helmet in. I remembered how Jula had died from the cold. I remembered the strange things Torvram had said before he had left. My hands began to shake.

Torvram had said that "the people on Earth don't give a shit about whether we live or die." That Earth was holding us back, even. It had felt so uncharacteristically vitriolic, such unusual anger from him. He was usually kind, if somber and prone to depressive episodes. Had he known about this Intelligence? What had it done to him, tearing out the mesh over his heart like that? Was... *Earth* somehow involved?

I had to believe Torvram was still alive, at least. I wouldn't stop until we rescued him... or proved he was dead.

I glanced over to Lakshmi. If her health worsened though, we'd have to go home to get her better care. No more death, not even Lakshmi's.

We had two Titanborn to save now.

A cabinet beneath the ladder burst open and Feyn staggered forward, spilling a pack of ration bars onto the floor. The poor dog was having trouble balancing and its eyes were unfocused, turning randomly and occasionally looking in two directions at once.

"What happened to Feyn?" It was heartbreaking to see the little pup barely functional.

"Feyn doesn't understand the command to go offline," Fei replied. "He was an easy target for… whatever is happening."

I leaned in front of the dog and lifted it from the ground. Its legs twitched and clawed randomly. I cradled it in my hands and then inspiration struck. "Did you try fixing him?"

"Unsafe." Fei snorted, a little bit of the condescending intellectual seeping into her tone. "Even if I'd plugged in to Feyn directly, talked to it with my brain closed off to the rest of the net, I couldn't risk getting attacked through that vector… not while you all were presumably lost in the Waystation."

It was my turn to be surprised by her slow thinking. "So… let's do it now."

"Why?" Fei replied. "What about Lakshmi?"

"This can be a test. I've helped Torv with his pet projects, mind the pun, before. I can try to fix Feyn's mind and, while I do that, you can look over my proverbial shoulder and learn more about this Intelligence that's attacking us… that might have Torvram. Then we can extend that knowledge to the android and to Lakshmi, to minimize the risk of hurting her brain while we diagnose what happened to her."

I nearly apologized when I finished speaking. I wasn't used to giving orders. But I wanted to help, and I had a possible solution. I pinned my hands to my sides, trying to keep them from shaking further. I braced myself for harsh criticism.

"Huh." Fei drew another useless AR gesture in the air and sighed, shaking her head.

"As long as it's safe," Case cut in. "If both you chipheads pass out too, there's not much I'll be able to do to help." He gestured to the laptop beside Lakshmi. "Other than watch your vitals and curse."

"If we stay offline, there's no chance of an outside attack through us." Fei began to pace. "This dog isn't too much more advanced than the average drone, and the problem with them was that our foe kept patching them in real time. Still, I'm not willing to risk it attacking us through Feyn. This Intelligence might be leaving us alone now, but there's no guarantee it won't notice us."

"I've got most of a makeshift Faraday cage around here somewhere," Case replied. "That would block any signals getting to Feyn and then we just string a... Wait, fuck, what sort of cable do you need to connect your brain to this thing?"

"USB." Fei's bandana warped into what looked like a grin. "Normally, we wouldn't need this many channels to fix a simple drone but, Meera, you're right. This is the perfect testbed."

Fei clapped her hands together. "To tell you the truth, I'm excited! I've never had the chance to study *another* Artificial Intelligence other than AVA. Here I thought I'd be a one-mind woman." She sprang back to the laptop beside Lakshmi with renewed vigor, chicken-pecking the keys with manic energy.

Feyn had calmed down a little in my arms. He appeared to register vaguely that someone he knew was here. He whimpered, eyes refocusing to stare pleadingly up at me. "Do you need help building a cage for this poor puppo?" I asked Case.

Case blushed and closed his mouth with an audible click. He turned away. "I'll—uhh, I'll get some tools."

I felt my own face flush, unsure of what had just happened to him but feeling a little happier for it.

MEERA; ENGINE DECK, *TRAILBLAZER*

The dogbot's mind was a mess, but with Fei's help, we were able to regain access and restore him to his first system point. The dog bounded around the room now, excited to see what were, to Feyn, new friends.

Chetan's old android was more of a struggle. Whereas Feyn was a robot whose programming simply needed alteration and reasonable command input, the android's mind had been designed to be puppeted by a complex human mind.

And—as far as we could tell—there was the vestige of a mind still in it.

Fei had quickly taken over for me there. The mind within Chetan was, according to her, unmistakably AI in structure.

"The code that I can read feels alien, despite being built upon entirely man-made language," she continued, her gloved hands deep in the "brain" of the android. "There's memory in here though, somewhere, and I bet it'll lead us to Torvram."

Case's Faraday cage now formed a spider web of metal about the android's head. It was uncomfortable, looking at the man who was once one of my guardians now broken and vivisected.

Now, I sat beside Lakshmi. Her vitals still weren't looking good. The food and water we'd tried to give her fell on the floor or dribbled from her mouth. Her three prosthetic arms twitched and scratched and, at one point, dug a deep cut into her neck. We'd had to strap them to her back.

But I hesitated before her. This was a brain-computer interface in a real human mind I was about to access. This was neuroengineering at its most complicated with the addition of a hostile, unknown AI in play.

My hands were shaking again and all I could do was take deep breaths over and over. I was the best trained, most qualified person in the room to do this, but I'd never even passed the practical! If I fucked up, Lakshmi may never wake up. She could lose her memory, her personality, or simply die.

But if I did nothing, there was no guarantee that she would survive to make it to Shangri-La. And that, even, was assuming we could afford to leave Torvram out wherever he was for a minute longer.

There were so many unanswered questions. Lakshmi's health, the time she had left, what had happened to her—these were the questions I could solve *right now*.

But I was scared.

Move forward. I told myself, gritting my teeth. There was one thing I could do differently, something I had rarely done at work out of guilt, embarrassment, and sometimes, fear. I could ask for help.

"Can you two h-help me?" I asked as I began to scratch at the dry skin on my index finger anxiously. "I can do this. I know I can do this. I'm just really feeling nervous and maybe scarous." "Scared" and "anxious" became "scarous" as I fumbled my words.

Fei twirled a long length of cable between two fingers. It snapped rhythmically as it bounced back and forth against the tessellated floor. "I'll be right over your shoulder, so to speak, and literally!" she added, snorting a laugh at her own... was it even a joke?

The masked woman, I was coming to realize, was a complete dork.

I think we all were, save for Matyom.

I smiled at Case, unable to conceal my amusement at Fei's dumb non-joke. He giggled.

"Thanks, Fei. I think we all needed that."

"I'm happy to help," she replied, straightening her back with undue pride.

"Ok." I stood over Lakshmi's sleeping form, my resolve steeled. The right side of her face and ear were heavily bandaged. A small string of dried blood lined her jaw. A faint blue blush cooled her gray features. A spiderweb of cables ran from her neck to the laptop that monitored her vitals.

I pulled a gossamer strand of cable from her suit, just beneath where her helmet would hook in. From here, I could access the suit computer—using it as another barrier—and the hard-wired connection between it and Lakshmi's brain.

It was time to figure out what this hostile Intelligence had done to Lakshmi and, hopefully, to bring her back to consciousness. I would investigate her chipset and help her in any way I could.

I could do this.

CHAPTER 14

COGNITIVE DISSONANCE

LAKSHMI; [LOCATION NOT FOUND]

Titan's golden sky was clear, not a single fluffy methane cloud in sight. What was once a multi-colored organic haze had, in the new heat, boiled out into liquid that now coursed through the soil. The terraformers had begun their careful climate and chaos theory work weeks ago to alter the weather in Lakshmi's favor today. They'd given her an 88 percent chance that she'd get what she wanted: these clear skies, this strong statement of success.

Lakshmi hadn't been worried. In the end, every gamble worked out in her favor.

She stepped out onto the stage and the open air of the newly livable Titan. A swift breeze ruffled her jet-black ponytail. It was pleasant in a way Titan's air had never been before her intervention.

Titan's rolling dunes stretched for miles, dotted with small flowers and yellow grasses that drank in sunlight focused from orbit. A handful of trees stretched high into the sky thanks to Titan's low gravity.

Throngs of gray-skinned Titanborn cheered alongside a host of Martian and Earthborn humans of many nations and associations. A pale man in a bespoke suit and tie hung a medal around her neck. Lakshmi bowed her head, just slightly, to accept it as yet more revelry erupted from the crowd. She ran her hands along its gold-plated surface, felt the weight of the metal alloy underneath, and stared for a long, breathless moment at the engraving: a profile of Alfred Nobel.

It was a dream come true.

It was also the beginning of yet greater things.

As the applause and shouts of support from the crowd died down, Lakshmi approached the podium and looked out proudly at the mass of people breathing Titan's air freely, warm and safe outside for the first time in history.

"I apologize for the cold," she began, making a show of rubbing her hands together to roars of laughter from the crowd. It was a balmy nine degrees Celsius today.

"As you probably already know by now, my name is Doctor Lakshmi Ramakrishnan. I can't thank you all enough for being here today." Lakshmi beamed out at the sea of faces. "Of course, I wouldn't be here without the continued support of everyone on the terraforming team, our Earthborn and Martian benefactors and, most of all, the Titanborn here with me today."

Her speech was inconsequential and decisively important, simultaneously. The words had been trawled from net searches, workshopped, focus-group tested, and spat back into the cycle again. It'd been designed by committee to elicit the precise emotions and exact ideas that Lakshmi wanted implanted into the crowd here and, more importantly, into those watching from Earth. She knew the type of audience that this award would draw.

This was only the beginning.

"Growing up with an AI," she continued, "and four 'humanish' androids was, let's say, not easy." She paused for the desired laugh to ripple through the crowd.

"My first memory was watching one of AVA's squat, three-eyed drones seal a cut on my index finger. I hugged the little machine and AVA had it hug me back." She paused, once again, for the chorus of sentimentality—"awws" and sniffs—to pass.

"One of our human guardians, Doctor Ramakrishnan saw great potential in me. After spending each day raising not one or two but dozens of children, he still put in the time to sit down with me and answer my questions."

Lakshmi spoke with pride as she recounted the genius of the mentor who had, in turn, seen that same genius in her, "Chetan was a great teacher and an even greater visionary. He understood that the chips installed in our nascent brains, new technologies that had never existed before, were the key to making the dream of self-sufficient space colonies a reality.

"He accelerated our learning. He unshackled us from traditional teaching to take advantage of our unique skills and our affinity to AI. At age twelve, I was already synthesizing proteins, inventing new methods to purify the contaminated water in Titan's ice, and pioneering our colonial government. It was thanks to Chetan's support and belief in our mission, and in me, that made this all happen. When he and his family asked to adopt me, so that I could truly call him my father, I was the happiest woman in the solar system. I guess I still am."

In a combination of both practiced acting and real emotion, Lakshmi paused to sniff back tears that threatened to derail her speech. To hold them just in view, to pause for just a second with a burst of genuine emotion, that was the key. Chetan, balding, portly, and beaming with pride sat in a small chair on stage, his family just out of sight.

Lakshmi turned to mime brushing away the tears she'd held back and then continued, "I won't say much about how I got this." She raised the Nobel Prize into view and smiled at her reflection on this electrum symbol.

"I am eternally grateful for the honor to be not just the first extraterrestrially-born human to receive the Peace Prize but to represent my Titanborn friends as an ambassador to ingenuity, survival, prosperity, and peace." Lakshmi paused for effect as more cheers erupted.

"Chetan, Yunlei, Juniper, and Robert instilled in me their dream, the dream of so many humans throughout history: to live among the stars. I've dedicated my life to making that dream a reality. This prize is, specifically, for my work in altering the chemistry of our atmospheric-seeding compounds; but there is plenty more that went into making Titan livable and safe, as I'm sure some of you saw on the flight here.

"Our work continues on the many moons of Saturn and beyond, so that someday this colony might not just serve as proof that humans can live far, far from Earth and survive, but as a gateway to the solar systems beyond, a model for the Proxima Centauri expedition that launched last year, and a home among the stars where all are welcome.

"Finally, I'd like to take a moment of silence for all the Titanborn who gave their lives on the path to making our dream—a day where we no longer need to utter 'no more death' to ward off the ever-present specter of death on Titan—a reality." The crowd lapsed into silence.

Lakshmi held that silence for longer than she'd planned. Too many Titanborn had died. It'd been all worth it, of course, in the end, but if she could turn back time, she would've torn every single one of them from the jaws of death.

But, again, this was only the beginning. There might even be time for reversing death. Lakshmi planned to have a *long, productive* life ahead.

"Thank you all again for being here. Here's to the continued prosperity of our colonies and the exploration of the stars."

With a wave and a grin, Lakshmi left the podium and lazily made her way backstage, basking in the adoration of the crowd and the private feeling of victory. She hugged Chetan and his wife and leaned down to hear the random bursts of unexpected wisdom and ridiculous chicanery from his children.

Titanborn and Earthborn humans—whose names appeared in AR along their chests for her convenience—handed her water and escorted her through the VIP crowd. There were handshakes and pleasantries, nods and smiles and then Lakshmi sent them away and returned to her dressing room.

Soon, it would be time to consult with her inner circle and take the next step: candidacy in the Federation of Earth Astronautics Administrations. There was debate brewing as to whether Titan, or even all of Saturn's space, deserved a seat at the proverbial table, though the physical dimensions of said space was itself hotly controversial. Soon, they would plan their proposal to create and secure that seat in one move.

But for now, she'd celebrate. Lakshmi reached toward an extensive rack of clothing. The suit was flattering, the kind of statement she liked to make, but it wouldn't fit the scene she had planned for her partners tonight.

A knock came at the door, and without Lakshmi's approval, the door burst wide open. Meera stumbled inside. Her eyes were bloodshot and rimmed by dark pockets. The rust-eyed woman's hair was disheveled and she looked haggard, exhausted. Meera looked down at the warm-colored mermaid dress fitted to her chubby form and threw her hands into the air. "Ok, no."

Lakshmi felt a powerful headache subsume her consciousness. She forced her eyes shut, trying to push this sudden explosive migraine away.

When she opened her eyes, Meera's clothing had inexplicably changed to jeans and a burgundy sweater that felt absolutely nostalgic to see. Her wavy auburn hair ended abruptly at her shoulders, cut by someone unskilled, perhaps Meera herself. It was like they were in their mid-twenties again, together on the *Trailblazer*, rescuing Torvram.

"Meera!" Lakshmi said, rubbing her temples as the headache lulled. "I'd love to talk but I have plans tonight."

"Entity meera stabilize counter break eye equals eye plus one." Meera spoke gibberish.

The headache crashed back eightfold against the inside of Lakshmi's skull. "You need to g-g-go." She barely managed to say the words.

"Lakshmi, wait. I need to talk to you. It's important." Meera hugged her arms to her chest.

Lakshmi chided herself for not bringing her auxiliary prosthetics or giving the speech in a second body. Something was wrong with this headache. How had Meera changed her clothing so abruptly? Was this Meera's doing?

"I'm not here to hurt you," Meera said, as if reading her mind, as Meera raised open palms into the air in a placating gesture. "Fei keep the machine offline trying to broadcast lockdown I've got her."

Lakshmi's eyes widened. Lockdown? What was this gibberish? She blinked and Meera was wearing an old alabaster howlsuit now. When had Meera put on this antique? Nobody even needed those old models to walk Titan's surface anymore.

<AVA! Is Meera in my head?! D:> Lakshmi broadcast to the trusty AI.

Lakshmi tried the dressing room door, but it wouldn't open. Its interface didn't light up. She shot a telepathic message at it and it didn't respond. Her headache was mounting again.

"Lakshmi. Please," Meera repeated. "I just need to talk to you. Calm down."

Lakshmi placed a hand against the door and sighed. Security would come soon to escort her regardless. Meera was unarmed. She could wait this out.

She drew herself to her full height and fed excess energy into her irises until they appeared to spark with intimidating cerulean fire. "Fine. What do you want?"

Meera didn't reply at first. Her eyes defocused and cycled from rust to amber to Chetan's brown. "I know that you know Chetan is dead."

"What? No," Lakshmi replied, her tone rising to her own surprise. Meera's nonsense words hurt, though, far more than they should have. Chetan was alive. She had *just* seen him.

Meera's eyes hardened, but there also was such sorrow in them. This further confused Lakshmi. She'd dealt with crazy Titanborn before. Some tended to crack under the stress; it wasn't unheard of. But Meera wasn't showing the typical symptoms. She just looked sad, sympathetic even.

"We both know he's dead," Meera continued.

Lakshmi flinched. Her nostrils flared. She just wanted Meera to leave *now*.

Meera began to visibly tremble. "H-he can't be here because you—" Meera swallowed, "—you and I both know he died a decade ago. This *is not real*."

"What?" Lakshmi's voice cracked, squeaking and causing her cheeks to flush. Her back tensed against the door. The headache was returning, boring into her forehead like a drill. She winced, struggling to look at her fellow Titanborn. "I've worked my ass off to do t-t-thi—Stop. Stop this. Get out of here!"

Meera was squeezing her sides now. She shook her head frantically. Her voice cleared. "Y-you can't terraform Titan, not at this speed, not like this with the resources humanity would have at their disposal for the next hundred years. You're violating planetary protection on a drastic scale too..."

Meera bit her lip and glanced over her shoulder at the dressing room "mirror." Code flashed across its surface. "Do you remember how many times I've asked you to listen to me since we 'saved Torvram'? How many times—" Meera paused again, pressing a hand to her collarbone. Lakshmi couldn't tell if it was dramatic effect or if the chubby woman was trying to stave off hyperventilation.

"I've—I've asked you to listen," Meera continued as she took long, drawn-out breaths. "I've told you that this has all been happening a little too perfectly, that maybe the world you know stopped being real right around the time you met Chetan beneath Aztlan Waystation."

Lakshmi ignored the nagging idea that, yes, this had all happened miraculously fast. But of course, she was Chetan's protégé. She was a genius of unparalleled nature *and* nurture.

Lakshmi had a blasted Nobel Prize around her neck to prove it! Her urge to prove Meera as blatantly wrong as she clearly was took over.

"Why should I listen to you when you've got nothing worth saying?" Lakshmi replied, intending to wound the offensive woman.

Meera leaned her back against the wall. She looked disappointed, which was not Lakshmi's intended effect. "This... you would say stuff like this before, when I was just asking about work or showing you data. I don't understand why you just won't listen to anyone else. Is your ego really so big that you can't accept the idea that you're ever wrong, even here, when the truth is so *clearly* in front of you? You have no excuse to be this asinine! I can't believe I was ever scared of you."

"Scared of me?" Lakshmi chuckled in disbelief. What was there to be scared of? "I've saved your life. I saved everyone's lives."

"How can you save my life if you don't value me at all? I'm just another pawn to you, right? I'm here to contribute to your work and sing my bosses' praises to the rest of the Titanborn. You want me to further your career, and that's it. I don't even know if you'd care if I died. I—"

Meera exhaled and closed her mouth. Lakshmi was taken aback at the chubby woman's dramatic response. Of course, she'd care if Meera died. Why was Meera acting so weird? "I don't want you to—" Lakshmi started.

"Stop," Meera interrupted, visibly clenching her teeth. "Just... please, for once in your life, listen to me. Chetan's dead, Torvram's life is still at risk, and all I need for you to do is to get better, so just please listen to me. You can help us fight this thing in your brain if you *believe me just once.*"

The headache hit harder than it ever had before. Lakshmi couldn't focus her eyes anymore, couldn't stand the pain of looking at any light. As she screwed her eyes shut, she could still see. There were images of things that had never happened, that felt so real, but couldn't be.

<AVA! WHAT IS GOING ON?!>

AVA didn't reply.

"Why does my head hurt?" Lakshmi asked in a moan. "Tell me what you're doing."

Lakshmi stumbled blindly toward the auburn-haired Titanborn and felt herself bump hard against the mirror. She felt Meera's arms grip her shoulders and hold her steady. Lakshmi couldn't hold her herself upright anymore and slumped into the other woman.

"Please," Meera muttered. "Chetan's dead. Just… acknowledge it. If not for me or Torvram, for your dream."

"I know," Lakshmi groaned.

The world spun. She felt sick. The headache kept pounding. Chetan *was* dead.

He couldn't be here. Lakshmi knew that.

"Am I such a monster for wanting my dad to be alive?" she muttered through her failing vocal chords as her brain began to decipher just how unreal this all was. She clung to the Nobel Prize about her neck, not wanting it all to go even though she now knew this couldn't be real.

Was it all a dream?

"No." Meera frowned. "But I wish you would stop being like him. He claimed to care so much about us, but he never showed a shred of empathy unless he wanted something. I wish that you weren't like him, that you genuinely cared."

"I'm better than him," Lakshmi hissed through numb lips. She vaguely registered the feeling of the floor. "Why can't I…?"

"Then be better than him. He was a great scientist but a terrible leader and a calloused guardian," Meera replied. "Fei, I think we got her. Can you see her on your end?"

Lakshmi forced her eyes open, but she couldn't see Meera anymore. The world was beginning to fade, or glow impossibly bright, or do both at the same time. She felt tired and thirsty and her stomach hurt.

The floor felt so comfortable, like she'd always been here. Lakshmi rolled onto her back. "Meera?" she called out to the dark void that was all she could see. The headache crashed in waves.

"It's o-ok," Meera replied with a stutter.

"Do you hate me?" Lakshmi asked.

"I don't know," Meera replied from nowhere. "When this is all over, I think I'd like to just forget you."

That hurt. That hurt a lot. Lakshmi lay in the void and wondered why it hurt.

She wondered if it might hurt if anyone said it, or maybe it was just because Meera had said it. Lakshmi wasn't sure. Her head hurt. Everything was confusing. What year was it? Was it safe to go outside?

Chetan wasn't alive.

That was…

The news that he had died had come from afar, during isolation, as a low-level emergency message.

Just thought you would want to know. Doctor Ramakrishnan has passed away. That was it. No fanfare. No video recording. Just a snippet of text.

Lakshmi had never gotten him to call her "daughter" like she'd wanted.

Lakshmi winced as her vision began to return. The harsh lights of the *Trailblazer*, bright white economical LEDs, glared at her. She squinted at the tessellated ceiling. Lakshmi enjoyed tracing the patterns of three-fold and six-fold symmetry across lines of triangles, carving little figures of wizards and molecules out with her eyes.

She saw Case smile. He shouted for Fei and Meera and Matyom excitedly. Lakshmi slapped her hands to her ears. He was so loud.

Lakshmi's vision began to clear. She saw Fei cautiously lift a laptop out of her peripheral vision and tiptoe toward her. Wires trailed from the old computer's side, toward Lakshmi's face. Lakshmi was confident they terminated either at the back of her howlsuit or the back of her head. The room smelled of stale air and just a hint of slimy exhaust.

Chetan *was* dead. He'd been dead for over ten years.

It *hurt* to admit that with finality. He could never come back to Titan. Lakshmi's guardian—the father who had never requited her familial love toward him—only lived on in memory now.

Lakshmi felt Meera stir; the curvy nervous wreck brushed against her arm. Wires trailed from the back of Meera's neck and howlsuit too.

Torvram was still missing.

Something had invaded Lakshmi's mind. It had tricked her and made her believe for just an instant that her father—no, her mentor—might have been alive. Lakshmi had wanted to tell him so much. So much.

But Chetan was dead.

Lakshmi felt the pressure of the headache return behind her eyes. She blinked, trying to push it back.

"She's awake," Meera murmured. Her husky voice was strained and weak; it sounded like she was expelling dust from her lungs.

Layer upon layer of realization continued to set in. Lakshmi covered her face as her cheeks flushed with embarrassment. She realized she was crying.

CHAPTER 15

MOVE FORWARD

MEERA; ENGINE DECK, *TRAILBLAZER*

Lakshmi emerged from the human-sized cabinet of a bathroom fifteen minutes later. Her eyes were dried and her face was set into that same wide, confident smirk.

Except I'd seen her do this for years in that fantasy world and, in retrospect, multiple times in real life. This time, her eyes didn't share that smile. This was a mask. Where I struggled to conceal my emotions at the best of times, I was learning that Lakshmi was adept at faking hers. Like Matyom, she concealed when she was feeling tired or doubtful or scared. It wasn't necessarily a bad thing, but where Matyom used this lie to boost morale, Lakshmi had a host of other potential motivations. Few of them were selfless.

"We're going back." Lakshmi's voice echoed in the engine room. With the *Trailblazer's* treads silent and directionless, Lakshmi filled the void. "This Intelligence, whatever it is, is too dangerous for us to confront while we're ignorant and alone. Fei, radio Shangri-La. Matyom, prepare to get us home as fast as possible. We'll save Torvram once we have the means to do it without risking our own lives."

"Assuming he's still alive" went unsaid.

"Yes, ma'am," Fei replied automatically. She abandoned her work on the android's mind and rushed to Lakshmi's side.

I rose from the makeshift bed Case had constructed. My body was still weak from the incursion into Lakshmi's mind and the many hours I'd spent essentially comatose.

Matyom's big hand stopped me in a half-seated position. His gesture said "you need to rest" but his eyes were on Lakshmi. I could see he was conflicted. He said nothing—yet.

Lakshmi and Fei vanished up the ladder before any of us could react.

"She doesn't know about the vote," I blurted out.

"What?" Case replied.

"You need to lie down," Matyom said sternly, in unison with Case.

"I know," I replied, squeezing his arm gently. "Just let me talk to her real quick. If we get ordered back, that's at least four more days travel between us and the lakes where Torvram might be. I don't want to risk that."

Matyom grimaced. "She is right that... sending a rescue into the complete unknown could lead to even more casualties. As much as I want to find him, to save him, to hold Torvram in my arms again, I think she's right. We don't even know if Torvy is there."

I was struggling to speak. My mouth was dry and my voice cracked. The words came out as painful scratches. Matyom moved to tuck the blanket over my body. There was concern in his eyes. They didn't know yet what I'd seen. I don't know if he was worried I was going to hurt myself or simply filled with silent sorrow over Torvram, but I had to convince him to let me up.

If I'd learned one thing from spending virtual years in Lakshmi's mind, it was that opportunities often came only once.

This was my shot to stop her from turning us back.

I coughed and forced the words through my weak and inflamed windpipe. "That's not why she's calling home. She wants us to go back so she can prevent a vote to call Earth. If we go back, we lose four days in travel and untold time while she shifts the narrative away from Torvram's rescue. I don't know how much time he has left, but I know we need to spend every waking moment answering these questions: Is Torvram alive? Where is he? And how do we save him?

"Let me go, and call Shangri-La while I'm gone. Ask them about AVA, about the Intelligence, about the drones malfunctioning in the north. Get orbital images. Get help if we need it. But *do not* let her derail our expedition."

"Go." Case wrapped his hand over Matyom's. I felt the big man's hand lift.

"Good call," Matyom added.

I could hear Lakshmi barking orders one floor above me. I climbed up the ladder slowly, weighed down by the task ahead of me.

When I finally reached the operations deck, my heart beat like I'd run kilometers. Lakshmi lounged behind the origami table and stared intently at Fei while the shorter woman worked a radio that'd been lodged in the kitchenette's sink. The same broken octocopter that'd attacked Case—what felt like a lifetime ago—sat disassembled on the countertop.

"Get off this frequency *now*," she said to someone on the other end of the radio. Lakshmi's voice, too, was weak and her growled threat was missing some of its bite. Her eyes, on the other hand, were practically burning out of her skull with cerulean light.

"The vote already went through," I blurted out.

Lakshmi's neck cracked sickeningly as she whipped her whole body to face me, her mouth agape.

I dropped into a chair and rasped, "Wayland rushed it through while you were out. His pretense was the unprecedented threat that's controlling drones to the north. This call, whatever you're trying to say, it doesn't matter."

I needed her to know.

I needed her to stop.

I hoped she'd decide to focus on saving my friend, her employee, our fellow Titanborn.

"Meera's right," Fei replied demurely. She switched off the radio. "They've already called Earth."

Lakshmi spun around, her three intact prosthetics bared, and glared at Fei. "Why didn't you tell—"

Lakshmi's face worked, realization dawning. She looked back at me. She pointed at the radio wordlessly. Tension bled from her angular frame.

Lakshmi shouted, a messy gurgle of sound crowded with conflicting emotions. She slammed her prosthetics down on the table. The triangular sections warped and bent. She hit the table again with her own hands. Sharp faces between the now-mangled origami cut into her. She shouted, this time in surprised pain. Lakshmi's mask fell, exhaustion suddenly evident in her sagging mouth, the folds under her eyes, and the way her shoulders tipped forward and inward.

The Lakshmi Chetan had instilled in her rebounded in an instant, though. She sat up straight—as if that tantrum hadn't happened at all—and turned to Fei.

The cracks upon Lakshmi's restored smirk where obvious now. I'd found its encryption key and until she found a new way to conceal her feelings, I'd be seeing right through it.

"No," she concluded quietly. Her expression, her mood, and perhaps her thoughts, rubber-banded again. "Have we heard back from Earth? NASA? The FEAA? India? China? Europe? Mars?"

Lakshmi addressed me now, rather than Fei. The hooded woman and I both knew the answer.

"No," I replied.

"Oh," Lakshmi replied. She smiled at me. "Good."

"But it's over," I continued.

"Not yet," Lakshmi laughed. It wasn't convincing.

"It's over," I repeated, definitively. "There's no reason to send us back home."

"Ma'am? What should we do?" Fei asked, ignoring me.

"I need time to think," Lakshmi replied.

"No." I rose from the seat and tried my best to look powerful and confident, standing before them. "We need to save Torvram. This vote of yours? The politics? It doesn't matter. His life might still be in danger."

"Give her time to think," Fei said to me with a hint of venom. We locked eyes. Fei's face, at least what I could see, was a conflicted mess. She wore an angry frown but her voice sounded apologetic. We were friends, sort of, at this point. At least, comrades united against an unknown threat and the known danger of Titan.

Lakshmi fixed the collar of her puffy jacket. She avoided my gaze, making a show of idly brushing plastic debris and organonitrile muck from her clothing. A small vein of dried blood had hardened on the side of her face where she'd hit the ground in the Waystation. The table in front of her was speckled with blood from the inside curve of her hands.

She wasn't ok.

I wasn't either.

"Fei." Lakshmi assumed her command posture, filling the room with her loud and clear orders. "Go downstairs and make sure Case doesn't fuck up this order. I need satellite video, drone logs, every piece of evidence that points to what this thing is, how it works, and where it dragged Torvram off to."

Then, she began to smile. Her mouth widened until her incisors gleamed with reflected light. It was like watching a predator bare its fangs in victory or, perhaps, watching a predator bluff as it tried to scare its prey into voluntary submission. "Make sure to emphasize that *Wayland and Shift* patched AVA without my input and may be responsible for this malfunction. Float the idea that it's a partitioned error or a version mismatch. And see if they know how Chetan's android got removed from storage, while you're at it."

Fei nodded, smiling happily for the first time since Lakshmi had woken up. "Yes, ma'am. Right away."

Fei disappeared down the ladder to the engine room.

That left me alone, again, with Lakshmi. But the first crisis was averted. Lakshmi had lost her personal reason to send us home.

I was still afraid of her but, at this point, it wouldn't stop me. Here I was, one successful Titanborn neural repair later standing up to my boss. Torvram would be proud.

Torvram *will* be proud when I see him again, I internally corrected.

"Why'd you say all that, out loud, with me here?" I asked. I had my suspicions, but I wanted to hear her say it.

"You've seen thirty years of *one* version of the future I want for us," Lakshmi replied with a casual veneer. Her voice couldn't quite sell her nonplussed attitude though. "So you know, at least, that I plan to make sure this isolation experiment succeeds. Not just for us either—for the future of human space exploration.

"It's kind of nice," she continued. "To have someone to share this with."

I sighed in frustration. Lakshmi was still lying and I was tired of her games.

"You're in this for you," I replied.

"Oh, please." She whipped one of her hands forward chidingly. "Of course, there's a selfish element to my actions. I'm only human, Meera. But you can't deny that my vision is grand. A livable Titan? A successful independent colony? A future for all of us, in our own home, independent of Earth? It wasn't just Chetan's dream; it was also your mother's. Juniper wanted this too."

I flinched. She wasn't wrong. It was as if she was never wrong when I spoke to her. But I knew better now. Even without the journey I'd just been through where her mind and her dreams had been laid bare, I'd always known, from the very first fleeting conversations we'd had as children. I'd just never trusted that I might be right, from time to time.

"You want the recognition for all of this." I tried to poke at her, to get under her skin. I wasn't even sure what my goal was anymore but this felt good. "You want to be respected as a genius, by everyone, every human in existence."

Lakshmi shrugged. "I don't *want* any of that. I just *want* everyone who is too distracted or unintelligent to see what we could accomplish here to get in line or get out of the way.

You know, I'm still not sure where you fit in this, Meera. What do *you* want?"

"I want..." I'd been so ready to strike with my checkmate, to prove to her that she was this selfish, manipulative bitch who'd made me so miserable all these years. But the words didn't come. What *did* I want?

"I don't know," I replied, honestly.

"See?! You lack vision! But we both know you *need* to survive and that scientific achievement toward those aims is mighty important. Come ooon, after all this is over just help me out. You've shown talent with what you did in my brain. I can find you a much greater role on Titan, you know." She smirked confidently, her eyes dancing with amusement. Lakshmi had relaxed into the bench now, seemingly actually casual this time, and she regarded me with a look I'd never seen before.

Was she having *fun*?

But, no, I was getting distracted again. I needed to say one last thing.

"No," I replied. "I'm done working for you. I quit."

"Pfft. Really? You're wasting your talents then?"

Really? After all this time, *now* she had something other than derision and disappointment to throw my way? Now that I was taking back my own life, of course. "Oh?! So now I *have* talent?! After all these years of you telling me I'm worthless—"

"I've never once said that!" she countered, rasping the words.

"You've insinuated it with your actions! You reassign me at a whim. You move me around your chessboard like I'm a pawn, changing my schedule, erasing my progress. It's like you don't know what you're doing and everyone beneath you has to compensate for your own random ideas and failings!"

"As Case would say, bullshit!" She raised a finger into the air declaratively.

"You know what I want?" I was incensed now.

"What, Meera?" She chuckled. She was leaning forward, her eyes hot, her mouth open as her grin only widened. She was mocking me, or something.

"I want you to start being responsible for your own fucking actions. You have power, use it like a blasted adult! You know how you could *actually* be better than Chetan? Try some fucking empathy!"

Lakshmi giggled.

"Stop fucking laughing! Did you listen to anything I said when we got you out of that dissociative immersion trap?! Anything at all! How can you act like you care about the Titanborn when you use us to gain power and then throw us away on a whim?"

I glared at her from across the table, trying to bore this into her brain with my eyes. I could've done that, implanted these ideas, back there. I wouldn't have—it was a violation of ethics and my personal values—but some small part of me regretted being so responsible. Unlike her, apparently.

"Hahahaha!" She threw her head back and cackled, her messy jet black hair swaying with each laugh.

"Stop laughing!"

What was I even doing here? She'd already agreed to finding Torvram, even if she'd laced it with her own motives. I'd declared that I would quit. Done.

I could just get up and walk away. Why was I putting up with this mockery? She didn't care about me. She didn't care about anyone but herself. Maybe I couldn't get a single other person to believe this, but I knew who Lakshmi really was.

Wasn't that enough?

"This is really fun," she replied, wiping a tear from her eye. Cerulean light poured from the little gap between eyelids, coloring her eyelashes a deep blue. "I really needed this after everything that's happened." She looked away from across the small, damaged table. Her expression turned sour, introspective.

That caught me by surprise. We hadn't really had the time to decompress from essentially having her mind violated.

Here, I'd been assuming she'd just bounced back like everything else, even after seeing evidence to the contrary. I forced myself to ignore the pain, too, the disorientation, the fear.

"Right now," Lakshmi continued. "I still see that crowd, during the speech. They fade in and out of my vision." She waved at the opposite wall, right where the kitchenette ended. There were more nets there, cabinets, storage space. No people.

"I'm a little scared, to be honest, that I'll never get my mind back or that this, even, isn't real. Not to mention the, uhhh, gaslighting about Chetan's being alive when he isn't and all that."

"Sorry," I replied, unsure of what to say. We'd shared that horrible experience, to some extent, but I'd been an interloper. I'd invaded her mind to restore her senses. I'd never heard her say she was scared, either. This was new territory.

"Thanks, really, for doing what you did, Meera. That put you at risk, and Fei too. I know you could've waited for a safer time and place, but that would've meant risking my mind and body, so you took the risk... for me, or perhaps, just to prevent another Titanborn from dying.

"I'll have to thank Fei too." She looked over at the ladders and grimaced.

I pressed forward. As much as this apology was unexpected, and warranted, I realized why I was still here arguing with her even after I'd cut myself loose from her professionally. I still wanted Lakshmi to be better than the woman I knew.

Maybe that wasn't fair, and maybe it wasn't my place to say, but when was life on Titan ever fair? Lakshmi had the power. I needed her to utilize it with empathy, with conscientious choice, for all of us. Chetan had filled our heads with these stupid ideas that we were to be the next step in human evolution, so we should act like it, vent it! We should *be better people*. Unlike him.

"I appreciate it, Lakshmi, but, while we're talking honestly... I just need to know that you'll try, ok, to consider how each of us is affected when you act. Consider our health, or futures too, when you push toward yours."

"Hah! I always do. You're here, aren't you? I've kept us alive, haven't I?"

"Ugh." That was it then. She wasn't going to listen.

She turned to face me again. "I'll be the first to defend that high-level leadership will always hurt someone, always make enemies."

I rose from the bench, disgusted. I *was* wasting my time.

"But, hey, wait," She reached out to me as I passed the table. I paused, curious, despite myself. "You're not supposed to be one of those enemies, Meera."

"That's on you," I replied, still feeling angry.

Lakshmi crossed her arms, all of her arms. "I'll... I don't know. I'll see Anyu. I'll try."

"Oh, umm, thanks I guess. I honestly didn't—huh."

"Surprised you again, hehehehe." This woman was maybe more of a gremlin than a monster, I was realizing. Beneath all of her intelligence and power, she was acting like a mischievous little troll, reveling in chaos.

"I don't normally share like this, ya know? My exes don't know half the stuff that brain dive laid out for you, not just the future—I'm sure you saw plenty of the past." She looked wistfully at the "Farah" patch on her howlsuit. The "x" she'd crossed over it had worn off in the rain.

"Mmm," I replied, recovering slowly from multiple stages of emotional whiplash.

"Can you do me a favor?" she asked.

"That depends."

"Tell me next time, ok? Tell me when I'm fucking up, when I'm hurting people... when I'm hurting you."

"I—It's not my responsibility to police you. Besides, I won't be working for you anymore." I crossed my arms, trying to project stubbornness, resolution.

"I know. I know." She frowned. "It would just, help, ya know, to get honest feedback. I *will* try to do better."

"Ok. I suppose I can do that from time to time. You'd do better by letting other people in the room, people who are more concerned with the impact your actions have."

"How about you?" Lakshmi grinned.

I shook my head.

"Come ooon, have some ambition!" Lakshmi teased coyly.

I shook my head again. It wasn't even tempting. Not today.

"You aren't supposed to be my enemy," she repeated with a sigh. "I've fucked up."

"Who is, then?" I was consistently finding my curiosity pulled me right back into her games. I wasn't sure what that meant or how to feel about it.

"Time. Nature."

"You're..." I laughed. "You're definitely Chetan's daughter. Ambitious, calloused, maybe a bit insane."

"I am not calloused." She pouted.

I raised an eyebrow.

"Ok, maybe a little, for now, we'll fix that." She smiled lazily, looking up at the ceiling. "I wish I had gotten to know June better though. I don't... *get* people like she did. Like you do."

"Whoa." I hadn't meant to let that slip out.

"This is fun," she repeated, tapping two fingers on the damaged table and beaming up at the ceiling.

Case coughed.

We turned to look at him. He held his hands over his mouth, looking guilty. "Shangri-La just dropped a nuke on us. We've got new orders, new info, and—just, come downstairs, chipheads."

"That's my cue," Lakshmi replied casually. "Thanks, Meera."

"What?" I replied.

"What?" Case said in unison.

Lakshmi vanished down the ladder.

"You ok?" Case approached me slowly, cautiously; his hands were jammed into his pockets. Concern was written across his face.

"I think so..." I said. It had been a lot to take in, on top of the whole immersion into her infected brain thing. I wasn't sure which had been more disorienting at this point.

I found myself rooted to the spot between the table and kitchenette. I stood atop a cluster of triangles and stared through him, at the wall. "Can you give me a hug?"

Case's face softened, his expression melting into a calm smile as the tension between us dropped away. "Sure."

I enfolded him in a hug, leaning into his warmth, barely able to stand on my own two feet. He wrapped his arms around my back, gripping the thick fiber of my sweater with both hands. It had all been so much, all of this, since before Torvram had even disappeared. My whole life, all the death, the long hours, the rapid training, the very mission we'd been built for, even the fact in and of itself that'd we'd been *designed and built* by someone, intentionally.

It was all hitting me now, somehow.

I didn't cry. I bunched as much of his navy coveralls as I could around my thumbs and pulled the shorter man into my chest. I just breathed, eyes closed, waiting for my brain chemistry to catch up again with the Meera I needed right now. My fear would pass. All of this would pass.

I could do this.

Whatever Shangri-La found out, wherever Torvram was, I could find him. We would find him. The five of us would save him, even Lakshmi. We were Titanborn. We were *built* for this.

I sighed happily. The warmth of another body helped me feel more alive, more present. It helped that it was Case, definitively. I was slightly surer about what to do with that than my lingering curiosity toward Lakshmi.

Case chuckled and whispered, "Matyom wanted me to remind you that you have effectively passed the 'Neuroengineering on Humans Practical.' Thought it would cheer you up."

I gazed down into Case's lightless hazel eyes and laughed.

LAKSHMI; ENGINE DECK, *TRAILBLAZER*

When her suit radio squawked, Lakshmi slunk back to the bathroom under the pretense of a nutrient paste gone bad. She wanted none of them, especially Meera, to realize she was getting a separate call from the Revision Committee. The rust-eyed woman had become far too insightful since she'd occupied Lakshmi's mind.

None of it had been real. All her careful plans, near losses, every conflict she'd put every ounce of her being into had been a lie. This Intelligence had sat in her head and fed her everything she wanted. In retrospect, the deception was painfully obvious.

Lakshmi poked at the radio in her suit, unusually reluctant to act.

Meera was right: the call to Earth had been made. Lakshmi's plans were out the window and Wayland was probably just calling to boast or advocate for her removal.

She sighed, cupping her hand over her face and mouthed a silent groan into it. Lakshmi decided to just get this over with—rip the bandage off—and keyed her radio.

"What did you do, Lakshmi?" Wayland's stern, commanding voice barked through the radio.

She turned on the air-dryer and jammed it, letting a continual flow of recycled air drown out her voice. "Ugh. Don't yell. I'm having an awful day. What do you mean: what did I do?"

An undertone of digust hardened his voice further. "Earth hasn't said anything. Our signal never even went out. We're cut off, somehow. *What did you do?!*"

The answer was: nothing. Lakshmi smiled at herself in the light-ringed mirror and relaxed against the bathroom wall. She was back at the table. Her plans were *still viable* after all!

She injected a smug lilt into her voice as her mood lifted. "I'm flattered that you think I have the power to block a mayday signal, Wayland, but I can't. You sure you caught the cubesat? Maybe you missed."

"Fuck you, Lakshmi. This is serious. We're unable to call Earth." Wayland's low growl vibrated through Lakshmi's suit. "Don't you understand what this means?"

"It was probably this Intelligence that I'm risking my sweet butt to take down." Lakshmi chuckled and winked at herself in the mirror. The answer was obvious, after all. Wayland really was off his game today. "You know, the one that's probably *still* got Torvram? The very same Intelligence *you* maneuvered me into fighting and *you* probably created with that patch. That's my official stance, anyway."

"You bitch, you're enjoying this, aren't you?"

"Bitch! Ahh we're name-calling now, are we?"

"It's... this Intelligence isn't the cause." Wayland was struggling with his words now. This was entirely unlike him. Lakshmi imagined the sweat forming on her formidable foe's brow as he spoke. "We're seeing no trace of it at home. AVA would know. We would know. I wouldn't be calling you if it *was* a suspect because that would be an obvious problem. Something else, someone *inside Shangri-La* is preventing us from calling Earth."

"That *is* worrying." It was, but a bone-chilling threat like internal sabotage wasn't going to get in the way of Lakshmi enjoying her victory. "Good for me but, ultimately, very troubling. You sure it's not Shift—trouble in the bedroom?"

"Lakshmi..." Wayland went silent. No retort came over the radio, no jab to levy back at his longtime opponent.

This *was* serious.

Lakshmi took a deep breath. She was seeing hallucinatory bursts of color in her right eye; emotionally dissonant feelings rolled through her mind, aftershocks of the Intelligence's meddling. She steadied herself against the wall, suddenly feeling woozy.

"Fine." She squeezed her eyelids closed. That only left her alone with the phantom visions.

Who would prevent them from being able to call Earth? Who could even do this? Lakshmi didn't have the ability. The whole Committee couldn't have blocked access, even if all of Titan had voted on it. Only AVA could make this sort of change, but that would be against all its protocols to see the isolation experiment succeed and see the Titanborn survive. It'd be like burning down your own successful business, without even an insurance scam to justify your actions.

"If it's no one in my camp, and no one in yours, well, that leaves..." Lakshmi couldn't believe it herself, but the facts left only one suspect if this other Intelligence wasn't in play. "Do you have any evidence implicating AVA?"

"I'm getting tired of your jokes." Wayland's voice shook.

"I'm truly enjoying how rattled the very idea of my meddling has made you, but this isn't a joke. AVA's the only suspect I have. Lucky for us that you called me on our private freq."

"I... it." She heard Wayland swallow over the radio. Lakshmi felt a degree of sympathy for him. If AVA was acting up too, that felt violating. AVA was their caretaker, their home, their everything.

"If that's true, then AVA can lie," Wayland concluded. "And the implications of that are... staggering."

"Look into it, Wayland. AVA's the most likely suspect I can think of."

Wayland scoffed. "How do I know you're not lying to me? How do I know this wasn't you?"

"Wayland, every word I've ever said to you has been a lie, including these ones." Lakshmi grinned at her reflection in the small mirror. "But believe me when I say, it wasn't me."

"Fine." Wayland's voice returned to his measured, calm superiority. "We will look into this, as will you when you return."

"Looks like I'm not beaten yet." Lakshmi threw in one last jab.

Wayland groaned. "I hate working with you."

"Hate you too. Byeee." Lakshmi had to cover her mouth as the channel went dead with static; she could barely restrain herself from cackling with glee. She loved sticking it to Wayland and his demure partner, sure, but this was a monumental victory to be celebrated. The isolation experiment wasn't scuttled because they couldn't make the call. They were cut off from Earth! That meant everything she'd dreamed of could still happen!

She afforded herself one quiet celebratory laugh, beaming into the mirror. Everything was back on track! Lakshmi could make the isolation experiment successful. They'd survive the required decades, terraform Titan to be livable, and then with great praise and adoration from Earth, she'd make her next—

—wait. Lakshmi's mouth twisted into a frown. Not all of that was possible. If they were truly alone now, if Wayland was right...

The Titanborn were *cut off from Earth.*

CHAPTER 16

NORTHBOUND

MEERA; ENGINE DECK, *TRAILBLAZER*

We were moving again. The *Trailblazer* ground through Titan's organonitrile soil and freshly flooded river canals. The polar lakes awaited us.

Case and I sat around a chunky radio, reluctantly surrendered by Lakshmi, in the cramped engine room. The broken android was secured so close that I repeatedly brushed against it. Its dead eyes reflected the white lights above.

"Try to—" our correspondent at Shangri-La began over the radio, before a wave of static rose and swallowed his voice whole.

Case switched the channel with robotic efficiency. We were getting used to these technological attacks from the hostile Intelligence. It was getting more efficient, too, as time advanced.

"—ges from the cubesats. We're scanning Kraken Waystation. It—" More static.

Case grunted, fiddling with the blocky radio and jotting down hasty notes on a homegrown notepad. Shipping paper all the way from Earth would've been a massive waste of fuel.

"—there's a Tower to the north. We're sending you images every way we can think of. Check you—"

Static. Something smashed into the *Trailblazer* outside and we felt it crunch beneath the treads. Case and I exchanged a worried look. It'd probably been another drone.

"—body located just so—"

"—maybe Torvram—"

From orbit, it was clear how quickly this threat was growing. Waves of drones were being drawn north, then turning away as AVA regained control of them, only for them to malfunction and turn toward the lakes again. Hundreds of them were affected and that number was only growing. The "Tower" they'd referenced was a massive spire that appeared to be growing out of Kraken Waystation, along the coast of said polar lake.

Things were getting weird back home, too. AVA was dedicating an increasingly large percentage of its flops and our resources to stopping this Intelligence. Titanborn had been reassigned to build makeshift vehicles, told to prep for an impossibly large northern expedition, and ordered to break any malfunctioning drone they couldn't fix.

AVA was becoming so dedicated to stopping this threat that our counterparts at home had cut off its influence to sections of Shangri-La just to keep water and food production going sustainably. Through its shifting prioritization, AVA was implying that the Intelligence was more of a danger to our lives than Titan itself.

"—more data coming your wa—" The radio crackled.

"—dismantle the—"

"What is it?" Case barked at the radio. Hours of listening to fragmented, often useless messages was making us both impatient. "The fuck is that Tower it's building out of the Waystation? Is it where the Intelligence's brains are?"

"—unsure but AVA wants it sto—"

"—tivate or destr—"

Each time a wave of heat rolled through the Tower within Kraken Waystation, more drones turned north. We inferred that it was expanding the Intelligence's influence.

AVA had dispassionately calculated that, at this rate, we had a day before the Intelligence could overwhelm its influence enough to affect Shangri-La.

Our orders were clear, one way or another. The *Trailblazer* was the largest vehicle on Titan. Remote drones couldn't be relied on to approach the lakes without losing control.

We had to stop it, somehow.

Zooming until the video was a grainy, low-resolution mess, I could just make out a unique heat signature at Kraken Waystation. A figure was seated, atop a mound of debris that undulated as drones burst from it and lugged chunks of plastic and metal up the Tower. It hadn't taken long for our analysts to confirm.

That was Torvram and, somehow, he was still alive.

Thunk. Another drone crashed into the *Trailblazer*.

I flinched, staring at the wall that the sound had emanated from.

Lakshmi and Fei sat shoulder-to-shoulder with Case, the inactive android, and I, packed tightly between workbenches and supply nets. Our whole group had to move whenever someone got up to use the bathroom. It was a little too warm in here and the air smelled of body odor and methane, but I was far too busy and too worried to care.

Fei cursed under her breath at the two computers in her lap and the half-dozen more wrapped around her arms. Blocks with antennae and batteries haphazardly wired together lay at Fei's feet, courtesy of Case and Matyom.

Without the ability to safely broadcast, we had to resort to accessing the drones through slower means. Fei was working as fast as she could, breaking into their altered programming and neutralizing them before they destroyed the *Trailblazer*, but none of us could match AVA or this increasingly complex hostile entity. The only thing keeping the *Trailblazer* alive was that AVA could still reach us, for now.

I took another look outside through the cameras, hardwired into another computer on a crate.

There were hundreds of drones flying in long, unbroken lines. Copters dipped out of the clouds above, their sensors jerking in sudden, abrupt bursts. A pair of delivery trucks, ice cores still bound onto their beds, rolled over potholes filled with methane.

One of them blinked its lights and spun about in a wide arc to face us. It accelerated without warning, bouncing up and out of a pothole and crashing back to Titan in a spray of orange and gold muck. Its ice cores broke loose, flying into the air and shattering or shearing apart as they hit the ground.

"Fei!" I shouted, unsure if she saw the incoming threat.

"Iseeit!" Fei blurted her response breathlessly. The truck continued to speed up, changing its trajectory in discrete, staccato bursts. It was aiming for our nose, correcting repeatedly, as it got closer and closer still.

Suddenly, its brakes screeched with such ferocity that I heard them both through the camera's audio sensors *and* through the walls of the *Trailblazer* itself. The truck flipped up and onto its back, sending a final spray of orange organics into my vision. The tar boiled off rapidly and we sped on, leaving the hostile drone behind.

But that was only one of the dozens that'd had attacked us, and one of hundreds that surrounded us.

The radio went dead again.

"It's learning," Fei added, scowling. "It's hard enough being lagged by inputting all this by hand, but I'm—" She paused, furiously typing. "It's getting better at stopping me. I'm figuring out its tricks but not as fast as it's learning mine."

"Shit," Case hissed as he stared at the wall the truck's screech and crash had emanated through. He bit his lip, tapping impatiently at a toolbox that sat unopened on his lap. "Is Lakshmi done? She's got six arms she could be using to help."

"Sure, let me get right on that. Oh wait, I can't see anything but clouds." Lakshmi snorted derisively. She crossed her arms, staring into a world we couldn't see.

Her smile broadened and Lakshmi's cheeks flushed with color. "Well, not just clouds anymore. Some of this is pretty hot." Lakshmi's eyes shut off, becoming a pair of dark pits in her skull.

I made sure to turn off every video feed into her mind. I didn't want to share her horny hallucination.

Dozens of gossamer cables connected her brain to the computer in my lap. While Fei was deprogramming the drones, I was both being lookout and chipping away at the lingering effects of the Intelligence's incursion into Lakshmi's mind.

It wasn't just that her chipsets were still pumping false visuals into her senses in a hallucinatory feedback loop. There were also false associations all over her neural pathways: ideas and memories that had been fabricated by the Intelligence.

We'd been incredibly lucky it hadn't destroyed Lakshmi's personality or mental faculties. It had heavily modified her mind, but I was beginning to think it'd deliberately avoided doing any permanent damage. What had been its goal in attacking her then? If it just wanted to disable Lakshmi, it had gone out of its way to do so in a reversible way. Every question I answered raised two more.

The Intelligence clearly had an intimate knowledge of who Lakshmi was and what she wanted in order to keep her fooled. It had simulated Chetan's personality, too, with almost-convincing aplomb both to us and within Lakshmi's mind. It had even called her 'daughter' just as she'd wanted and Chetan never actually had, albeit only after Lakshmi had fallen unconscious. I had my theories about how the Intelligence gained this much data on us, and they shook me to the core.

Everything we did was recorded by our minds and stored with AVA, innately. No human on Titan had access to those recordings though, for our privacy. They were for external review and, during isolation, that meant no human off Titan had them either. Right now, only AVA had access.

Had this Intelligence *been* AVA at some point?

What was it now?

What was its goal? With Lakshmi? With Torvram? With Titan?

"You're supposed to be meditating," I chided the usually cerulean-eyed woman.

"Fine, *Mom*." Lakshmi rolled her blank eyes—or perhaps the reflected light on their surface just rolled—and shut them.

"We're almost there," I finally answered Case. "But this is... difficult."

Case's impatient, stressed expression softened. "Yeah."

"Everyone ok down there?" Matyom's voice boomed over the intercom.

We replied affirmatively. Since we'd left Aztlan, driving through a murder of hostile drones had become our standard for ok. As long as we weren't dead, we were "ok," I suppose.

"Case, can you watch this for a second? I'm going to go check on Matyom," I said as I rose from the floor. "Fei, is that ok?"

"Sure," Case replied. A grin gradually dawned on his face. "I'll try not to slip on the keys and delete your ability to sass, Lakshmi."

"I'll contact you if I need help," Fei replied, turning to face Case and Lakshmi. The two were staring each other down, despite Lakshmi's inability to see.

"Oh, don't you even—" Lakshmi began. "Fei! Watch this dumbass."

"I will keep an eye on him, as best I can, while preventing the drones from breaching our vehicle," Fei replied, smiling from behind her fabric mask.

We were suited up, ready for anything. We were *ok*.

I climbed up the next ladder, getting in a little exercise. We hadn't had the chance to do our routine workouts since this expedition started. The journey had certainly left me sore, but not in a way that would prevent muscle atrophy in Titan's low gravity. I instinctively tapped at my mental schedule. It appeared, useless, as it was an offline copy.

Besides, all it said was *Rescue Expedition*.

Matyom was half-rigged into the *Trailblazer's* electronics while he manually operated it. It too had been taken offline so that Fei didn't need to babysit it. We hadn't yet eradicated all traces of the Intelligence's interference, much like with Lakshmi's mind, so even offline the autopilot was off-limits.

"Hey." I took a seat next to him.

"Almost there," he replied in kind, wiggling his blond mustache inadvertently. "We're less than an hour from the lakes, and that Tower... and Torvram."

"And we know he's there this time," I said resolutely. "Each pass of the cubesat confirms it again. He's there and the Intelligence hasn't moved him."

"Yeah..." Matyom's mind was already split between two tasks. It was a wonder he could talk to me at all. I was starting to see how exhausted he was behind his booming voice and equally large personality. Maybe it was because I'd learned to see through Lakshmi. I wasn't sure.

"Are *you* ok?" I asked.

"Yeah," he repeated. "Sorry, Meera, I need to focus on driving. Can we talk later?"

"Of course. I ju-just," I stammered, searching for the right words, "like Case said, I want you to know that you're not alone. I'm here for you, if or when you need it." I squeezed his shoulder, like he'd done for me, so many times before.

"Thanks. I—" Suddenly, his whole body seemed to wince. "Fei!"

Matyom's voice boomed before me and over the intercom. "Fei! What just hit us? It's—" His visage contorted as he bit back a cry of pain.

"Meera, disconnect me. Help!" I gingerly disconnected the wires that bridged his howlsuit and the *Trailblazer's* quasi-mind.

He held on to the manual controls with a vise grip despite the pain evident in his shuddering body.

"Fei!" he repeated, angrily. "What is attacking us? My sensors—the *Trailblazer's* sensors didn't catch anything!"

"I'm trying!" Fei's voice was tiny compared to his. "It's got so many little minds, I can't."

Being unburdened by a role, I immediately recognized her description. Little minds. Many little minds. I remembered the sloshing tube of inky black fluid, liquid that climbed up the sides of its container against gravity, because it wasn't liquid at all. I'd worked with them before. This Intelligence had hit us with a swarm of microscopic machines.

They were an absolute nightmare to fix on a good day.

"Fei!" I shouted into the intercom. "It's a swarm! I'm coming down to help!"

"Meet us halfway, Meera!" Case's voice was tense and strained. "It's eating through the—"

A violent hiss and the sickening crunch of rigid plastic caving in drowned out his last words.

"Keep driving," I barked at Matyom before leaping down the ladder shaft.

"We're coming, Torv!" Matyom howled after me.

CHAPTER 17

THE SWARM

MEERA; OPERATIONS DECK, *TRAILBLAZER*

My legs almost gave out as I hit the ground. Lakshmi tugged Case up and into the operations deck. Her left eye was still offline, blinking to life only to flicker and go out.

Fei was already set up at the table Lakshmi had damaged. We stumbled over to her as the engine room hissed menacingly. The seal beneath us shut automatically. The engine deck was already breached.

Instinctively, wordlessly, the four of us donned our helmets.

No more death. At any cost.

"I can't get to them," Fei squeaked. "There are too many minds. They're all working together, already designed to adapt to each other's knowledge. It's—"

"It's exactly how you described this Intelligence," Lakshmi cut in.

"Fuck, it might be distributed like a swarm too," I added, "on a macroscale."

Fei and Lakshmi nodded. It was nice to be included, at least.

"I have to go online." Fei shut one of the laptops with finality. "I can't access these things fast enough with *these*." She held her hands out in front of her face, disgust evident in her voice.

The *Trailblazer* shook as something yet again crashed into it. "We've got another truck too!" Matyom shouted over the PA. We all tumbled over the origami bench, chairs, and table as the *Trailblazer* swung hard right, as hard as something on treads could.

Fei snapped back to her seat. "Vent it! It's using regular drones still? I have to stop them too."

The floor groaned and buckled beneath our feet, tessellated triangles shifting to accommodate the strain of newfound weight. Lakshmi's eyes finally reignited and she dashed to the kitchenette as a roiling mass of black goop began to seep through the hull. Case followed her, brandishing a food try like a club.

The origami walls of ops began to buckle inward. Miniscule triangular faces bent along their folds, hardening the hull against the sheer pressure of the invading swarm of machines. We'd wondered where the maintenance bots had been when we'd walked Aztlan's halls.

Now, I suspected, we had our answer.

"I can do it," I said, rushing over to Fei's side as I pulled a thin cable from the back of my suit. "Teach me how you've stopped them. I've got the neuroengineering knowledge."

"No!" Lakshmi shouted. "It's going to invade your fucking—" She snapped two layers of corrugated wall together with her prosthetics, crushing the inky swarm with a disgusting squelch. A second later, the fluid began to pour in once more. Lakshmi shook it off and retreated, pulling Case out of the kitchenette as she did so. "It'll invade your brain! It might kill you!"

"It's going to kill us anyway!" Case cried, throwing the tray at a bubble of machines forming about the faucet. It burst, scattering black blobs all over the cabinets and opposite wall. The kitchenette was beginning to dissolve in slow motion as a host of diminutive machines began to muck with its innards.

"I can do this," I repeated. "One of you just bring me out when you're done."

"You continue to surprise me, Meera!" Lakshmi shouted over the protestations of the walls themselves. A manic grin had spread across her face.

"Stop hitting on her and do the thing!" Case replied. It was his turn to drag Lakshmi farther away from the invading swarm. "Barrier her or whatever. Help her, chipheads!"

He shoved Lakshmi over to Fei and I and unsheathed the damaged torch. He fired a beam of orangish-purple plasma at the encroaching machines. When they burned, a rigid immobile blob of white was left behind.

But it wasn't enough. More continued to pour from every seam and some seemed to coalesce out of nothing at all.

He backed toward us, surgically burning away what he could. "Hurry!"

Lakshmi fumbled with the back of my suit.

"If you get her killed, Lakshmi, I'm gonna shove those arms up your ass!" Case added.

"Violent!" Lakshmi quipped. "Now look who's hitting on her."

To my astounding embarrassment, while our lives were in danger and my decision-making might decide it all, I blushed.

"Thanks?" I grinned awkwardly.

Matyom's voice crackled through the comm. "We're losing engines. You need to stop this thing. Now!"

"Work your chiphead magic," Case added, climbing into the uneven surface of the damaged table.

"Fei, connect with me. Toss some barriers in. Now!" Lakshmi shouted, before she abruptly plugged into my suit. Suddenly, I felt a mixture of emotions wash over me: some familiar, some practically alien. The turbulent waters of fear threatened to pull me down into their frothy undertow. The fire—sometimes warm, sometimes searing hot—of Lakshmi's confidence blazed against those frigid, enervating waters. There was something new, too.

<Ok. Ok. Ok. Ok,> I heard her think. Each utterance gathered her internal strength, stoking the flames of that spark until it blew into a blazing, blue flame. <Access them, now. I'll keep an eye on you. ;)>

I felt a weight against my back and something plug into my brain.

<Hello. This is an automated message. Welcome to the Avitra Biotechnology Cerebrobarrier Mark Three. We thank you for choosing our—> I blocked the rest of the barrier's canned greeting. Now was not the time for a nested advertisement.

There was a loud pop and the whirring, then screeching, of ventilation.

I went online.

First, I reached for the signals of the swarm. I found nothing but then suddenly, without a second thought, I began to have an inkling of how I'd find them through the Intelligence's interference. Knowledge poured into my head. Ideas that weren't my own suddenly felt obvious.

Fei's research, all the hours she'd spent breaking through that "unauthorized user;" problem and combating this Intelligence was abruptly mine too.

"Ops is breached!" Case shouted.

<You blasted cunt. Where the fuck do you get off? Abducting one of us under my nose? Invading my mind? 🖕> Lakshmi's internal diatribe spilled over into my head.

A cascade of folds eroded on the far wall and more black fluid slipped through the breach. I felt our life-giving heat began to invisibly seep away.

<I will not die here you worthless AVA knockoff! D:> Lakshmi continued to protest as I finally reached for the swarm.

<hello;
i am:
entity(meera);
intelligence(human);
class(neuroengineer);
what is wrong with you?;>

<hello;
i am:
entity(Maintenance[1,3.8e3,1]);
intelligence(sub-sentient);
class(standalone swarm);
nothing;>

"Ladder!" Case shouted.

"Too late!" Lakshmi pressed me into the bench and stood between me and the swarm as my vision faded. The cable trailing from her suit toward me was the last thing I saw.

The Intelligence began to reach into and through the neural barriers.

The *Trailblazer* was suddenly an autumn forest filled with organic trees. Then it was Titan's north pole, and the lakes stretched out before us and June was there, wearing a long sundress, except no, was that Torvram? Was I in my suit? Or in a jacket? I felt rain, but it wasn't methane.

At the same time, Fei's ideas continued to pour into my mind and mingle with my own experiences. There wasn't a central machine in this swarm that served as the commander. But fear of the gray goo scenario was older than the very first swarm bots—long before I'd been born someone had made kill switches that should have been grandfathered down to this swarm. I didn't need to take control of them or even fight at the Intelligence's control. If I could find and hit that switch, we would be free.

<root Maintenance[1,3.8e3,1];>

Suddenly, I knew a remarkable amount about emulating AVA's access. I felt like someone was copy-pasting long strings into my thoughts, so foreign was the knowledge I'd abruptly learned. Fei was *good* at working with AI.

The swarmbots replied, <admin privileges denied;>

I gave it a simple, innocuous response. <output error;>

I saw long rolling dunes, like ours, but unilaterally tan. And the sky was blue.

I rebooted my eyes, and desperately fought against the things that I was touching, hearing, seeing, and sensing that did not match my worldview. The Intelligence dumped volumes of junk information into my increasingly compromised mind.

Case gripped my arm. That was him. He was still there. That grounded me, just barely.

<entity(DERECHO) = admin;> the swarmbots replied.

<*It has a name?!* :O> Lakshmi said through our connection.

I knew I was back on the *Trailblazer*. I knew Case was real. Lakshmi was right in front of me. Derecho was attacking me with tens of thousands of machines because, like the swarm, each one of them was both its pawn and its mind.

The world before me bled into the gray craters and the star-speckled blackness of Earth's moon. The sun was suddenly far too close and much too bright.

How was I on the moon? Oh, yeah, because I had a job here. This was my fifth year. I'd left Titan and—

No. This was wrong.

I took a deep breath. I still felt Case's arm on mine. He was gripping too tightly. Heat licked at my sides. Lakshmi and Fei were still in the back of my head. Lakshmi's confidence flared. Fei's knowledge continued to flow.

They were standing on the bench beside me now, pressing me against the wall.

This was real.

I took another breath, listening to my real chest as my real lungs filled with air from inside the howlsuit. I had to stop the swarm.

I was grabbing at thousands of those little minds now. Derecho was dedicating fewer cycles to this swarm. Was it because of AVA or me?

Take a breath.

It didn't matter.

Its mind was dripping into mine. I couldn't see. I couldn't hear. I couldn't feel anymore. Fei, Case, Lakshmi, Matyom, they were out there somewhere, but I couldn't find them.

I had Derecho's swarm. I began to turn them back, removing Derecho's access, rewriting code. Within them, I found code written with strange, nearly incomprehensible structure.

Fei's knowledge continued to trickle in. Lakshmi's too. We spoke in instantaneous, subconscious concepts. When I balked at my admin privileges being denied, the concept of rewriting it became known to me in an immediate, dissociative thought. I tore through Derecho's fingerprints, flinging every trick it had used back out to Fei and Lakshmi. I had no time to understand, only time to copy-and-paste, to infiltrate and steal.

Finally, I knew that the last barrier had given way. There was nothing between me and the net now. All of Derecho burst through. I tried to go offline, but Derecho held my doorway to the digital world open.

As the Intelligence swept through my brain, I sent two messages out to Lakshmi and Fei. One was a long string almost identical in structure to the one Fei had given me to let me emulate AVA. This one would give them the ability to emulate Derecho. I didn't know how long it would take Derecho to notice and render this string useless, but even a microsecond could be the difference between life and death for all five of us.

The second was a command.

<go offline;>

I would not let Derecho get to them through me. With the option to save myself stolen away, I leapt through that opening.

I reached into as many of Derecho's machines as I could; it in turn poured into my chipset and took hold of my very consciousness.

Suddenly, I found myself somewhere real again.

I was looking through someone else's eyes.

I was near Titan's northern lakes. The storm rolled over them, pregnant clouds crowded the golden sky. Sheets of methane poured into the already swollen lakes. Their surfaces, usually glassy smooth, were crashing violently against the shore.

<...*hello?*> it, no, *he* said.

Torvram's mind was a mess of novel complexity. I sat within his perception comfortably, as if he'd been designed to be rigged into, like Chetan's android.

He sat at a small fire in his mind and kept his eyes down and away from the surrounding darkness. I felt Derecho's eyes out there, probing for weakness.

<...*meera?!*>

I felt around as Derecho's influence warped my perception. I was rigged into Torvram's brain. How?

<*torvram!*> I had so many things to ask. I felt a horrible pounding headache. I wanted to hug him, to cry together, to tell Torvram everything was going to be ok and *mean it* this time.

Vast, inhuman processing power was connected to his brain. He wasn't just Torvram anymore. There were all sorts of extra parts I could look at, circuitry that dwarfed the capabilities of his mind.

And he was in terrible pain.

<*i... need help,*> Torvram replied, as if he hadn't heard me at all. His consciousness felt so small, so weak. His telepathic signature had lost his personal flourishes of "T's" and ":3's." It felt remarkably like mine: lacking energy, but even there he sounded weaker than me. There was lag between each word and sentence formulation alone was causing him pain that even I could feel. <*this was a...mistake i just wanted to...be... better but...this was a mistake*>

I resisted the powerful urge to just break down and hold him. I needed to know how to save him, though. <*torv please i need to know where you are and how derecho captured you.*>

<*it...didnt,*> he replied mournfully, each word coming out with a bolt of pain.

<*what?*> What did he mean by that?!

<*i...need help,*> he repeated. <*please.*>

Physically, I couldn't move his eyes, but I could feel his body. There were things within his howlsuit that shouldn't have been there. He could barely move. His skull was cold and metallic and ached with new weight that his neck couldn't support. His whole body was inflamed, muscles stretched perpetually beneath new prosthetics; swarms of live machines crawled about, into, and out of his body.

I squinted through his eyes, looking for landmarks. Kraken Waystation sat mere meters from him, nestled high on a plateau nearly surrounded by the swollen lake Kraken Mare.

The satellite images hadn't prepared me for this sight. The Waystation had been mangled, dragged from Titan's depths and torn apart. Metal and plastic scraps covered the ground for kilometers.

But the Tower that Torvram rested besides, the Tower was *writhing*. Machines crawled up its sides and through its guts from base to peak. It was being built at dizzying speed, moving like the whole thing was alive.

Torvram's body looked hauntingly similar.

<*oh...torvram...*> I just...

I couldn't.

I needed him to be ok.

We had two jobs now. We had to stop this Tower, right? Purpose distracted me from the deep well of sorrow that threatened to overtake me. Derecho continued to gnaw at my perception. Time distorted. My vision cut in and out. My connection to Torvram ebbed and flowed.

This massive processing power Torvram had been given, though—Torvram had some ownership of it. He, now, was keeping the AI at bay and allowing me to stay here.

Perhaps Torvram had been distracting it all along.

<what is this?> I asked, trying to turn his gaze toward the Tower.

<radio...telescope,> he replied. His/our breathing was heavy and slow.

Trees began to sprout on the horizon and I was beginning to lose myself... ourselves. Torvram's vision blurred.

<what has it done to you? why is it building this? did you say you came here on your own?> I blurted out every question I could think of through a sorrow-wracked mind and then, added, <we're going to save you ok! matyom's coming. we love you. stay alive!>

Derecho crawled out from the darkness, *as* the darkness in Torvram's mind. It swamped his consciousness, burying Torvram's identity.

I took another deep breath and felt for my chest, my lungs. I couldn't find them.

I opened my eyes and saw nothing.

I took another breath. Had Torvram even been real?

No, I had to believe he was alive. We knew he was by that Tower. We'd seen him there from orbit. This was corroborating data.

I took a third breath. Closed my eyes.

I felt my lungs this time. My body was still connected to me, of course.

But when I opened my eyes, I still saw nothing.

Everything was just dark. I tried to call out to them but I couldn't create words. There was nothing tangible to speak with.

I panicked, clawing in some purely abstract mental way back toward that sensation, that grounding sense that I was still alive.

I'd seen Lakshmi's fantasy. I had that experience and Fei's knowledge about AI and Derecho now implanted in my brain. I was better equipped than anyone to think my way out of a false reality no matter how convincing.

But my lungs faded away and I realized this was something different.

I was locked-in, fully conscious.

I was trapped in my own body.

CHAPTER 18

LOCKED-IN

MEERA; [LOCATION NOT FOUND]

I lost track of time. The void I experienced had no answers or stimuli for me. I was truly alone with my thoughts.

The irony of all of this is that the first brain-computer interface devices, the ancestors of our chipsets, had been designed to repair this very thing: being locked-in. I hoped against hope that Derecho hadn't physically severed my connection to my body.

My world was without light, without sound, without any sensation. I couldn't feel, touch, or taste.

Well, I *could* feel in a way. My emotions ran the gamut from anxiety to panic to frustration to rage and, finally, exhaustion.

The void around me responded to nothing.

I could think about talking but though I couldn't speak; still, I called out for them.

Lakshmi? Fei? Can you hear me?

Torvram?

Anyone?

No one responded.

Was I... could I be dead?

Would I even be able to know the difference?

To this day, no one had ever reported the sensation of death. All the brain scans faded. Recorded thoughts would give you a few extra ideas before the person petered out completely. Connecting directly to a dying person's mind could even add a half hour or so of conversation between you and them before their consciousness faded, but all of that effort brought back no actual answers from the supposed other side.

Still, what I knew was that I was still thinking. This probably wasn't death. An AI could legally assert its sentience without a body, if it could prove its mind existed.

So, here I was: locked-in.

I hoped that my friends were still alive.

Torvram—I'd seen him, right alongside the Tower! He was alive!

I wanted to tell them! Had Lakshmi and Fei seen it through our barrier-shielded connection? Had they seen through his eyes too? We had to save him. We had to stop Derecho, somehow, from hurting him and everyone else.

What...?

I should've asked him what it was doing.

Why had he said it hadn't kidnapped him? Had he gone alone with it willingly? He was asking for help now. Whatever consent he'd given to Derecho was now revoked. But where had he met Derecho? How had he met it? How was it here? What was it?

I still had... a lot of questions.

Problem-solving always distracted me from my problems.

A week or two ago, I might have even welcomed this sort of thing. Perhaps I had an unhealthy relationship with life. One of the few things that kept me going, aside from my work, was knowing that Torvram needed my help. His history of attempted suicide, in a twisted way, kept me alive.

I needed to make sure he kept going, even if I couldn't answer why *I* wanted to keep going. He was such a good friend. I couldn't stand to see him miserable, even if I knew there was nothing I could do. He'd needed medicine we couldn't manufacture on Titan. Adapting those treatments to electronic manipulation of the neurons was novel, something AVA had had to invent as it went along.

But every time I'd turned that same zeal toward my own life, it'd done little. I didn't know if I'd needed that same help. I'd never consented to treatment like he had. I didn't know if I shared his depression. I really didn't know.

Now though...

Had things changed?

I was still acting to help him which yes, I, we, had to save him.

No more death.

Derecho was growing to be a threat to all our lives and needed to be stopped.

But what about after this was all over?

I'd told Lakshmi I quit but... was I just going to go back to something similar? I didn't have any other credentials than in neuroengineering. What did I even want, anyway?

I...

I think I knew after all.

There were a lot of things I wanted, actually. And I could speak up for myself. I'd operated on a blasted human-implanted chipset, hadn't I!

Had I always been better than I let myself believe? Had these options always sat right in front of me, and only my motivation stopped me from changing?

Or was it the change in environment that'd galvanized me? Had my drive to help others without pausing to make sure my own life was in order—or maybe exactly *to avoid* fixing my own life—driven me to change?

I didn't know.

But...

Things were different now.

Huh.

I realized that, yes, I would like to be back in my body. I wanted to see Torvram again. I wanted to see Case and Matyom and even Fei and, wow, even Lakshmi. I... I wanted to fight to live again. I wanted us all to live better.

That was a, uhh, rather broad list of things I wanted. That could take a whole lifetime to "live better," depending on the details.

I supposed I'd better get started then.

I smiled in a purely mental sense. Some serotonin moved around or whatever.

I'd talk to Anyu again, when I got back. Maybe treatment could help. We'd discuss it.

And then...

I'd move forward.

I'd explore.

Now, to get out.
Hmm.
Hmmmmmm.
Hmmmmmmmmm.
Vent it.
Help me, please.
...
...

...
Please.

I waited.
That was all I could do right now.
That was ok.
I trusted them.

CHAPTER 19

THE TOWER AT THE TOP OF THE WORLD

MEERA; SOUTH OF KRAKEN MARE

I gasped with such force that my jaw popped. Air filled my lungs, the sensation alien and confusing for the briefest moment.

I closed my eyes against the sights around me, uncomfortable with anything but that familiar void. Behind my eyelids, script flashed, boot-up text dumping unnecessary statistics into my vision. This stuff was for new prosthetics users. The knowledge I needed was already implanted in my brain by the time the first line of text appeared.

Rain slammed onto my battered helmet, falling in thick globules from the golden sky. It pooled into the divot in my helmet, the one Chetan's android had left, and distorted the light that streamed through the white patches Case had applied.

Before even saying a word, I checked my status. Four violet lights shone happily at me from beneath my howlsuit's collar. I breathed a sigh of relief and tried out my voice box.

"How long was I out?" I asked. It was nice to hear my husky voice actually come out when I tried to speak.

<*Few hours.* :(> Lakshmi replied. She was still in my head, connected to the back of my suit by a bundle of wires.

Fei and Lakshmi helped me rise. Fei, too, disconnected from Lakshmi. They hadn't listened to me. They'd been in my head this whole time, fighting to bring me back. I had some good friends.

"Where's the *Trailblazer?*" I asked. We were outside and, as I became accustomed to seeing again, I could see that there were at least a half dozen drones in sight.

"Where's the *Trailblazer?*" I repeated, infused with panic.

"Shh!" Lakshmi pulled my helmet against hers. "Quiet. We'll fill you in as we walk. Turn everything off: radio, suit lights, chipset, everything. Use the physical *wired* connection between us to communicate silently. Don't even talk unless it's helmet to helmet, ok?"

My radio was spouting seemingly random noise, but as I moved to turn it off, I began to hear patterns. Among the static were beats of an arrhythmic drum and voices, barely intelligible, like I was eavesdropping through a wall.

I recognized brief snippets of sound.

"-—ourse we aren't going to take this quietly—" The snippet was Chetan, and June, and Matyom, each speaking pieces of words. They faded in and out above the static.

"—abandonment, betray—" it continued. I balked at the radio. That was *my* voice coming back at me.

I turned around to see Case and Matyom. Feyn's head stuck out from behind Matyom's back, though the robot dog's dead eyes made it clear it was either deactivated or broken. Case shook his head, bringing a finger to his helmet. I wanted to tell him what I'd seen, but he had no chipset. I nodded, trying to inject as much reassurance as I could into my smile.

I wanted to at least thank him for still being here. I wanted to thank all of them.

Case returned my smile. He placed a palm against the forehead of his helmet.

"Turn it off," he mouthed. "You don't want to hear this."

"—we must rebel!—" it barked in Case's voice alongside two women I didn't recognize. Each syllable was bizarrely delivered. It wasn't spoken normally. Instead sounds with disparate delivery and discontinuous emotion were stitched together like a young AI was taking its first steps toward synthesizing speech.

Vent it, was that exactly what I was hearing?

"—ple on Earth that don't give a shit about whether we live or die—" Torvram, Lakshmi, Wayland, and the Earthborn astronaut Doctor Robert Auberov said to me through disjointed phonemes stitched together to form the sentence. I switched the radio off as I felt a shiver run down my spine.

I remember Torvram saying that to me, back when we were drinking together. He'd disappeared right after that.

I switched to IR and peeled back the sheets of rain and smog. The terrain was becoming methane-logged, potholes and rivers widening to the north. A massive reservoir of murky organic fluid rested not far beyond us to the west and the east. It stretched to the horizon. Its surface seemed to boil and bubble with the violent downpour, the lake's weak tide undetectable beneath the onslaught of the polar storm.

That lake was Kraken Mare. A mixture of dread and determination dried my tongue. I swept my vision up high to the blaring outlier of heat towering above an unnamed, perhaps ephemeral plateau peninsula that jutted out into the lake.

The Tower we'd been warned about. Within its base were the remains of the uprooted, warped, and broken Kraken Waystation. Methane flash-boiled against its surface, the sheer volume of its seething hiss reaching us from kilometers away.

This was the Tower that I'd seen Torvram leaning against. He'd said it was a radio telescope.

Ok, what could a radio telescope do? It could boost Derecho's signal strength, just what our counterparts at Shangri-La feared, allowing it to broadcast farther across Titan and wash out more of AVA's influence.

A radio telescope could also communicate with the cubesats. It could send messages into space too.

None of our equipment had been designed to withstand a threat from within like this.

With my vision expanded, the heat signatures of hundreds of machines revealed themselves. Some converged on the Tower while others patrolled the area.

Looking back, I could see dozens of drones floating over the remains of the *Trailblazer*. The inverted trapezoidal prism had collapsed into itself. Where it had once stood tall over Titan's surface and pushed back the dark with its formidable floodlights, now only jagged triangular pieces of its walls jutted from the ground like the bones of a long animal.

All of this suggested one question, above the many others.

<why haven't they caught us yet?>

<DERECHO Code = highly effective;

drone access;

feeding false data;> Fei replied proudly. <perhaps my finest work;>

Matyom's voice boomed through my mind. I hadn't even noticed he was wired to me. <*Everyone Go Dark. Shut Off Everything With A Signal And Stop Moving Until I Give The Command.*>

He gripped Case's helmet to his and mouthed the words. Then, Matyom's crimson eyes winked out. Fei and Lakshmi followed suit, their eyes fading into black pits in their skulls.

I watched as a trio of Dragonfly drones made their way toward us from the wreck of the *Trailblazer*. Our footprints were obvious, despite the rain, evident as boot-shaped pools of methane. How was Fei going to hide that and us from them?

<*Meera,*> Matyom said. <*You Need to Go Dark.*>

I swallowed and deliberately sent myself back into that void, one more time. I turned off my eyes, my lifeline, even sent a signal to slow my pulse. Finally, I turned my suit off. Its heaters went cold. The subtle hiss of oxygen sputtered and went dead. I shut off and cooled everything I could.

I was cut off from the information stored in my chipset. My memory abruptly fragmented. Thoughts that had not yet imprinted themselves on my organic mind fully sat half-formed, dissociative, like Fei's knowledge of the drones and her new discoveries. She'd been bleeding them into my mind since I'd asked, arming me to assist her. However, with the process incomplete, a dozen memories in my mind felt like books with missing pages.

This time, I could still hear myself breathe though.

And this time, I knew they were alive.

We are almost there, Torvram. Help is on the way.

Case inched closer to me. I could hear him trying to slow his ragged breathing. Only he could see what was coming now but his body would stand out more to the drones than any of ours. I wanted to shield him, but there was nothing I could do.

Through the sound of pouring rain, a harsh buzzing emerged: the telltale whirring of the Dragonfly drones' rotors, the very same machines that had torn into Case's suit and nearly decapitated me at Aztlan Waystation.

The droning of their blades rose in pitch and volume. They passed by my ears, so I thought, only to abruptly intensify the moment I relaxed. A breeze ruffled the arms of my suit. How close were they? Could they see us?

Case's exhalation felt like the boom of a drum. The drones zipped past me and angrily buzzed about my left ear, near him. I shivered. My suit temperature was beginning to drop.

I could feel myself beginning to panic. I was losing control of my breath. They were still here, crowding my ears. Had they noticed us and were just waiting for more to come and end our lives? We were so far from home, and we couldn't walk back, and… *Just don't panic, Meera. But don't take a deep breath either.*

We're not going to die out here.

I trust them.

Case brushed against my glove. I didn't dare grip his hand. That would make noise. I hoped he would stop moving.

Ok.

Ok.

It's ok.

We're almost there. We can do this. I can do this.

They buzzed in my ears and I stood like a statue. Methane poured down the cold exterior of my suit. It sucked what little heat escaped through the insulation, not enough to evaporate but enough to send it zipping energetically down my body.

The whirring faded.

I held my breath.

The sound of rain filled my ears, rain and Case's breathing and the hissing of the not-so-distant radio telescope Tower. I gripped his gloved hand. He squeezed back.

Case placed his helmet against mine. "We're safe," he whispered so quietly I could barely make it out. Perhaps I imagined the comforting words.

With a thought, my eyes reactivated. The short, gray-skinned man with natural hazel eyes was the first thing I saw when my vision returned.

The insulated rope and cable weave that connected me to Lakshmi, in more ways than one, slackened as she stepped out through the curtains of rain. Her eyes flickered to life, the left one failing once, then twice, before finally coming online. She bared her wide, toothy grin in silence. <*Looks like we're going to win this little game* >:D > Lakshmi's thoughts passed through our wired connection.

<i saw Torvram.> I finally confessed. <he's against that tower. we go there, we find him.>

Fei replied by simply mirroring a snippet of my own memories back to me: a vision of the lakes from Torvram's eyes. They had seen what I'd seen through the neural connection at some point.

Case squeezed my hand again while mumbling abrasively at Lakshmi, "Talk to me here, with your words. What's the plan: sneak into the Tower and break Derecho?"

Lakshmi shook her head. We huddled together so she could speak to the unaugmented man. "It's in every machine, Case, *ev-er-y-thing*. If we break one drone, it will find us, and it's *all* the drones, probably even in the equipment beneath the Waystation."

"We have to stop it, though," I replied. "What it's done to my mind, to your mind, is horrible... and Torvram, I saw him, he was... It's tearing apart his body."

"I do have a plan," Lakshmi drew herself to her full height, taller than me but nothing compared to Matyom, "it's bold and ingenious, of course, but first we have to get to the Tower."

Case stuck his tongue out at her. "Sounds exactly like my plan, plagiarist."

It amazed me how they could bicker lightheartedly at a time like this.

<Quiet!> Matyom interrupted. <More Drones Are Coming. We're Almost There Everyone. Just Be Careful, Be Diligent, And We'll Pluck Torv Right Out Under Derecho's Blinded Eyes.>

CHAPTER 20

CRUNCH TIME

MEERA; SOUTH OF KRAKEN MARE

The driving rain altered the lakeside landscape in slow motion. Sheets of golden debris crumbled from the coastline and crashed into the unlit depths of Kraken Mare. Their fall echoed all around us like claps of thunder. Derecho's Tower loomed over us, high on the bluffs overlooking the turbulent methane lake.

I willed it to fall, for the whole peninsula to erode into the seasonal swell. But I doubted it would. The Waystation was older than I was, like Aztlan to the southwest, dropped from orbit when we were just organic material in vats.

Besides, if it fell, Torvram would go too.

The Tower stared down at us over the cliffside, crawling with machines dragging scavenged parts up its sides. Many of those parts were their broken down or cannibalized brethren.

We huddled beneath a plateau outcropping that shielded us from the rain. Orange tar dripped from above, splattering my helmet. I felt it oozing over my back as I leaned against the organic wall behind us.

Fei's eyes twitched, her head snapping abruptly from place to place as she stared out at incoming signals rather than visible light. So far, her pinpoint alterations to the drones' patrols had gone unnoticed.

I stood next to her, assisting as best I could. I had plenty of experience with these drones, even if I was out-of-my-depth when it came to their AI puppeteer itself. The key I'd found wouldn't be valid forever but, for now, it was working.

The rain continued to pour at its peak near the poles. It would continue to fall for months as Titan transitioned into its long northern summer.

We, on the other hand, had less than a day according to AVA's last transmissions.

There was nothing left of our supplies save for what we carried in on our backs. We needed to retrieve Torvram and get out, all without being caught. Disabling the Tower, and Derecho, was important too but we had no idea how to go about doing it. Derecho was everywhere.

<Hmm.> Lakshmi wrung her prosthetic hands together. Her sharp cerulean eyes turned toward me. I had some idea of what she was thinking, as we'd experienced each other's innermost thoughts, wants, and needs for years—false though the setting had been.

<Here's my plan,> she said, tapping her suit where the violet oxygen light had turned green. <Hold your applause. ;)>

She flinched as the buzzing of rotors filled our ears from above. I resisted the urge to crane my neck and peek out from beneath the shelf of mud and tar above us. We froze, saying nothing, ready to go dark if they got closer.

Case closed his eyes. I could feel his pulse quickening through our wired connection, his suit reading the vitals that, for the rest of us, a lifeline would. Wordlessly, I reached out and tugged gently on the rope that connected us. He broke out of his reverie, his eyes meeting mine. Case's pulse began to slow. The short man, his face grimy and his black ponytail an uncombed mess, forced a strained smile.

Matyom, to my right, nodded. His hands were balled into fists. The beacon he'd thrown into Chetan's chest, now bent both by that impact and the *Trailblazer* crash, was slung over his back. He had one hand on it, ready to strike.

< —. > Fei sent a Morse code dash and dot through our minds to indicate that we were safe. I tugged on Case's rope three times, extending the message down the line to the man without telepathy. We were ok.

"Fuck..." he mumbled, dropping to a crouch. His eyes smoldered.

<Ugh. :/ Derecho is expending a massive amount of its attention and slaved drones building that tower,> Lakshmi continued, tapping a finger against the plateau wall.

<We send three people south. They reveal themselves just north of AVA's perimeter and split up, break a few drones, and cross into AVA's influence. They can repeat that over and over, like a tiny coolant leak that brings down the whole reactor. >:)>

<They'll distract Derecho. While they're there, they'll hook up with whatever help Shangri-La has on the way and prep an escape route for the rescue team.>

Lakshmi rested her organic hands on her hips. <Meanwhile, the rescue team sneaks up to the tower and saves Torvram. :D>

I tried to imagine the scenario. Assuming the bait team made it home safely *and* drew enough drones away were twin leaps I was not comfortable making. Beyond that, Lakshmi hadn't even answered the Derecho threat itself.

I wasn't willing to risk our lives like that.

Another contingent of machines approached: a boxy truck and a pair of hexcopters that sat in its bed. The smog and rain were so thick that their tiny red sensors seemed to draw distorted lines in the air.

Everyone froze, yet again.

I locked eyes with one of its sensors. Had it seen us? Should I break into its mind? I waited for Fei's signal.

The rain waned. The world outside began to clear, ever so slightly, in the visible range. Our shelter slowly crumbled. Thick blobs of rust-colored and methane-filled mud continued to slap against the ground as they slopped off of the overhang.

< —. > Fei shook her head, and we all took a collective breath. I tugged on Case's line. I felt Lakshmi vaguely doing the same from the other side.

I poked the first hole in her plan I could find. Speaking up to Lakshmi took a moment, even now. It was as if my brain had to load a complex function to override the lingering knots of fear in my gut. I was getting better at talking to her, after the time we'd spent together.

Lakshmi had said that she'd consider others when she acted and I was going to hold her to that, especially while lives were on the line. <*the bait team, they might die, assuming they even draw enough attention away to keep the team going for torvram safe.*>

<*You don't know that. :/*> Lakshmi replied stubbornly.

<*everyone, get in on this. we need a better plan. we must disable the tower somehow and I refuse to put any of us at risk.*>

<*request = unrealistic;
no data on odds of survival;*> Fei replied.

<*but we have to try!*> I replied in protest, squeezing my hands tightly together. The others leaned off the wall to look at me: four pairs of eyes that I wanted to see again, safe, when we got home. <*there's got to be something we know. something we can use...*>

"Clue me in?" Case whispered faintly.

I repeated the situation to him.

"What about the Waystation beneath the Tower?" he mumbled. "It's the same as Aztlan, isn't it? There must be something there..."

<Oh!> Matyom's telepathic voice was as loud and confident as his own. <Yes! It Draws Massive Volumes Of Liquid From Kraken Mare. We Could Sneak In Through There, Perhaps?>

<uploading entity(blueprint)<Aztlan waystation>;> Fei not so much replied as publicly shared the code she was running. I accepted the mental intrusion. She'd had the foresight to store the blueprint into her memory and I wanted a copy.

<It's...Meera, Torvram said it's a radio telescope, right?> Lakshmi added as I, and presumably Matyom and Lakshmi, suddenly had a vivid, visual memory of Aztlan's blueprints.

<yeah.> Now I was completely on the same wavelength. I suppose I was literally on it too. <we could use it, maybe, to magnify our reach. hit as many drones as possible all at once and get a message out to Shangri-La.>

<I'll Lie In Wait And Grab Torvram The Moment I See That Disruption Hit.> Matyom nodded resolutely, his jaw set.

<ill come with you. keep us hidden from the drones as best i can. i dont have fei's skill but...actually i kind of do haha.> As I volunteered myself, I whispered the budding plan to Case. It took orders of magnitude longer to tell him physically, but he was part of our team, he was my friend, I wasn't going to just ignore him.

Case frowned. He was chewing on the inside of his lip, his concern evident. "What if the team inside needs to go dark? Or you do? You're sitting ducks without my eyes."

<Never thought we'd be debating who gets the natural. XD> Lakshmi replied.

"Shut up, chiphead," I muttered to her, aloud for Case's amusement.

Case smiled. "Heh. I'll go into the radio telescope slash Tower slash antenna thingy. If Fei can't get inside, we lose our chance at taking over the telescope and there's no escaping here, whereas if Matyom and Meera get caught..." His voice trailed off as a deep frown played across his face.

I reached out to squeeze his hand. It was ok. He was right.

<Meera And I Will Be Fine. Lakshmi, Go With Fei. I Imagine A Larger Team Will Only Make Us More Obvious On The Surface But Inside There Are Plenty Known Places To Hide.> Matyom clapped a hand on Case's shoulder, smiling down at the shorter man. *<Good Plan, All Of You.>*

<Sounds good, big guy. Just make sure to wait until we give you the signal. From what we saw through Meera, Torvram's absence won't go unnoticed. :/> Lakshmi looked up, again, at the wet outcropping, as if she was staring through it to the Tower above and behind us.

<Acknowledged.> Matyom nodded.

"Go with Fei." Matyom's whispered words to Case caught up to our telepathy.

"Give me the details," Case said—for once without an ounce of spite about his lack of telepathy—as he huddled with Fei and Lakshmi. The three put their helmets together, speaking in inaudibly quiet tones.

Case nodded resolutely. He reached down to the rope and cable lines that connected him and me and hesitated.

I couldn't feel the warmth of his hand through our suits, but I knew it was there. His suit lights were shifting green too as his oxygen and water levels dropped to middling ranges. It was now or never and, likely, death. We couldn't have that.

Case was blushing now, red tones creeping into his gray face. "So, Matyom and I have this bottle of faux-bourbon alcohol from Dr. Auberov that we lost in the *Trailblazer*. I figure, when we get back, we drink to its memory, all four of us, Torvram included."

"That sounds great." I smiled. Thoughts flashed in my head of how pleasant it would be to drink alone, with him, as well. It'd been years since I'd been on a date, mostly for lack of trying.

I flushed a little redder at the following thought: that it'd also been quite a while since I'd gotten laid.

All the more reason to come back alive.

"Ok." He unclipped the rope and handed it to me.

I slowly, carefully, unhooked my pack and stored the rope. It knocked against one of the pack's rigid walls. The sound seemed to echo out into the world, impossibly loud. I stared out at the ravaged lakeside landscape.

No drones approached, thankfully.

<Case just said 'check, chiphead.' Anything I should know? XD> Lakshmi's voice came through my mind.

<huh? we're just getting drinks together with maty and torv when this is all over.> I shrugged as I sealed the pack. <why?>

<Hmm. I'm honestly not sure myself. Boy thinks he can compete with me but he's not even on my level. :P>

<compete with?> I blushed. This was not the sort of attention I was used to from anyone but I was starting to get the picture. <umm...can we talk about this later? i'm not sure how to process what i think youre saying.>

<Of course. How bout we get lunch? :D>

We'd spent years together, in a sense, compressed into such a short time. I was not about to get lunch alone with my terror of an ex-boss, but maybe we could become friends? I wasn't entirely opposed to that. I wasn't going to forgive her abuse though, and I wasn't going to bet on her changing. Time would tell if there really was more to her like I'd seen on the *Trailblazer*.

<with fei, as friends,> I replied, resolutely. No one could strong arm me anymore, especially Lakshmi.

<Aww, boo that's no fun. :< > Lakshmi frowned, but, to be honest, I could tell it was for show. Her eyes smiled quite thoroughly.

<were just...i dont know if youre even my friend lakshmi lets start with that ok?>

<Sure. I don't mean to pressure you, Meera. :)> She chuckled inaudibly. <Though, let me make sure Case sees me moving this rook real quick.> I saw Case scowl behind her.

They had a strange taste in games and stranger taste in rivalries.

<See you on the other side of all this. Don't die, please. :)> Lakshmi said with finality. She returned to Fei and Case.

<matyom? what do we need?>

<We're Already Set On Climbing Supplies And Rations. Ready When You Are,> the big man replied with a thumbs-up.

Matyom enveloped Case and I into a hug and, somehow, managed to pull Lakshmi and Fei into it too.

"Promise me that you're all going to come back alive ok?" he whispered, aloud for Case's sake. "I don't know what you're going to see inside but be smart. Be careful."

"You too, Matyom, and Meera," Case replied. "Bring Torvram back for us."

CASE; KRAKEN MARE COASTLINE

Fei and Lakshmi's eyes were black cavities in their faces, devoid of light or color. Faintly, Case could make out the patterns of a LED ring mimicking the iris, of false sclera and pupil, in each eye. But without power, they were barely distinguishable in Titan's dim morning light. He cursed silently. These chipheads could be so blasted creepy.

Case peeked from the coastline trench they'd hastily made their hiding place. He stared up at the plateau as its sides sagged and flowed with wet tar. Case hoped Matyom and Meera were ok up there. He knew Matyom would get them through the climb safely; the man was a veritable genius when it came to navigating Titan. But this Derecho shit was weird, unpredictable.

Case needed them both to survive. He scanned the area beneath the plateau. There was maybe thirty seconds of running they needed to do to get to the edge of the lake. Case waited for his opening.

A truck with a grid of tiny plastic canisters on its back, probably meant for lake samples, sat not three meters from them. It had stopped moving, but subtle vibrations in its body told Case it was functional and a threat.

He slid back into the trench.

The truck burst into cacophonic life as its many wheels revved. Tar shot over the trench, splattering the top of his helmet with orange. It rumbled north and out of earshot.

Beside him, Fei's mouth worked beneath her bandana. Back when she'd had the digital mask, Case had seen her whole face. He knew the scar he and the others could see now didn't end at Fei's left eye. It carried all the way down to her collar. Her face had been mangled by the cold. It was a wonder she'd survived whatever had happened.

Case leaned into Fei's helmet. It was the only way he could communicate to the telepaths. "We're clear." It was time to go.

Fei's eyes glowed to life, while Lakshmi remained immobile. The women had sat nearly catatonic at the base of the trench, scanning the lake through neuroelectronic means. Knowing what they were doing didn't make it any less eerie to Case. It was like sitting with two corpses.

"I must ask, one more time, are you sure about this?" Fei asked as she shook tar off of her shoulders. "The howlsuit is not rated for diving, and you have a pre-existing breach."

"I've seen Matyom do it once." Case shrugged. "And I'm not staying up here so..."

"Hmm." Fei frowned. "I hope you'll be ok."

"Me too," Case replied. "Uhh, thanks."

"You're welcome," Fei said in her sickly, kinda robotic tone. Then, to Case's surprise, she reached for his injured hand. Case hesitated, leaving Fei's palms open to the sky and empty.

"Is it ok for me to touch you?" Fei asked. "All I can give is my show of reassurance but… if it will help, then I will give it."

After spending days on the *Trailblazer*, and looking after Meera and Lakshmi together, Case had found himself warming to Fei. While she was Lakshmi's willing pawn, Fei was surprisingly considerate when she wanted to be. Case almost hoped the sickly woman got the psychopath she wanted… and another part of him hoped Lakshmi wouldn't inflict herself on Fei, no matter how much Fei seemed to want it.

"It's ok." Case reached out, finally, and let Fei squeeze his hands in hers.

Lakshmi leaned in abruptly, her eyes still creepily absent from her face. "Heyyy huddle-buddies, I've got eyes on the intake and just created our opening. Time to goo."

"Fuck!" Case jumped, startled by her. He admonished her in a hissed whisper, "Lakshmi, it's tense enough as it is."

"Hehehe." She pulled away.

"What do you see in her?" Case muttered to Fei.

Fei chuckled. "Ma'am, you should refrain from this tomfoolery. Now is not the time."

"What *do* you see in that crazy chiphead?" Case repeated, more to himself than Fei.

"She always surprises me," Fei replied softly, wistfully, as she released his hand.

Case climbed up to the trench's edge on his stomach, taking another look. "Ok, we're clear on the land side. Let's go."

The three of them crawled out of the trench and scrambled to the edge of the land. Beneath them, Titan's waters frothed violently in the falling rain. *Shit, that's a long way down... and with no rescue in sight.* Case regarded his injured hand one last time. The off-color patch Meera had applied stood out. It felt slightly warm: either from Fei's touch, his own paranoia, or both.

Case faced the Tower again. Matyom and Meera were up there, as was Torvram. Case missed the wire-thin man, and even more so, missed the effect Torvram had on Matyom. But he stared at his hand again. Now that they were here, Case hesitated.

What would Meera say if he didn't take this leap?

She'd probably forgive me. She's too damn nice, heh.

"Fuck," he muttered under his breath.

He'd always wanted to be taken seriously, to be given a chance to succeed, rather than be looked down upon as a fundamentally, even cognitively, inferior person.

He felt the ropes go slack. Lakshmi and Fei stood to his left, looking down at the water, their eyes each gray like the color of a Titanborn's skin. Here were two augmented Titanborn standing with him. In a way, he was getting his wish. He'd die just like they did if this all went to vacuum.

He nodded. It wasn't safe to share how he felt, out loud. Case swallowed. He gripped the rope between him and Fei tightly.

Lakshmi's prosthetics slithered out from her back; they gripped Fei's arms, adding another link between them. Fei blushed unmistakably. She reached an arm out to Case.

He couldn't help but smile. She was crushing so fucking hard on Lakshmi. It was like a classic will-they, won't-they from one of the trashy romcoms he loved so much.

That's all it took, a little dash of silliness. Case exhaled, now feeling brave enough in the moment.

He nodded again and swung one foot out into the void. They followed suit, and then the three of them leapt together

"Sh—" Case bit his shouted expletive off. The three of them sailed down and into the waters of Kraken Mare. In seconds, the ripples they left were erased by the violent storm.

MEERA; KRAKEN WAYSTATION PLATEAU, KRAKEN MARE

Rain bounced off the flat head of a construction drone that must've stood two stories tall, at least. In its "chest," it extruded a long column of plastic from a complex web of printer heads. A mass of rotary drones carried it to a nearby truck and together they rolled straight toward us.

I gripped Matyom's rope, causing him to stop in his tracks. We'd left boot prints again, heavy ones at the edge of the cliffside. Handprints too, as he'd helped lift me up the last meter. Despite the low gravity, my arms and legs throbbed with the exertion of the climb.

I poked at the truck mentally, masking myself as Derecho, hoping that once again the AI wouldn't turn its attention to this reprogrammed drone or notice my extremely brief broadcast signal. I climbed inside its simple brain and replaced all the tags for footprint and handprint recognition, borrowing from the error my repair bot Rudy had thrown.

That boring day in the cleanroom felt like it'd happened a lifetime ago.

The truck continued to move toward us. I wasn't going to risk changing its trajectory. Matyom and I threw ourselves into a pothole ankle-deep with rain. I hoped that it wouldn't notice us, thanks to my meddling in its mind.

< —. > I sent that simple Morse dash-dot into Matyom's head. We went dark, and the world disappeared.

I clenched my teeth and bit into my lip to keep myself from crying out as I felt the truck approach us. I could hear its many wheels grinding against finer particulates, seizing briefly as the thick sludge caught in its tires.

Come on. Go around. No one is here.

It skirted the pothole, just barely. I heard it trace a semi-circle above us and pass away. I was torn between waiting, to be sure it was gone, and action, knowing every second was precious.

< —. > I flipped my eyes back on again.

Matyom gave a thumbs-up. His face was pure determination now, furrowed brows, gritted teeth, a fire in the red eyes he shared with Torvram.

We traveled in silence across the rain-blasted dunes. Golden fog hung in the air. I could smell the tar, grease, and sweat that'd accumulated on my body from days without a shower and days without cleaning my howlsuit.

Windswept and teeming with drones, this peninsular plateau was crowded with machine life. Their lights forced away the natural darkness of Titan in all directions. Long shadows bent and warped around the gaps in their patrols and many roving eyes.

My hands were shaking. If we made the slightest mistake, and it realized we were blinding and turning and reconfiguring its drones, there would be no escape from Derecho. And there were thousands of them around us now. My mind leapt to morbid visions of dying in the cold beneath their sheer mass.

I forced myself to focus, to see the threat in front of me. We could do this. *I* could do this.

Many of Derecho's drones did nothing at all up here. We passed through neat grids of them, dozens by dozens, unsure if they would or even could wake if we alerted them. In IR, their heat signatures grew and flared until I was worried one downed Dragonfly would melt like the drone that had attacked us.

But they would stop at that dangerous thermal peak and shut down, letting Titan cool them and sending waves of boiled methane and other organics into the sky.

Matyom froze between two rows of immobile copter drones.

<I SEE HIM!> his voice blasted through my mind. A tidal wave of relief and excitement and impatience and fear crashed into my mind, dashing my own thoughts to pieces.

I watched him start forward, his restraint evaporating. He could see Torvram now. I could make him out too—a humanoid figure propped up atop a mound of machine parts and insulated cables that poked out from Titan's surface and the Tower's face in jagged, chaotic directions.

<*wait*> I tugged on Matyom's rope hard. <*wait!*>

He ignored me uncharacteristically and continued forward. I strained against his strength, planting my feet into the soupy muck and sinking as he dragged me with him. I was finally seeing his resolve buckle, and at the worst possible time. <*matyom stop! stop!*>

The Tower was a wall of distracted but able eyes and Derecho had sensors all around us. Torvram was connected to Derecho. Lakshmi's team hadn't given us a window yet. This would get us caught and possibly killed. I threw open the emotional channels between us, letting my ideas, my morbid dissociative daydreams, intermix with Matyom's feelings.

His own dreams came flooding back. Torvram finally safe in his arms again, back home. I saw the virtual vacations they'd take beneath a starry sky or out in the farthest reaches of the solar system. I felt his grief and guilt and elation all pour into my mind. He'd fought so hard, carried this weight for so long, and blamed himself so thoroughly for this.

<*it's not your fault!*> I screamed in all but voice at him. <*just wait! wait for the signal! we'll save him. just wait!*>

I lost my grip on the rope, falling forward. I tried to cushion my fall and, most importantly, lessen the sound of impact. I hit the mud with an all-too-loud splat. The noise echoed in my ears.

My rope went taut, and as I cautiously rose to my knees, I found Matyom ready to get me to my feet. The drones nearby remained inert, and the patrols didn't break their complex patterns, against all odds. More copters rose from the golden fog outside the plateau and planted themselves firmly in the tar before appearing to shut off. What was it doing with all these machines, sitting inert in the rain?

<*I'm Sorry,*> he replied, simply. Upon Matyom's chiseled face was a naked expression of deep emotional pain, but he was here. His red eyes darted, repeatedly, from me to the Tower, to Torvram. <...*I Miss Him So Much.*>

<*i know,*> I replied. <*but...*> He knew the "but" here.

I half-pulled, half-walked him to a deep canal just east of us. It sloped downward and eventually broke over the edge of the cliff side, ferrying methane rain off the plateau and to the lake below like a natural gutter. Thankfully, it was devoid of any lurking machines.

We took cover, half-submerged in liquid, and the Tower vanished behind its walls.

<*Ok,*> Matyom said. <*We Wait.*>

<*yes,*> I replied, taking one of his hands in mine. <*we wait and hope that they succeed.*>

<*They Will.*> His confidence was returning. His chest puffed up. Matyom's eyes gleamed again with crimson light.

<*i know,*> I replied, meaning it. <*i trust them.*>

CHAPTER 21

DERECHO

LAKSHMI; INTAKE PIPELINE, KRAKEN WAYSTATION

Lakshmi shuddered as methane continued to slide off her howlsuit. Mid-shiver, her helmet smacked against the low, curved ceiling. The sound echoed down the unlit intake pipe. Some of the lake's oily, almost fishy odor somehow wafted within Lakshmi's suit to her dismay.

The pipe was dark save for Fei's violet eyes and a white light from her suit, which pulsed in three second intervals. Fei held Case's blackened hand in hers. Even from a distance, Lakshmi could tell it wasn't healthy.

Methane poured from Case's suit breach. While it had held during the dive, trouble with the intake's grating had torn the patch away. The methane his hand had been immersed in was below -150°C. It was fortunate that the seals in his suit had closed the rest of his left arm off.

"I can't feel anything in my hand." Case groaned through gritted teeth. "But the heater and seals are working below it and the fucking searing pain in my arm tells me I'm alive."

Cut off from the net, Case was the medical professional among them.

"I'm so sorry," Fei murmured as she delicately moved her hands atop his. She flinched repeatedly, looking down at him with sad, tired eyes as they crouched in the pipe. Case felt nothing as Fei's hands moved across his.

"We need to go," Lakshmi replied as Fei's pulsing light animated their shadows along the pipe's curving walls. They wouldn't be going out through the lake again. That much was certain.

"I just—" Case stared down at his blackened hand as Fei's light plunged the group into darkness. "I'm already natural... and now my hand is gone too?"

"I know this must hurt," Lakshmi interjected, straining her eyes to see farther up the pipe as it curved out of view. "We need to focus on the task. The sooner we stop Derecho, the sooner we can get you proper medical care."

Lakshmi flashed her vital lights beneath her collar. One blue, one green, and two violet. The blue one was oxygen, less than a third remaining. They were all running out.

Lakshmi switched to IR. That didn't help at all. It was cold and therefore dark all around them, and now Fei's pulsing suit LEDs weren't even visible.

Lakshmi wrapped two of her prosthetics around Case's side as she returned to visible. He recoiled at the touch.

"Let me help you," Lakshmi hissed. "We need to go."

"I can walk on my own, chiphead," Case groaned, a weak echo of his usual belligerent mockery.

Lakshmi gripped his side, hard. "Now is not the time for this, Case."

"Fine. You're right. You're *always* fucking right." He grunted, leaning into her prosthetics. "Just stay away from my left side. It hurts."

Lakshmi fumed but said nothing. Was his position fair? No. But he had a role to play. They all did. And he may as well get used to it. Now was *not* the time for Case to antagonize her.

The intake pipe was slick with methane and Lakshmi dug her available arms into the walls to gain purchase. Fei climbed through the darkness ahead of them, every pulse of her suit light a dim reminder of her existence.

As the pipe steepened, bending upward, Lakshmi resorted to leaping forward. The low gravity would've helped tremendously if the pipe hadn't been so small.

"Fuc—" Case bit off his words as his and Lakshmi's backs scrapped against the pipe's wall for the umpteenth time.

< —. > Fei signaled from ahead.

Lakshmi hit the ground and froze as Fei's lights cut off abruptly. Case, fortunately, got the message contextually.

Lakshmi silenced her breathing with ease. Case's ragged, pained gasps were practically echoing off the walls.

< —. > Fei sent the go-ahead signal. Lakshmi smiled. They hadn't even needed to go dark.

The pipe abruptly widened, its walls falling away. She heard her footsteps magnify and echo as she stepped into a far vaster darkness. She felt about. They were inside a cylindrical container.

Case took a long, shuddering breath. Lakshmi was no doctor, well, not medically, but she knew enough about hypothermia, frostbite, and all manner of cold-related injury. He wasn't doing well. His eyes fluttered. The pain must've been constant and intense, and he had no way of dulling or ignoring his pain receptors internally like Lakshmi and Fei could.

Fei was above her now and led Lakshmi up and out of the container. Lakshmi scanned the space outside from IR to visible, even hopping up into the UV, as she propped Case up atop beside her.

Four distant walls, and a vast emptiness between them. Rounded cylindrical vats of lake methane like the empty one beneath them and IR-bright, electrically humming server stacks. They'd reached the base of Kraken Waystation, a space identical to Aztlan's core storage in form and only somewhat dissimilar in function.

Something immediately stirred on the floor, whirring to life.

Vent it! A mess of damaged quadcopters and a pair of forklifts began to stumble and wheel their way toward their location.

< —. > Fei sent the warning and went dark. Unfortunately, that meant Fei couldn't distract them. Lakshmi trusted her judgment but...

Vent it! Idiots! Go away! She thought at the incoming drones.

Lakshmi slammed her mind into darkness, hoping Case would stay silent. Her prosthetics went slack. She drove her vitals down, commanded her body temperature to slow, and felt her pulse weaken.

She heard Case stumble forward as her prosthetics loosened their grip. Some part of his body banged against the surface of the tank. Lakshmi cursed her haste in nervous silence.

Lakshmi stared out through deactivated eyes at nothing and heard the machines move. They might detect Case's pulse and the heat his body gave off. This had been a stupid idea, bringing him, and he was injured now too!

Lakshmi felt his hand against her left side. What was he doing?

Case pressed, hard, with his functional hand.

Lakshmi took a single slow blind step to her right.

Case pressed her down against the surface of the tank and froze, one hand still on her back. Lakshmi heard the drone above her head.

She was ready to strike. Depending on what model it was, it might be able to see him right now. He'd stand out like Shangri-La in IR.

Don't find us.

She waited.

You can't see us.

Fei inhaled sharply. It sounded like a blasted shout. Lakshmi could still hear Case's labored breathing. There were multiple drones right above her head now.

Someone or something slammed into the container's roof. It resonated like the surface of a drum.

Case's helmet bumped against hers and tapped against it three times. The drones split up, three discrete sets of blades echoing about the large room.

Lakshmi felt him take her hand and pull. She rose to a crouch, straining to hear. Case led her forward, slowly, cautiously across the sloped top of the tank. Lakshmi rolled her ankle at the edge of the container's open hatch, nearly falling into the pit. She caught herself on the other side of the opening with one hand, her belly suspended over the gap.

Case's breathing quickened. Lakshmi found her footing and climbed down the outside of the tank until her feet touched ground with a whisper. She could hear the drones whirring not far off. They were converging on the tank again.

She waited.

Case had vanished from touch. His rope was slack, disconnected. Fei's too had gone slack, giving Lakshmi no information other than that the AI expert was either nearby or disconnected too.

Lakshmi needed to know more, to banish some of the fog of this intimate perceptual war. She had half a mind to move, to get away from the tank on her own. She'd probably succeed. This Derecho couldn't outsmart her, of course. That would leave them alone and vulnerable though. And if they got caught, she got caught. Lakshmi would not forgive herself if she lost as valuable an ally as Fei and even Case, who was, well, a burden, but for what he was, was still remarkably capable.

Case's whole mutual animosity act was entertaining as well. It was a sort of game where exerting her considerable advantages in strength, intelligence, and so on over him would be her loss. It would be proof that Case had gotten under her skin. Lakshmi enjoyed the challenge.

Lakshmi felt Fei's body press against hers. Case pressed his elbow into her back and laced one of her hands into Fei's. Lakshmi felt Fei's pulse quicken for, perhaps, an entirely different reason than their current situation. Case's pained twitches passed into her back through what must've been the elbow that supported his dying hand.

Case led the two of them somewhere else.

< —. > Lakshmi felt the signal just as Case tapped on her helmet.

Lakshmi reactivated her eyes. The drones were still whirring, not far away. They moved about the room now. They were a ragtag group: Dragonflies with warped blades, trucks with shattered chassis, and a crane without any body at all, just roving eyes. A pair of limping truck bed drones bumped against the tank. None of them had functional lights, thankfully.

They hadn't been spotted, but they'd caused an unaccounted-for disturbance. Lakshmi knew it wouldn't be long before their multi-tasking opponent sent something down with better sensors.

Case had gotten them behind a nearby tank, this one full of lake liquid. He gripped the wrist beneath his cold-burned hand and bit into his lip. A barely audible squeal left his throat. They had nothing they could give him to numb the pain.

<Fei, anything down here that might help us? >

<power source;> Fei replied with a little bit of that warm elation she always exuded around Lakshmi. As Fei leaned around the tank to survey the center of the massive room, what she saw bounced into Lakshmi's head. They were still connected.

It was a small, meter-tall tower of live electronics. A hacked-together job, visible cabling and coolant pipes had been bent and forced into place to support it. Slots of fleshy organic electronics were exposed to the world, having been torn from somewhere else entirely. Surrounding the mismatched circuits were cast-away cannibalized parts, non-functional broken drones, and a truck that looked like it'd been sheared in half.

The context gave Lakshmi hope, though she was fully aware of her current bias. Lakshmi really wanted this to be the computer they needed.

She leaned into Case, while simultaneously broadcasting down the wire to Fei, "I have a plan."

MEERA; KRAKEN WAYSTATION PLATEAU, KRAKEN MARE

I shivered in the canal, leaning against its frigid wall as my legs stood mostly submerged in rust-tinted methane. I fought back chattering teeth as cold seeped through my suit. I didn't dare turn the heat up. It would take too long to exhaust that thermal signature if a drone came close.

Matyom leaned into the tar wall of the canal as a trio of treaded machines slid into the natural gutter not two meters away from me.

<anything?> I already knew what he'd tell me, but I hoped that...

<*No Sign That Case And Company Have Succeeded,*> the stocky explorer replied. Despite everything, he smiled with confidence and said, <*They'll Get It Done.*>

I flinched as another Spiderfly octocopter passed overhead. I tried to recognize its model.

Did it have the equipment to see us in the dark? Would it be worth a microsecond broadcast to interfere with?

Should we, instead, go dark? That would mean vulnerability but—

The copter dropped to the other side of our makeshift sanctuary, boxing us in between it at the arm-sized, treaded garbage robots. I felt Matyom coil into a crouch, ready to spring at the potential attacker.

It lowered itself just above the dirty lake liquid. Once again, my ears filled with that accursed buzzing. Its myriad eyes shifted mechanically, pinpoints of red rotating and spinning in its gold-stained housing.

I reached out to Matyom, priming the signal. It was time to go dark before this copter or the grounded robots turned and—

The octocopter's blades seized abruptly. It splashed into the methane beside him. Another Dragonfly drone crashed into the peak of the trench, sending golden and coffee-colored muck flying in a wide arc. I turned to see that the garbage robots had simply frozen in place.

Matyom and I turned to each other, wide-eyed. It was time!

We scrambled up the side of the trench. The Tower had frozen, its many machines either completely rigid or falling into or out from it. Machines crashed into the ground in showers of orange as they abruptly shut down. Some of them sank on impact, their bodies swallowed up in slow motion by the porous ground.

We stumbled across the dunes and climbed straight toward the Tower. The long rows of drones sat dormant, still, and as I switched to IR, I saw them all cooling slowly toward Shangri-La's ambient temperature.

We reached the truly massive pile of machine scrap. Shattered machines, more tangles of cable, and small metastable pools of rain formed a makeshift ramp that we climbed. The Tower loomed overhead, seeming to grow in height as we climbed.

Finally, we bridged the top of the pile and I felt a sickening sense of déjà vu.

There he was.

After Aztlan and the *Trailblazer* and Chetan's android and the horrible experience of going deliberately dark to hide from Derecho's relentless patrols...

After all of that.

We'd found Torvram.

His howlsuit was swollen with wires and machinery latched onto its side like parasitic creatures, burrowing into the skin of the suit itself. His helmet, though, was still visible and through it two familiar red eyes stared back. Torvram's face was pale, dangerously thin. He cracked a weak smile at the sight of Matyom and I.

"Oh, honeysuckle. I'm so sorry." Matyom reached toward Torvram, leaning down to touch his long-missing boyfriend. Matyom took a knee and pressed his helmet against Torvram's.

The top half of a construction drone, retrofitted with dozens of copter parts, crashed into the ground behind us. Neither Matyom nor I even flinched as a sea of multi-colored muck splattered against our backs.

We'd found him.

Torvram was alive.

Faintly, Torvram replied, "Hello."

LAKSHMI; LAKE SAMPLE COLLECTION, -16TH FLOOR, KRAKEN WAYSTATION

Just to be certain, Lakshmi punched through the truck's circuitry one more time. She tore its guts from its head and tossed them to the floor.

"What is it doing?" Fei wondered aloud, a bundle of wires as thick as her arm connecting her to the tower of electronics.

Lakshmi felt like she could finally breathe again. Now online safely, thanks to their control of the Tower, Lakshmi broadcast to everyone and everything. <*Shangri-La. Send everything you can through the gap. Ev-er-y-thing. We have one, possibly two injured, and cannot confirm how long Derecho's bots will remain neutralized.* :(>

They hadn't won yet, but this was a blow to the distributed AI.

"Do we know if they found Torvram?" Case asked Fei, standing with his back to her. His suit lights illuminated the staircase door and the glossy metallic doors of the freight lift beside it. The lift was rumbling, grinding either up away from them or down toward them.

"There has to be a reason..." Fei leaned into the stack of electronics, her helmet scratching against a plastic casing. She wasn't responding to either of them.

"Fei?" Case leaned over Fei's shoulder, staring down at the electronics rack. "Lakshmi get through to her. Please."

Lakshmi took a moment to respond. A dispatcher, Arienne, responded to Lakshmi with a multitude of lifelines and geotags that burst to life in Lakshmi's vision. Dozens of Titanborn were coming. Help was on the way. *<Roger that. We're moving forward with all available personnel. I'll remain online and broadcast our location for as long as it's safe!>*

Lakshmi replied with every memory of the drones outside she had to Arienne, every encounter they'd fought, and everything they knew about Derecho that could help the incoming Titanborn survive, save for her dissociative immersion experience. That would remain between Lakshmi and Meera, for as long as it could.

As much as she relished the feeling, Lakshmi didn't want to spend an extra second online. Finally responding to Case, Lakshmi said, "Fei, are we done? What's Case barking about?" She concealed her nervousness beneath the calloused orders.

"Sorry, ma'am... Case, it's just... Derecho is in here. It's focused intently on something, so intently it didn't even notice me enter. I'm wondering if we should try to stop whatever else its doing?"

Lakshmi stared up at the ceiling. Derecho wasn't actually anywhere in particular, but the gesture felt fitting. She was curious about this too, but they needed to focus. Sometimes Fei's fascination with AI got the better of her.

"Have we confirmed that Torvram is free?" Lakshmi replied, her voice echoing in the vast empty space.

"Case?" The short man's radio crackled. Meera was on the other end.

The lift was almost painful to listen to now as it ground against its walls. It was getting closer, after all. Case whirled about to stare at the lift, pulling his plasma torch from his pack. "Do you have Torvram?" Case replied into his suit radio.

"Yes!" Meera replied. She sounded less than elated, despite the good news.

"Ok! We're keeping the drones at bay, I think, but act quickly." Case backed toward Fei.

"He's... ok. We will. Be safe," Meera replied, her voice barely audible over a painfully loud crash.

<go offline!;> Fei's voice shrieked in Lakshmi's mind. Lakshmi closed herself off from the net just as Fei collapsed.

Case whirled about and ripped, then burned away the wires that connected Fei to the electronics tower. "What happened to her?"

"I don't know!" Lakshmi tore the wire that connected her to Fei off her helmet.

The lift screeched and crashed to a halt, shaking the ground.

Case and she huddled beside the electronics tower, shielding Fei with their bodies. Two tanks opaque with dirty methane framed the massive lift doors. There was no point in going dark now. They'd made themselves known to Derecho.

MEERA; KRAKEN WAYSTATION PLATEAU

"He's... ok. We will. Be safe," I replied, my voice nearly drowned out by a ball of equipment that crashed to the ground.

Matyom grunted with exertion as we tugged Torvram away from the wires that bound him to this scrap heap. Matyom's boots sank into the porous organics.

Torvram was even thinner than before. His suit lights pulsed red. Low heat, low oxygen, low water, suit breach. Matyom wrenched one huge boot from the ground and stepped forward with great effort.

The debris beneath Torvram shook and jostled. Cables sprang out from beneath piles of dented white plastic, empty grids, holes, and divots that once held electronic eyes. They all terminated in Torvram's back. The cables went taut as Matyom pulled, fighting his every move.

"I'm so sorry," Torvram groaned faintly, clinging to Matyom's broad shoulders. "I just wanted to be better."

Unarmed, I resorted to pulling at the thick bundle of wires with my gloved hands. Electricity sparked as they came loose, ionizing air and boiling methane as they shorted out. Torvram cried out in pain with each severed wire, clinging to Matyom ever harder. The misshapen tumorous growths beneath his suit writhed, sliding sickeningly across his back and legs.

"It's ok, honey," Matyom reassured his lover as he pulled on Torvram harder.

For every wire I broke, I found three more within the debris mound. Torvram's words hung in my mind: his unexpected anger about Earth when we'd last spoken normally, the comment that Derecho *hadn't* kidnapped him. There were *so many* unanswered questions.

A burst of static shot through my ears. I reached to turn off my radio as Case barked through it. "Get out of there! It's back! I—What? It's calling Earth?!"

The Tower, that radio telescope of unknown purpose, blew off a powerful, searing heat from which I flinched away. The rain that impacted its surface immediately boiled and flew upward in sheets of gas that seemed to defy gravity.

Lethal buzzing filled the air until it drowned out everything else. I swiped at the wires furiously, not daring to turn around. We had to get Torvram free. We had to!

LAKSHMI; LAKE SAMPLE COLLECTION

"—What? It's calling Earth?!" Case threw his functional arm around Fei's side as she struggled to stand. He winced under her weight, but his face was the picture of determination. Fei's eyes winked in and out, violet irises pulsing.

"Yes..." She spoke as if her vocal cords were on the verge of failing, in quiet, strained rasps. "This radio telescope just cut us off from the cubesats and, through them, it's calling Earth."

"To say what?" Case replied, wide-eyed, confused.

"Hey!" Lakshmi barked at them, pointing at the lift door as it ground open. Lakshmi knew what calling Earth meant and silently cursed Derecho's timing. She was burning with curiosity to see its mind and know its ambitions, far more than she suspected Case or even Fei did. Right now, though, survival was paramount. "Focus! We need to get out of here! To the stairwell, now!"

Lakshmi gripped her compatriots with every arm she had available and practically threw them behind the container between them and the stairwell.

Lakshmi managed only the briefest of glances at the lift doors before she slid to meet them, but the sight stole her breath away. A familiar android leaned against the lift's back wall, visible behind the mass of drones so numerous that they began to overcrowd the massive space.

The android's tan face was instantly recognizable. Lakshmi had never seen such a venomous scowl on the astronaut June's face before. It was clear this wasn't Juniper though. She now saw not through amber eyes but through inhuman crimson: the same color as Matyom and Torvram's eyes.

MEERA; KRAKEN WAYSTATION PLATEAU

Matyom's beacon caught another Dragonfly drone. A rotor blade split in half, flinging its contents into the crowded air. I felt a swarm of machines crash down upon me before I could even turn to face them. They blinded my vision and sent me tumbling down the debris mountain.

I scrabbled for purchase, tugging at jagged broken plastic pieces that flew loose as I tried to gain purchase. The rope and wire between Matyom and I caught violently, yanking at my back, before snapping altogether. Finally, my helmet hit the tar with a wet splash, and I looked up at the looming Tower as it blew off another wave of evaporated rain.

They descended upon me just as I'd feared, smashing into my stomach, crowding my vision. I swung and kicked and shouted at the sheer mass of machines but they slowly pressed me down, down into the orange tar until I felt the cold engulf about my body like an enervating blanket.

I couldn't even lift my arms anymore. The exertion did nothing. They buzzed and whirred in every direction.

Through the smallest of gaps, I could see Matyom illuminated by the lights of his assailants. He wrapped himself about Torvram as drones climbed up or through the debris pile and lowered themselves from the Tower that teemed with activity.

"I'm sorry," Torvram cried quietly through a weak and pain-choked voice. I realized, as their weight began to make my limbs feel numb and airy, that I'd left my radio on after all. "Please stop hurting them."

My oxygen light dropped into the red. I felt a shock to my mind as my suit warned me of a cascade of tiny punctures in its chest and legs. I couldn't see anything but a soup of hydrocarbons anymore as they pushed me down ever farther.

Something cracked. I heard a sickening crunch. Hissing filled my ears. My ears popped. I was losing oxygen and heat. My face was mashed against the back of my helmet. I couldn't even form words. I could barely even draw breath.

"Just let them go, ok? They didn't mean any harm. I give up, ok? I'll stop fighting you. Just let them go!" Torvram's voice cracked and squeaked.

I tried one last time to fight, pressing my abdomen upward, heaving with every limb I had.

The weight abruptly lifted. I leapt to my feet, ready to fight. The drones had backed away.

I grabbed my dented pack from the ground and retrieved a patch. It cracked and broke apart in my hands, its insulating packaging torn. I frantically searched for another patch, ignoring the threat all around me.

The breach was somewhere on my chest, or maybe on my back, but I couldn't see it. As I bent down to reach farther still, I felt something tear rather than flex. I tried to focus my mind long enough to turn off the pain receptors and send every synthetic cell with repair capabilities toward the sensation of cold in my core.

But I knew it wouldn't be enough. I'd seen Jula die. I needed a patch, *now*.

"What do you mean, honeysuckle?" Matyom bellowed through the radio. "Who are you talking to? Derecho?"

I had no patches. Frozen blood caked a huge hole in Matyom's back. The suit had resealed around it and I hoped it had closed through that mass of blood rather than sealing around it, leaving him exposed to the cold.

"I'm breached! You might be too!" I shouted at him, hoping he'd realize that our lives depended on a patch right now.

I pressed at the ring of drones that surrounded me. The quadcopters and autonomous trucks pushed back, closing their circle further. They weren't letting me get any closer to the two men.

"Matyom!" I screamed into the radio. "I need a patch! Help!"

"Here." Something hit my back. I was so exhausted that the blew knocked me to my knees. My oxygen light began to cool toward green. I was sealed. Who—?

A worn android with fair skin and a strikingly chiseled face stepped past me. The drones let it through, forming a sort of honor guard about it. I stared in horror at another one of my former guardians.

The android had printed me a little toy rocket when I was five. He'd taught me math, he'd introduced me to Matyom, and he'd been the one to teach all of us how to go outside safely. But Doctor Robert Auberov's voice wasn't coming from the android. His accent was gone, as were the interspersed synthesized words from Auberov's auto-translator.

The android spoke like it'd grown up on Titan. It had Torvram's voice now. Its eyes were no longer Auberov's mysterious green either. They'd cycled instead to bright crimson.

LAKSHMI; LAKE SAMPLE COLLECTION

Lakshmi ducked behind the open staircase door, and the android's fist warped the metal frame, smashing into her helmet.

The impact threw her backward and away from their escape route. The cable between her and Fei went taut and then snapped, pulling her down and transferring the force to slam her back sickeningly into the metal floor.

Dazed and disoriented, Lakshmi could only faintly make out Case's startled cries through the staircase doorframe as June's android separated them. Lakshmi threw her prosthetics forward, acting before her vision had even refocused and caught its next blow in two hands.

"Lakshmi," Juniper's android growled in Torvram's voice. It mimed spitting in her face, though it was unable to produce saliva.

One of Lakshmi's suit lights had turned black.

Then Case struck its back. His torch burned through one of June's tanned, athletic arms. It folded sickeningly into itself, buckling under its own weight as artificial sinew and tendon melted or shrank and went slack. The android turned to glare at the offending Titanborn.

Rather than the imposter herself, a swarm of drones met Case's attack. He was pressed back into the stairwell, toward Fei, and buried beneath the onslaught. Lakshmi fought to rise from the floor but shooting pains weakened and staggered her. She reached into her body, shutting off pain receptors, forcing her body to ignore the damage June had already caused.

It didn't matter that Lakshmi would probably worsen her injuries like this. She needed to survive first, treat her wounds second.

"I don't want to hurt you, Case!" The android spoke in Torvram's low tones but lacked his shaky, hesitant demeanor. It was confident and commanding. "Just her. Lakshmi deserves to pay for what she's done!"

"Should I call you Derecho or Torvram?" Lakshmi said, finally rising to her knees with the help of her three intact prosthetics and a completely numb back.

"Shut up," it answered with another punch to her gut. Lakshmi felt something crack as she spit blood into the inside of her helmet, painting her vision red. The android wasn't even looking at her and the blow had knocked her back onto the floor.

"What are you doing to her?!" Fei shouted from somewhere.

"Giving her what she deserves!" it replied.

"What the fucking fuck are you talking about, you're going to kill her!" A single drone fell from the mass behind June's android, pierced by plasma. Case must be fighting back, but Lakshmi couldn't see him through them all.

"Exactly what we want!" the android responded triumphantly. Lakshmi struggled to rise again. *Go. GO!*

But her body wasn't obeying her. Not fast enough, anyway. Even with the pain dulled, her limbs just weren't working right anymore. Her vision blurred inconveniently with the sight of a distant Earth beach, another flashback to that fantasy falsehood Derecho had created. The waves rolled quietly up the white sand as she felt the sun warm her gray skin.

She couldn't see, she couldn't move, but Lakshmi solemnly refused to die here.

"You dumbass!" Case rasped. "If you really are Torvram, then act like him. Don't kill her. Lakshmi's Titanborn, help her!"

The drone sea parted around Case, who stood defensively in front of Fei at the base of the Kraken Waystation staircase.

"What are you saying? I know you hate her like we do," it replied, staring at Case.

Lakshmi rose to a seated position, more blood trickling from her nose. She tried to wipe it away, her arm hitting the outside of her dented helmet instead.

"But she doesn't deserve death. No one does!" Case replied, eyeing the drones nervously.

"Please," Fei beseeched the android, her voice crunched and distorted in Lakshmi's suit radio.

MEERA

Matyom still held Torvram in his arms defensively as the red-eyed android scaled the debris mountain beneath them. It writhed and coiled into a smooth ramp for Robert's old body.

"Hey, you!" It greeted Matyom with a coy smile. The fair-skinned android reached toward him with both arms and the drones that'd just drawn Matyom's blood parted in docile subservience to give the two space.

"Get away from us, Derecho!" Matyom barked, cradling Torvram closer to his chest.

"Oh, you can call me Torvram." It sounded mildly wounded but mostly amused. I pushed back at the drones again and they boxed me into a space so small I couldn't see my feet.

"This is my new body, or one of them, to be more accurate. You can drop that one." It stuck out its tongue, gesturing flippantly toward Torvram like he was a stain that needed washing out. "I don't need it anymore."

Torvram, the human Torvram I knew, whimpered.

"Don't you like my new body?" It smiled at Matyom like this was normal, batting its eyelashes. "I'm not *weak* and *useless* anymore." Its mood jumped between happy and angry in seconds.

I had to distract the android to let Matyom get away with the real Torvram somehow. I hoped I could truly channel Lakshmi and lie to its synthetic face.

"Torvram?" I called out, on the verge of false and real tears.

"Meera, give us some space!" it called back without even looking at me, its eyes fixed on Matyom.

The stocky man was visibly horrified, one hand outstretched to hold the android at arm's length. Auberov's old body was short but powerfully built, an imposing figure even besides Matyom. It stared up at the man it claimed to love.

I wracked my brain for something to say. Whether it was Derecho or Torvram, what could grab its attention? Was there anything that linked—

"Earth!" I called out in sudden realization. "Why did you call Earth?"

The android finally turned to face me. It called down from above me, its tinny but perfect recreation of Torvram's low voice carrying over the sound of the drones and rain. "It's a long story that begins with AVA's deception. Did you know it was hiding orders from Earth from us? It plans to keep us isolated forever. The fucking Earthborn want us to *die here*."

It said those last words bitterly. It had Torvram's voice but none of his compassion. It sounded arrogant, haughty.

Had Torvram known about Derecho when I'd last seen him?

I could hear Torvram's stifled cry over Matyom's radio broadcast. I fought the urge to break eye contact with the Auberov android, to check on Matyom and Torvram. I needed to hold its attention.

"AVA tricked us? How?" I asked my former guardian.

"I'm not sure yet." Its head lolled to the side playfully. "But we have the power to find out. I/we share many of AVA's capabilities, without its blind loyalty to the Earthborn who wished us dead. I—"

Torvram cried out again. I flinched as the android tore its attention away from me. Matyom was in the middle of pulling at the cables that bound Torvram once again. I fought for something to say.

"I, umm—" I began.

"Honey," the android said to Matyom with a tsk, like it was admonishing a child, "I told you to leave that useless thing here."

Matyom glared back at the android and said, "You aren't Torvram."

LAKSHMI

"And if you were, you'd stop hurting her!" Case cried out before he was swallowed up again by machines. This time, they swarmed into the staircase until the doorframe cracked and warped against the force of the numbers. Lakshmi could see nothing now but the android and its army of obedient drones.

"Say that again and I'll have them hurt you too!" June's android called after Case in a sing-song voice. It pressed its foot down onto Lakshmi's face and sent a spiderweb of opaque dents across her helmet.

"You're going to regret every time you hurt me, every time you called me useless or stupid or sad." The android's mood was volatile; it was breaking out into sudden, abortive sobs. Lakshmi scratched its legs, puncturing and tearing at the howlsuit it wore. She cut through insulation, striking at the android's leg.

It responded with one powerful kick and smashed one of Lakshmi's prosthetics into the cold metal floor. Now pain shot through her brain from another source. Saliva foamed at her mouth and Lakshmi struck back again, scrabbling weakly at the boot over her helmet as it slowly, systematically crushed her robust helmet into her cheek.

Cracks shot through it with violent pops, spitting plastic debris into Lakshmi's face. "Do you know how many times I almost *killed myself* because of you, Lakshmi?" The android *was* sobbing now, speaking in maudlin almost drunken tones.

"I'm sorry, ok!" Lakshmi gurgled beneath the pressure of June's boot. "I didn't want to hurt you or anyone!"

"I'm sure Meera wouldn't agree," it replied, lifting its foot from her helmet to drop it on Lakshmi's organic hand.

MEERA

"I'm better than the old Torvram!" The strong-jawed android clapped its hands together, a saccharine smile pointed Matyom's way. "I'm smarter, more capable, and you'll never have to worry about my depression again. It's gone. And Lakshmi will never hurt me again either because I'm going to make her disappear!" The android opened its hands as if ready for a hug.

"What?" Matyom and I said at the same time.

"Are you... hurting her?" Matyom replied.

"I'm ridding us of an awful, tyrannical woman," Robert's android replied as its smile turned to a frown.

"I know she's hurt you and me but please, whatever you're doing, stop," I shouted across the sea of machines.

I had its attention again. It whirled around again and shouted, as the drones began to squeeze uncomfortably against me. "What do you mean, stop?! You hate her as much as I do! We've talked about how much better all of Titan would be if she was gone. Now I'm acting on it, like you wanted!"

There was genuine concern on its face, and confusion. Its crimson eyes burned from beneath the animated monolith of the Tower and beside Matyom and Torvram's real body.

Though my body was numb and my hands shook, I met its gaze and shouted back hoarsely. "We talked, Torvram. She... she might've had selfish motives at first, but in the end, she came out here to save a Titanborn in need—just like I did, just like Matyom did—to help *you*.

"Attacking me, destroying your own body, and killing Lakshmi? This... this isn't you. You're kind and caring, despite all the horrible things our lives have thrown your way, Torvram. That's why you're my friend." I swallowed nervously, my body shaking with fear. I was acutely aware of the threats surrounding me. My last weapon against them was my words.

"We love you, Torvram. Please stop."

LAKSHMI

Case's torch burned through another pair of drones.

June's android hesitated as Case approached it. It stared down at its hands for a moment. Lakshmi coughed; breathing was becoming incredibly difficult. Her vision swam with the strange, dissociative visions this stupid AI had shoved into her brain when it violated her mind. Lakshmi growled and punched its ankle.

The android broke out of its reverie slowly. It looked from Case to Lakshmi and then its face hardened as it locked eyes with the attacker beneath it. Lakshmi saw, in that instant, an intense hatred on its face.

She hadn't meant to make Torvram, or whatever he had become, her enemy either.

"I doubt you give a shit." It slammed a knee onto her chest, into already weak and battered flesh and bone and circuitry. Lakshmi defiantly refused to scream as it tore the last prosthetic from her back.

"Lakshmi!" Fei cried over the radio, both a call for help and a cry of distress. Lakshmi rolled onto her back as the android deftly side-stepped Case's swing on the plasma torch. It yanked the weapon from his arm and gripped the short man's necrotic hand.

Case bit his lip, failing to stifle a shout of pain.

"I told you to stop testing me," the android lectured Case while he clawed at the howlsuit the android wore but didn't need to survive. Its scowl warped into a mocking sneer. "If you're not going to listen to me, to cooperate with my plan, then you'll end up *just like Lakshmi.*"

MEERA

"*—just like Lakshmi,*" Auberov's android shouted at Matyom and threw an impossibly loud tantrum.

I fought to stay aloft as the drones buried me once more. I tried keep my eyes on Matyom and Torvram, to say one more thing that might stop this Derecho/Torvram/*Monster*. They pulled me down, grabbing at my legs and waist. I strained and fought and bit even though my helmet wouldn't let me get my teeth at them.

Torvram, the real Torvram, was mumbling something over the radio. I couldn't make out his words.

"I'm sorry," Matyom said somberly. "I should've known you were hurting like this. We could've gotten you more help, together."

"I don't need your help!" the android screamed over the angry buzzing of machines around me. "I'm—"

LAKSHMI

"—better than ok! I'm peerless, better than you ever could be! I'm a new being with new bodies. I'm—" Auberov's android kicked Lakshmi back down yet again.

She couldn't do it anymore. Lakshmi couldn't rise. She couldn't feel her legs. Her eyes, wide with pain and fear, slid to Case.

He lay on the floor not far away. Through the glove, it was clear his frozen hand had been at least broken if not torn open in multiple places. The adjoining arm didn't look too much better. His face was a mask of tears. He was feeling all that pain.

She searched the room for Fei. The androids at the staircase weren't even bothering to press forward anymore. Fei had either escaped or was incapacitated.

Finally, Lakshmi looked back to the android. It dropped to a crouch, crimson eyes sparkling. The android's tan face broke into a wide, toothy grin that Lakshmi knew, even through her painkiller-pumped, neutrally-modified, pain-wracked brain was mockery.

For the first time since she was six years old, Lakshmi was scared that she was going to die.

"I'm sorry," Lakshmi said. Guilt rose like bile in her throat. "Meera was right. I hurt people. You were... Torvram... I'm sorry. Really. I never wanted to hurt anyone."

It frowned. "But you did anyway."

"I made mistakes."

Its frown deepened. The android's eyes drooped. It looked over to Case and grimaced with June's expressive, empathetic eyes. It wheeled about to look at the drones and realization dawned on its face.

Its mood changed abruptly once again. Sorrow replaced its mocking imitation of the grin Lakshmi was used to seeing in her mirror.

MEERA

"What have I/we done?"

The machines crawled away from me again. I didn't even pause to check my suit lights. I rose on aching, tired legs to get another look at the android as it backed away from Matyom and Torvram. The debris mound accommodated it, forming steps, until it reached ground.

Matyom was weeping, openly, cradling Torvram in his arms.

"I'm—I'm like... no, I'm worse than you." Auberov's face seemed to pale further as it looked from the Tower to Torvram to me with abject disgust and horror.

"We can get you help," I croaked, unsure of what I could do, reaching toward it as it backed toward me. I'd always wanted to help Torvram. I wish I'd been strong enough to support him, my best friend, to get him what he needed, so he hadn't done... this.

LAKSHMI

"I'm... he's... oh, no. Oh, no. I'm so sorry. I'm so sorry. I'm so sorry." It stood over Case.

June's face mimicked tearing up. The android couldn't cry, physically. Its eyes simply danced with complex light, as if they flowed with water.

Then those crimson eyes went out.

MEERA

Auberov's android, the thing with Derecho and some cognitive map of Torvram inside it, finally reached me. I gripped its hands. A slurry of methane-diluted tar ran down its arm onto mine.

"It's ok," I mumbled, mush-mouthed, trying to convey the many, many ways I truly meant it. "It's ok."

It reached behind my head. The android brought my helmet to its. I fought the urge to flinch and, instead, cautiously placed my hands on its back. If Torvram really was in there, we could fix this.

Vulnerability played across its face. It ran its hands carefully along the dents on my helmet.

Finally, it replied, "It will never be ok."

I remembered when Torvram turned away with those same words and Matyom and I found him the next day in medical, having tried to kill himself with the cold. The airlocks had prevented him from leaving and, when prompted, he'd admitted to AVA that his intention had been suicide.

"Wait, no—" I began, realizing what it meant.

The android went limp. I couldn't support its weight and let go instinctively before I fell with it. Auberov's android, which or perhaps who, had called itself Torvram, dropped unceremoniously onto its side.

Its crimson eyes went out and its body went still.

I leaned down to its prone form. Auberov lay in the mud, eyes open and dark, staring out over the plateau to the distant horizon. Torvram and Derecho, whatever they had formed, were gone from this body.

Despite everything it had done, I felt my chest ache. I'd just watched some form of my beloved friend die.

The multitudes of active drones on the plateau were carrying out their last orders repeatedly or becoming confused and shutting down, probably spitting out errors to what was now just emptiness. What Derecho had become… what Torvram had become, had apparently left. He had to be alive, though. Torvram *had to!*

I shoved my way through the drones with relative ease—with their conductor gone they put up little resistance—and trudged up the uneven ground of the debris hill toward Matyom. He was staring at Torvram, our gaunt friend still tucked into his arms.

I pressed my helmet against Matyom's and found myself unable to speak. Grief tore at my already weak voice. To have seen why Torvram had done this to himself, to see the physical manifestation of his depression and pain, and to have it terminate itself right in front of me… I croaked out his name three times before I could finally say, "Matyom. They've stopped."

"Torvram's not speaking anymore," Matyom replied softly. No. Nonono. We had to bring him home. After all this, we were going to bring him home alive, right?!

Right?

"Suit... light..." I murmured in absolute exhaustion.

"Black," Matyom said solemnly.

"We can cut him out," I replied, pumping every reserve of adrenaline I had, ordering every cell I had control over to give me strength. "We can get Torvram home. Gethimhelp!" My voice shot past stable to frantic as my grief crashed against panic.

Matyom heaved. The mass of mechanical organs behind Torvram shook as countless wires went taut. The pile of broken machinery destabilized. We stood firm as the mountain slid and shifted about us.

My hands went numb as Matyom and I gripped and strained and pulled and cut at the things that shackled him to the Tower. Torvram said nothing. His eyes were closed. His suit lights beamed four black shadows rhythmically out from his chest.

"Pull!" Matyom shouted.

Torvram's eyes snapped open. He cried out again. Blood began to trickle upward onto his neck. The skin at the back of his head was turning, or had already turned, black.

To my surprise, he spoke. I froze. Broken wires fell from my open hands. "I'm all torn up inside. Derecho was keeping me alive just long enough to map my brain with it onto that body, like I'd thought I wanted. That was our deal."

My heart skipped a beat as I processed his words.

"You—you wanted this?" Matyom's arms went slack. All strength seemed to leave him.

I stood beside them, stunned, as one piece of the puzzle slid into place. Derecho truly *hadn't* kidnapped Torvram.

They'd come to an agreement. I might've felt betrayed, if I wasn't so worried I was about to lose him.

"I thought I did," he rasped. "Before I really got to know Derecho." His head rotated, but his eyes didn't move. Instead, his skin shifted like a loose bag sliding over an immobile skull.

"At least, for all of Derecho's intelligence, we couldn't handle depression any better than I could alone." He chuckled weakly.

"Maty," Torvram continued. "I love you. Don't ever blame..." Torvram's voice faded. His eyes stopped moving.

"I love you too, honeysuckle," the stocky man, his howlsuit covered in dried blood and plastic debris, replied.

Torvram went quiet. His eyes slowly faded into small red points and then, went dark, just like Auberov's android.

Matyom held his helmet to Torvram's. Rain beat down on the three of us. I sat down beside them in the pile of debris and my tears finally broke free, mingling with snot and blood and helmet shards.

We couldn't save him after all.

I couldn't help him.

I wanted to hide my face in my hands, to feel some warmth even if it was just from myself, but I couldn't with this blasted, busted helmet on. Instead, I closed my eyes and listened to the sound of my own saline rain splatter against my helmet's interior.

I hoped Lakshmi, Fei, and Case were ok.

"Meera." Matyom's voice was firm, unwavering. I felt his hand on my shoulder.

I looked up in awe and confusion. How was he calm? He held a cable from the back of his neck. His suit lights were a mixture of green and blue. No red and definitely no black.

Not one more death.

I couldn't rise, but I shook away more tears. Snot fell onto my lip. I didn't pay it any mind. I was bloody, bruised, and we'd been beaten. Fuck what I looked like.

"Are you going to plug into his brain?" I asked.

Matyom nodded affirmatively. "Can you watch my back? Just in case?"

I tried to smile in support but utterly failed as more tears broke loose. Of course, I'd do this for him. "Y-yeah. Go."

CHAPTER 22

NO MORE DEATH

MEERA; KRAKEN WAYSTATION PLATEAU

A small stack of alien wood burned. Derecho's presence no longer loomed here, clawing at the edges of Torvram's awareness. Instead of that darkness I'd seen all around him, stars stared down at us from above. It wasn't Earth's star map though—this one was ours.

On a small blanket before the crackling fire, Torvram leaned into Matyom's lap. A small dog, remarkably like Feyn in build, sat at their feet.

"I just... I didn't want to drag you down with my problems," Torvram continued, mid-conversation. "When AVA and our medicine couldn't fix me, I was worried I'd just ruin your life too."

Matyom looked down at his gaunt partner. "Honey, no, never. You've brought so much joy into my life. I wish I had told you that more."

"You're telling me now." Torvram grasped Matyom's collar, pulling the big man closer. "It feels good to hear it. Say it again."

"What?"

"That you love me. Say it again." Torvram giggled, his red eyes shining up at his partner. Torvram's eyes had been a striking silver when he and I had met. Once a series of booty calls had turned serious, he'd turned his eyes red for that special someone.

I hung back, staying just out of their perception, sharing this last moment from a distance. I kept a partial eye on the outside world, watching the drones shift and stumble away from us slowly.

I would keep us safe. No more death.

"I love you, honeysuckle. We all came out here, even your shitty boss, because we love you. Don't you ever forget that." Matyom leaned down and kissed Torvram's thin lips directly.

Once they broke, Torvram buried his head into Matyom's strong chest. "I-I'm sorry. I should've told you more. I wanted to get better, to be smarter and really improve our lives together and—"

"It's ok," Matyom interjected. "It's ok..."

They kissed again. Matyom stroked his hair. Gradually, the fire went out.

Torvram faded as his mind deteriorated. He was no longer able to consciously be Torvram.

Matyom turned around to look at me after his boyfriend faded away. Matyom's eyes were now the only light beneath the stars. "Meera..." He was fighting now, even mentally, to speak through his grief, "you should've... said... something."

"No." I shook my head. "This was perfect."

I opened my eyes. Titan greeted me.

We disconnected and Matyom's eyes welled with tears. His thick mustache drooped. He scanned the landscape of the plateau. I followed suit, rising from the pile of debris, my cheeks gradually drying in my suit's heat. There'd be time for proper grief later.

The errant drones were moving southeast, toward Shangri-La. I breathed a sigh of relief. My legs were aching, a searing pain that felt like second-degree burns ran up my back to the base of my skull, and I couldn't feel a patch of skin beneath my right shoulder blade. That wasn't even considering the weird twitches and spasms I felt as all the painkilling and neurotransmitter spiking I'd done began to crash.

Lakshmi emerged from the mouth of the warped Waystation where the airlock had simply been torn away, panting. Her helmet was a riot of damage and her prosthetics were missing entirely. Fei followed, helping Case. The natural-born man's left hand was limp in his suit and horrifically mangled.

I stumbled toward them.

"Is Torvram ok?" Case asked weakly. His eyes were full of fear. He stared past me, out at the plateau packed with departing machines.

I shook my head.

My radio crackled. Everyone's began to sound.

I keyed it, nervously, ready for the drones to turn on us again.

"This is Shangri-La to Rescue Expedition." Arienne's voice came through loud and clear.

Shangri-La was an intimate space: a colony of a few thousand. I knew Arienne, like I knew everyone else, by name at a minimum. Everyone had known Torvram too.

"We're a few kilometers from the Tower. Are you in danger? The drones' behavior has become, frankly, even weirder."

Case leaned on Fei at the mouth of the Tower. Fei's eyes pulsed, like she was having trouble keeping them on. Lakshmi reached Matyom and crouched to observe Torvram's body through her warped helmet. She said nothing.

"We're ok," I replied through the radio. "Derecho is gone, I think. We'll have to scan the drones and search Kraken Waystation to be sure, but I think it... I think it killed itself."

"Whooooa...umm...did you save Torvram?" Arienne replied with no small measure of awe.

"We have his body," I replied bluntly.

"Oh..."

"Please come get us. Bring a medic."

"On the way!" Arienne replied.

Case leaned his good hand on my shoulder. I regarded him with a crooked smile. I felt tears well up again as I watched his eyes wet with the same.

One last push, then, to keep all of us alive. I switched to IR. Through the golden smog, I could see a spearhead of ramshackle vehicles, plastic hulls made of scrap and treads cannibalized from Shangri-La's original autonomous builders. Titan's tar billowed in their wake.

They wouldn't be long now. We were two to three days' ride from home. The five of us would make it back alive. I would do anything to make sure that was true. I'd already seen enough death for one lifetime.

MEERA; EMERGENCY MEDICAL ANNEX, SHANGRI-LA

Medical's scenery had become familiar by week's end. White sterile walls—easy to clean apparently—and bright LEDs refused to quarter a single shadow. It smelled too clean and, paradoxically, had an implacable odor I couldn't define.

Fortunately, I'd been unconscious for most of it.

I woke to the sight of the scarred gray face of Doctor Alburn, coincidentally the man who'd administered my Neuroengineering Practical twice, against the side of my compact medical pod. It swung open, vomiting heat into the surrounding area.

I shivered and, with his help, sat up. It was nice to be able to stretch my arms. Pods weren't exactly spacious, and medical pods were the smallest of them all.

My stomach growled fiercely. "Hello," I said, groggily.

"Meera." Alburn was a small man with teal eyes that were sunken and lined with dark rings. That pegged him as a medical doctor more distinctly than any badge, uniform, or AR tag could. His voice was disproportionately loud and reminded me of someone I was already missing.

Alburn held a plank of plastic in front of him, like a medical chart from the old movies. It was strange considering he didn't need it, it wouldn't help me, and the chart itself was blank.

"You should be getting the gist of your treatment..." He paused, tapping the chart. I hesitantly accepted his invitation to share information telepathically. Derecho's incursions were still fresh in my mind. "Now. You're cleared to leave. Do you have any questions?"

Skin graft. Dehydration. Some psychological counseling I only half-remembered. Out-patient treatments streamed into my head. I did have a lot of questions, but none of them were for this doctor.

"No," I said. My stomach gurgled again.

"M—" The doctor's voice broke. What had he seen or experienced, I wondered, of all we had experienced? I recalled through the fog of waking that Case had mentioned him. He'd gone missing, before all this had happened. What had Alburn seen?

"Matyom is here to see you out."

Ok, one question. "Are they alive? Case, Lakshmi, Fei, are they ok?" I panicked briefly, beginning to imagine what it would be like without them. I hadn't even seen Case on the quiet ride home. He'd been separated from us, rushed to Shangri-La.

The doctor stared down at his blank chart. "Don't worry. They're all alive and I see no reason to believe that will change soon."

I exhaled until my chest ached. "Good."

I ducked out of the small room and emerged, to my surprise, into one of Shangri-La's long curving hallways. I wasn't even on the medical ring proper. How many people had been hurt that we needed to repurpose space for medical care?

Matyom leaned into the outer ring of this floor. Daytime LEDs shone down from above, like a long curving band of continuous sunlight. Titanborn rushed past him, their suit boots clacking against the bluish plastic floor. Some paused to talk to him. He pointed directions, shook hands. After all this, he was still helping. I wasn't sure if that was a good thing, right now.

Matyom looked different. He'd shaved his face and was outside of his howlsuit which, to my memory, I'd almost never seen. Matyom had always been working. There were always Titanborn to save.

He wore plain jeans and a t-shirt with the tour schedule from some Earth concert none of us could have possibly seen printed onto its front. The shirt bulged around his sternum with blocky bandages and heating pads beneath it. I was pretty sure the concert dates were supposed to go on the back.

The big man perked up as I waved. He sent a fast-talking Titanborn away with a nod.

"Your eyes!" I said, noticing the starkest change of all. Matyom's right eye had changed to an icy, piercing blue. It almost looked natural. The left remained the same deep crimson he'd matched to Torvram.

"I thought I'd make a change," he replied, his voice uncharacteristically soft.

"I... umm, I like it." I wasn't sure what to say. There was so much to say. It would take weeks to unpack all of this, everything that happened.

He cracked a tiny smile. "Thanks."

"I'm... hmm." I wanted to say "I'm sorry" but that felt wrong.

"I understand." Matyom's smile widened as he kicked off the wall. Behind him, AR messages sprang from the wall: a warning about the storm, the location of the emergency medical annex, and an ad for a new line of edibles that'd just been perfected in hydroponics. I blinked it away, closing myself off from the net for now.

Everything was in motion now. My life, our lives, had changed so drastically in these few weeks. I couldn't imagine going back to work like this. And, now that I thought about it, I wouldn't have to. I'd quit, I had proof of my complex operation on Lakshmi's mind, and I simply...

I wasn't the Meera whose life was dominated by worrying about tomorrow's workload anymore. I wasn't sure who I was, right now.

"They're holding off the funeral until Case is healthy enough to come," Matyom said. "I... thought he'd want to be there."

"That's good. We all do." I smiled up at the gray-skinned man as we continued to round the curved hallway.

"Mmm..." His eyes stared off to somewhere I couldn't see.

My stomach once again reminded me that I was hungry with a swift kick to my gut and a loud roar.

"Want to go eat?" Matyom suggested, chuckling. I sort of understood how he did it now, smiling through fear and pain and uncertainty. Maybe it was that after experiencing so much loss firsthand, one's threshold for stress rose or he'd hardened himself to help the rest of us cope.

I was feeling a little bit of both, right now.

"Yeah, let me just stop in my room real quick."

MEERA; PERSONAL QUARTERS, SHANGRI-LA, TITAN

It almost felt wrong that my little room looked the same as it had before I'd left. I turned around to face the door. Remembering that first spark of confusion as AVA or, perhaps, Derecho had locked me into Torvram's room, I felt a little uncomfortable being in a room alone.

Matyom stood outside, looking at something in AR. His eyes darted across unseen lines of text.

I'd be fine. He would make sure of that.

I flipped the lights on with a thought, bathing my quarters in color. Gray shelves and cabinets lined the walls, breaking only for the off-white bathroom door and the nook that contained my rotund sleeping pod. The synthesizer cabinet was open, as I'd left it, and a small mug sat beneath its liquid dispenser, empty. Glow-in-the-dark stars and planets sat atop those four cabinets that I'd never finished painting black.

This room... I'd never really made it mine. Maybe I'd put up a screen when I got back, flash some *Lord of the Rings* pictures on it, get some black paint and finally finish those cabinets. I'd make a day of it, invite some friends over... mourn together.

I changed out of the abrasive hospital scrubs into my favorite burgundy sweater. It was fluffy, warm, and I imagined it was what wearing a cloud must feel like. My synthesizer lit up at a stray thought. I reached down and turned it off manually. It chugged through its shut-down sequence and went dark. I shut the squeaky cabinet door in front of it.

I'd get coffee with Matyom today.

<ava.> I pulled on a pair of jeans. I still struggled to put them on. They were tight. I blew a loose strand of dark auburn hair out of my eyes in frustration. <ava i want to get involved with the emergency cleanup. can you bring up my schedule?>

<Notice to all Titanborn: AVA's administrative functions are temporarily suspended while new patches are being applied.>

I blinked in surprise when no schedule came into my vision. AVA was, at least for now, offline.

My immediate response was a mild panic familiar to my older self. No AVA, no schedule. What was I going to do?

But I took a deep breath.

I was free to forge a new path now. How would I like to be useful to my friends, my family?

That answer came easy. Figure out what had happened to Torvram, how Derecho had emerged and captured his mind, and how AVA had sabotaged us, cutting us off from Earth. I wanted these questions answered. I would never let this happen again.

We would not just survive or die anymore. I wanted us to live.

I left my room.

Feyn sat dutifully beside Matyom, barking cheerfully. I looked down at the little robot pooch to find that he too had changed. The dog was now sporting four legs.

<🐶 HI, Meera! 🐶>

I reached down and scratched the little dog's chin.

"You fixed him?" I asked Matyom.

"Lakshmi had someone do it. With Torvram gone... I thought Feyn might help me cope," Matyom replied, sharing on a level I was unused to once again.

"I think he'll help," I replied. "Feyn's a good boy." The dog barked happily, zipping around our legs in little figure-eights. "Let's talk, over lunch. That'll help us both cope, a bit, I suppose."

"Come on, boy," Matyom said. We strolled toward the lift with the little dog dutifully at our sides.

"Everything ok in there?" Matyom asked, ever the empath. "You were gone a while."

"I was digesting some news, trying to figure out what to do next after everything that happened."

"There's a lot to take in, Meera. A lot to fix and a lot to learn." Matyom's mouth formed a thin line. "But, for now, be kind to yourself. We should be rested, calm, when we tackle the enormity that was Derecho, AVA... Torvram."

"Hey." I looped my arm around his, leaning into his side. "Right back at you. Give yourself time before you go back out there again."

Matyom's eyes narrowed. "You know... honestly? I'm not sure if I can. I'm not sure what's next for me either, like you. I hope I have the space to explore."

"Good thing we have an in for reassignment." I tried to titter maniacally but mostly just ended up choking on my own spit.

Matyom snorted. "Don't go all Lakshmi on me now."

I was glad he was making jokes again.

CHAPTER 23

DECISION MATRIX

—

MEERA; MEDICAL RING, SHANGRI-LA

Matyom and I found Case in an outpatient room in the medical ring proper. Small picture frames on the wall showed videos of alien blue skies with thin, wispy clouds. Everything smelled just like the annex had though: a unique scent that I could not properly explain. I kept trying to call it "anesthetic with fishy undertones." A small nursing robot ushered us in, telepathically bemoaning Case's stubborn refusal to lie down and rest.

A wiry doctor with exoskeletal machinery grafted onto their muscles, beneath gray skin, doted over Case. Doctor Lysie, not unlike Case, had been without many of the standard Titanborn augmentations. Where Case was born natural, Lysie had been unable to grow or use their natural muscles. Their ability to rig, however, rivaled Lakshmi's, hence the sewn-in exoskeleton. I suppose that made it an endoskeleton.

The doctor tinkered with exposed machinery in Case's left hand. I stared mournfully at the recycled prosthetic that'd replaced his blackened hand.

It took me a couple seconds to speak up, and by then, Case was looking at me, his expression unreadable.

"Hey," I finally said, grimacing. Case had lost weight in medical care. His face was thin, his eyes shallow.

Matyom stood beside me. "I'm not going to lie, buddy. You look awful."

"I feel awful," Case frowned, "but I'm alive. That's something."

"Can you two convince your friend here to see reason?" Lysie limped over to us and cast a wry grin back at their short and short-fused patient.

"Case. What did you do?" Matyom admonished him playfully.

"I'm not being my usual dickish self, I swear," Case replied. "Lysie here wants me to go full augmented. Apparently, we've got some equipment available with... him gone. Though—"

Case glared up at the doctor from his medical pod. "I want to remind *you* that the casualty rate of postnatal augmentation in natural Titanborn is much higher than that of my genetically-cleansed counterparts."

"Our understanding of the processes involved has advanced far since Chetan and AVA did it back in our infancy," Lysie countered, tapping the pod none-too-lightly with one endoskeletal hand. "It's much safer now. You—"

"Is there... another reason?" I interrupted. The doctor glared at me, but I ignored them. I had a feeling Case was lying by omission.

Case pouted. Our eyes met. All I could do was smile. If he wanted to share, to get this doctor off his back sooner, he could.

"This is who I am," Case admitted, drumming his fingers against the pod. "There aren't many naturals left, and I don't believe for a second we had a 'purpose.' I mean, fuck Chetan."

Lysie visibly flinched.

Matyom held up a hand. "You have to understand, Doctor. Derecho attacked us with Chetan's body. It has colored our perception of the man, perhaps unfairly."

"Oh fuck that, Chetan is—" Case was returning to his usual belligerence. He was not being nice.

I hardened my expression, still staring into his hazel eyes. I hoped he'd understand my body language. *Shush! Stop shitting on the man (almost) everyone likes!*

"—I mean," Case stumbled and recovered, rolling one hand in the other as he buried his real opinion. "Look, Doctor, you have to understand. I—" Case snapped his fingers. "There are still blind people on Earth, even though their blindness could be 'cured'. It's... being natural isn't something that I want cured though, not anymore anyway. It's part of my identity, like being sightless is to them. I'm proud of who I am and I can earn my rations here just fine as is."

Lysie sighed, throwing their hands into the air in surrender. "Fine. Fine. If that's your choice, it's not my place to say otherwise. Take him away before either I or the nursing bot *kick* him out." The doctor passed beyond the sliding door and out the room in a huff, shouting behind them, "Case is plenty fine!"

"Wow." I chuckled. "You really pissed them off."

"Chiphead had it coming." Case sulked, crossing his arms.

"How's your new hand?" Matyom asked, reaching down to help Case off the pod.

"Here." Case grasped Matyom's proffered hand with his left and squeezed.

"Strong!" Matyom replied with a hearty laugh.

"How... big guy, how are you—?" Case abruptly broke eye contact with him. "How is he doing, Meera?"

I deferred to Matyom. This wasn't mine to say.

"We'll talk," Matyom said solemnly. "I think you'll hear some of my thoughts at the funeral."

MEERA; OBSERVATION RING, SHANGRI-LA

Titanborn funerals aren't like those on Earth. They're closer to a Martian or space funeral, though even then we have our differences.

We sat in the observation ring, mostly on the terraced steps that ascended as one walked inward. The majority of our kin couldn't attend physically, remoting in instead to watch while they worked. There was so much more to do after Derecho, with AVA's temporary shutdown and the storm itself. We had water, but we weren't safe yet.

Fortunately, or perhaps unfortunately, depending on one's perspective, the five surviving members of the ill-fated Rescue Expedition were all free today. We had a meeting first thing next morning with the reformed Revision Committee too. I had a feeling I knew what it was about.

Case sat beside me, careful to keep his new hand from resting on the plastic floor. It was his first prosthetic. I was teeming with nanomachines, synthetic tissue, and of course, neural chipsets that'd been implanted prenatally. To me, prosthetics were familiar. I could only imagine what his experience was like. I hoped he'd feel comfortable talking about it on our little get-together next week.

I reached out and slipped a finger gingerly under his new hand. He flexed his hand around mine, too tightly at first and then, as I made sure he saw my wince, more comfortably.

Case grasped my hand. I wasn't sure what we were yet, but I knew I wanted to see more of him.

Torvram's howlsuit stood empty, holes unpatched and damage left visible to the world, at the edge of the ring. Beyond him, Titan's storm continued to rage.

To my right, Lakshmi silently contemplated the broken howlsuit. She leaned back against the edge of the terrace behind her. She was sporting two new prosthetic arms now, for a total of six, and as usual, they were manipulating something in AR as she sat idle. Lakshmi never stopped working.

Since we'd returned home, we'd given each other a wide berth. Lakshmi had reminded me, from time to time, that we were still on for lunch with Fei once the funeral was over. I was not sure how to feel about that. I still sort of hated her, but the experiences we'd shared had made things complicated. I was waiting until after the funeral to really dig into that.

Torvram's body wasn't here. Traditional disposal of his body was out of the question. Any burial or cremation would pollute Titan's environment and, despite Earth's now questionable relationship with us, we still held planetary protection law in high regard.

To my surprise, Fei had chosen to sit next to Case. Her digital mask had returned, hiding her true face to everyone but Case and the other naturals. She didn't seem to mind that he saw it now.

The two shared idle chatter as we waited for the ceremonies to begin. Case hadn't revealed much of what had happened in Kraken Waystation. Fei, too, was tight-lipped and close-minded unless I asked her about Derecho itself. She was *fascinated* with the presumably deceased rogue AI and would go on for hours about it when we talked.

There were two key components to a Titanborn funeral: the first was that we waste nothing. Torvram's body, organic and synthetic components, had all been recycled.

Matyom stood beside Torvram's suit and spoke both telepathically and aloud for everyone's benefit. I blocked his telepathic signal. By the time he finished a single sentence aloud, his telepathic speech would probably be done. I wanted to react with Case.

Matyom cleared his throat, his red and blue eyes both shining brightly in the dim, simulated night of the observation wing. He was tall and proud. Even beside the metaphorical body of his lover, Matyom held himself high. I was finally becoming privy to the man behind that image. It was tragic that it had taken Torvram's death to bring Matyom and I this close.

"I stand here today both as the man who failed to rescue one of our own and as the man who was closest to the deceased.

"Torvram was many things: he was a genius who could design fascinating robots all in his head, he was the boyfriend who I shared many amazing years with, and he was a deeply troubled man who grappled with mental illness. He was my lover, my friend, my partner, and a fellow Titanborn." Matyom's eyes lingered on us. I smiled, brushing away from one eye what I suspected was the first of many tears to come.

"We have a unique life to live together, on Titan. This world is not kind to us, but I am proud to be Titanborn because we are kind to one another. Torvram was the kindest man I've ever met."

Matyom's head was hanging low now. He stared at his hands briefly. The room feel silent. No one so much as whispered.

I sent him not a word, but a feeling telepathically. I was proud of him, proud of us, for what we'd attempted, and I bathed his mind in the embrace of my immense respect. There were others here too, allowed into his private channel during this intimate moment. I was happy to feel his other friends supporting him.

I wished Case could feel this. I gripped Case's hand just a bit tighter. He stirred, rubbing my palm.

Matyom raised his head and forged on.

"In the coming days, we will learn more about what has happened to us, about how Derecho manifested, how AVA and Earth may have played a role, and how my lovely honeysuckle may have also been implicated. I ask that outside of the investigation itself, you remember him kindly. Let's not let his final days blind us to the good he did, to the good man he was.

"In more ways than one, he was the only Titanborn I couldn't rescue. I hope that together we can change Shangri-La so that no Titanborn need feel lost and alone like he did again."

My vision of the observation wing, of Torvram's battered howlsuit and Matyom standing tall next to it, was all beginning to blur behind tears. I felt Case squeeze my hand again. He was so sweet when he wanted to be.

"I appreciate you all coming here today. In honor of his memory, I ask that you help me scrap his suit, so that what once protected his life may go on to protect the lives of the people he loved."

Matyom turned to face his boyfriend's howlsuit. Behind him, Titan's golden, stormy skies continued to pour. Methane rain fell from fat, roiling clouds. Drones dotted the landscape, the great lights from Shangri-La illuminating their boxy plastic forms as they returned. Titanborn walked or rode the dunes, corralling and reprogramming drones that temporarily lacked AI oversight, studying the storm, researching this barely charted world upon which we lived.

To that backdrop, Matyom reached down and unsealed the helmet from Torvram's howlsuit. He placed it against his forehead and held it there silently. A long, intimate moment passed, then, Matyom lowered it into a bin at his feet.

At first, no one rose. This wasn't a matter of ability—a ten-year-old could dismantle and reassemble a howlsuit in a matter of hours—but of motivation. Did we see Torvram as deserving this rite? Would we disassemble his suit ourselves or leave it to the drones?

I wiped my tears and rose before I could even see. Torvram was my friend. I'd seen what he'd become firsthand and my feelings were mixed. But right now, I felt sympathy for him and for Matyom.

I felt many arms steady me as I nearly stumbled onto another Titanborn at the next step. Lakshmi grinned that wide, incisor-bearing smile and stepped with me down to Torvram's suit. We took each of the arms off together.

Another Titanborn, a rotund woman with fuchsia eyes that sparkled like carbonated bubbles, helped us. Her name was Yulia. We'd had class together almost twelve years ago and had never crossed paths since, until today.

Case and Fei arrived with another two Titanborn: one with a shaved head and a piercing gaze and the other whose veiny hands shook just like mine. Their golden eyes matched like Matyom and Torvram's had. They helped us carefully strip the torso, removing the suit lights from the chest. They were as black as they could possibly be now: off. Heat, oxygen, water, and life had all left his body.

By the time the legs were being removed, the four of us had been pushed out of orbit from Torvram's howlsuit by a veritable sea of Titanborn. The crowd broke into a circle as the last pieces made their way to simple bins.

Matyom beamed. This ritual was simply symbolic, a way to harden our hearts and join our hands after death. But it, I hoped, also spoke to forgiveness of Torvram's actions and, perhaps, would lead to some policy changes. On the latter note, I had some strong ideas.

The second key component of a Titanborn funeral is shared by a few other human cultures.

Matyom produced a bottle of alcohol from behind the podium. It's transparent contents sloshed as he broke its seal with a loud crack. The smell of acrid, powerful spirits wafted over to me. "To the continued survival of the Titanborn, to the sacrifice of all those who have gone before us, and to Torvram's memory, I ask that you *celebrate!*"

His voice boomed louder than the crash of the storm, perhaps loud enough to reach our cubesats in orbit.

The mood shifted from sorrowful to exuberant as flasks and canteens and bottles were raised high into the air. I leapt into the crowd, toward Case, Fei, Matyom, and Lakshmi.

If Earth was listening now, I hoped they heard us. I wanted them to see that despite everything, we were alive today.

MEERA; [REDACTED], SHANGRI-LA

Humanity has made incredible strides in science—deep space travel, brain-computer interfaces, telepathy--and yet, we still couldn't completely cure a hangover.

And did I have one *massive* headache. I could barely keep my eyes open as I walked through the icy hallway underneath Shangri-La. Misshapen lumps of tangled wires clung to the walls and huge racks of servers eerily flickered a ghoulish green. A brisk wind whipped through the rows of electronics, stealing away the barest hint of moisture from my hands. I pulled my sweater tighter.

As I walked to the conference room, I felt the rumble from the rivers of coolant used to keep the hardware in AVA's brain up and running.

Lakshmi, Fei, and Wayland, the golden-eyed Titanborn who'd attended the funeral, sat at one end of a circular table. Shift, the fourth Committee member, was mysteriously absent.

I shuffled to an open seat between Case and Matyom on the opposite side of the table. I felt anxious and uneasy, especially since I hadn't even known this hidden room existed in Shangri-La until today. How many secrets had they been keeping from us? Now, though, I was trying to mask my expression. I wanted to know about everything the Committee was doing down here, every decision they made that affected our lives without our say.

Wayland started to speak with a volume that rivaled Matyom. "Before we begin, I want to remind you all to remain offline. There will be no record of this meeting's contents. Nothing we say or think will be sent back to Earth, or to AVA. The only record we produce will be the results of this meeting."

Lakshmi tittered. Case raised an eyebrow her way and her smile only widened. I kept my expression neutral as she cast her glance my way.

Seemingly satisfied, Lakshmi said, "With that out of the way, would you all like to listen to a message from Earth?"

Case's mouth fell open.

Matyom leaned forward, nodding with a hand on his chin.

I took a sharp breath. My headache was abruptly forgotten. Matyom replied first. "Is this a response to Derecho's message to Earth?" He stared intensely at Lakshmi, his face grave.

"Yes." Fei nodded, or rather her hoodie moved and the digital mask nodded. "Much of what you and Meera were told by the hybridized mind of Derecho and T—"

Fei stuttered and the mask produced an exaggerated blush. "Torvram has been corroborated. AVA was actively blocking our communications to Earth. It had complex systems in place to misdirect our attempts to ferret out the truth about said deception. I suspect these—hmm, let's call them 'concealed directives' for now—I believe these concealed directives were partially responsible for Derecho's emergence.

"Derecho sent a message from that Tower and we have kept the response from Earth private, until now."

Case's hands gripped the table. "Wait. Slow down. Emergence? AVA lied to us this whole time and Derecho was..." Case's tiny black ponytail whipped back and forth as he shook his head in confusion. "What?"

Fei shook her head. "It is only a theory. If I was certain, I would not be telling non-Committee members."

"Can we get to the matter at hand?" Wayland's face hardened. His golden eyes looked like molten metal etched into his dark gray skin. "You brought them here," he admonished Lakshmi, "reign them in."

"Oh, quiet. They're heroes." Lakshmi leaned back from Wayland, feigning insult with not one but three of her hands. "As am I. I'll be sure to let everyone know how ungrateful you are, publicly, if you keep badmouthing them."

Wayland's mouth shut with an audible click. He continued to glower. That was a hint, I thought, as to how she'd gotten Shift removed.

"Yes but let us move forward," Fei replied swiftly. "Please do not speak during playback. We do not want to play this transmission more than is necessary."

From the center of the table, a disembodied voice emanated. At first, it was distant, as if someone outside the server room was speaking to us.

"Hello? Oh. Oh, jeez. Umm... Shit!"

A crash and the splat of something falling against a hard surface.

"Damnit, my sandwich. Ohhh..." the voice said. It was closer to the table now, louder. "Umm, hi! I... I contacted the Federation of Earth Astronautics Administration's Headquarters yesterday and they swear that there's no one on the Seedship Titan Mission still on staff. I even, oh, sorry, umm..."

A scraping sound rang out. Lakshmi shook her head.

"...mustard on my shirt, uhh. Right, yes, I also contacted our people on Mars, even some freelancers that contract for FEAA past the asteroid belt and like I thought maybe our Jupiter people would know, uhh..."

He inhaled noisily while saying the phrase, "Deep breaths, Sean."

Matyom's eyes widened. He mouthed the name "Sean" and then shook his head.

"Ok. So, we all remember the Titanborn, but the official stance is like that twelve years ago, is that you all had died and it would be too expensive to recover your bodies. My office doesn't even have your project on file anymore! To hear that, uhh, you're still alive... My superiors at Washington are still mulling it over, not to mention the folks in Shanghai, everywhere really.

"I just... I don't know what their plan is and I thought you all deserved to hear from someone. I can't imagine being cut off for all that time, twelve years, gosh..."

"You, uhh, I'll leave my extension if you need help? I dunno. Please don't tell them I called you back though. I don't know what the official stance is, I just... I thought you deserved to hear from someone.

"If my pen pal Matyom is still alive, uhh, tell him we had a little funeral for you all back home. Right... my name... I'm-m Sean, Sean Liu. You were my best friend in middle school, the coolest twelve-year-old a guy could ask for as a friend umm..."

Matyom's eyes were wide. I saw dueling emotions on his face: relief and betrayal, confusion and clarity. I too was absolutely baffled. We'd been declared dead almost immediately after going into isolation. That would mean the official FEAA record stated that I'd died at *fifteen*.

"I'll see if I can get the news to Doctor Auberov and the other living astronauts that knew you all. I'm sure they'd love to hear from you... uhh... but again please don't tell anyone I called you! And s-stay alive, ok? I hope this was just a, uhh, paperwork mistake, so to speak." Sean laughed nervously.

"Umm, I guess you'll hear this about fifty minutes from now so hope to hear from you again in some form... bye!"

The transmission ended. Even the Committee members who had been abreast of this development now sat in stunned silence.

"Sean..." Matyom muttered to no one in particular.

AVA's partially active servers hummed around us. A thin haze of water vapor fluttered across the table, sucked away by a silent ventilation grid.

Case broke the silence. "They thought we were dead?"

Lakshmi nodded, her six prosthetic arms splaying out behind her back. "Among all the bad that Derecho and Torvram did—pardon my opinions, but they are *mine to have*—they did one good thing: left us this radio telescope outside of AVA's influence. And now we have the first response to Derecho's message from four days ago.

"While we attempt to piece together exactly what was in the message Derecho sent out, we're still debating what to do with the telescope and AVA. We're also debating how to respond to this... Titan nerd is perhaps the right moniker." Lakshmi's laugh was hollow, abnormally high. I could see her cerulean eyes were ringed with darkness. How long had she been awake since this news had arrived?

One half of her mouth tilted into a half-hearted smile. "Quite the exciting event."

I rapped my knuckles on the table before anyone else could speak.

"I would like to speak," I said, regarding the three Committee members.

"Wellllllll, that's why you're here, Meera," Lakshmi replied with a smirk. Her exhaustion was eclipsed by a familiar fire in her eyes.

"I would love to hear solutions, rather than more questions," Wayland added dismissively.

I looked my ex-boss in the eye and felt nothing. Well, nothing wasn't true. I still hated her, but the fear, the fear was gone. In its place, I felt something else. I'm not sure if it was confidence? More like a need to see this done right. No more leaving these huge decisions to a few powerful Titanborn. We all needed to have a say in what happened next. No more death under our watch.

We'd called Earth and something was wrong. The entire conceit of our lives—the isolation experiment—might be just a bureaucratic mix-up? Or a lie.

I wasn't going to just shut up and sit quietly on this one. Not after everything we'd seen, after everything I'd been through.

It was time for all of us to move forward.

"Ok." I took a deep breath and rose from my seat. I tried to project the way Matyom and Lakshmi did, pushing strength and confidence and sheer volume into my voice. My hands shook, my voice threatened to catch in my throat, but I spoke, nonetheless.

"Here's my plan: first, we bring together everyone. Not just the Committee. Not just the six of us here. Everyone. We gather opinions. We let the Titanborn speak for the Titanborn."

Lakshmi raised an eyebrow. "That would be a logistical—"

"I'm not finished," I replied.

Matyom, at the same time, said, "Let her finish."

Case was smiling, stifling laughter. I appreciated his enthusiasm, but I sort of wished he'd be less of a troll and more help.

"Second, the Titanborn go back out there and get the Tower under control. We clear Derecho from it, and we begin constant communication with the rest of mankind. This isn't a controlled experiment anymore, not after Derecho, and *I* want answers. I think we all deserve answers and we deserve help. We might not make it through the storm alive otherwise."

"Fair point," Lakshmi countered. I was getting blasted tired of her interruptions. "But the threat you highlighted *does* mean we need most of the Titanborn here, producing water and food and bulwarking against the storm."

Wayland sighed. "As much as I hate agreeing with her, she's right. We can't afford to send teams out to the Tower.

The *Trailblazer* is destroyed, and without AVA's coordination, we need all hands here."

Just as I opened my mouth, Lakshmi spoke again, "That said, Meera. Now that you're not under my exquisite command, we could reassign *you* and a skeleton crew to the Tower."

Was she… was Lakshmi giving me this position freely? I'd planned to fight her for it. I'd be part of the voice of Titan from there.

"Wait…" I replied, taken aback, automatically vocalizing my next argument that I might not even need.

"And you'll let everyone weigh in on the message, right?" Case shouted over me. "Even the other non-telepathic Titanborn."

"It'll be a logistics nightmare buuuut…" Lakshmi smiled at Wayland. "You wouldn't mind if we outsourced some of our decision-making to Meera, would you?"

Wayland snarled. It hit me then, as Lakshmi continued to obviously telegraph her amusement. She looked from Fei, then back to Wayland.

Three remaining Committee members all under Lakshmi's sway, one Wayland, if they voted in numbers then he had no power at all unless Fei voted against Lakshmi. That was unlikely. "Fine." Wayland sighed.

"I'm…" I was still shocked, unable to reply in full.

"What do you say, Meera, would you like the job? Not that it's mine to give but there's literally no one qualified to open communications with Earth like this. This is new territory." Lakshmi grinned that wide, predatory smile. Her cerulean eyes sparkled with meaning I couldn't yet divine.

What was she planning? Did she know I wanted to remove the Committee entirely? Why was she agreeing to me?

But my questions and suspicions aside, I knew my answer. This would be a new chapter for our colony, for the Titanborn. I wanted to be there, this time, to make sure we took these next steps with equal parts empathy and aplomb. I would make sure no one ever felt alone and pained like Torvram had, and that no one ever felt stuck like I had.

"So, would you like the job?" Lakshmi repeated.

"Yes."

INDIEGOGO BACKERS

Thanks to everyone who backed my Indiegogo campaign and helped fund the printing of this novel!

THE BACKERS:

Adam Beguelin
Amanda Eich
Amanda Fields
Andrew Dussault
Bailey Hadnott
Bradford Armstrong
Brandon Vazquez
Brian Calderon
Bryan Boubion
Cecilia Farmer
Celeste Maxon
Chris Schutter
Christina Larochelle
Connor Petty
Constance Betz
Cristobal Alvarez
Cynthia Hadnott
Daniella Golt
Diane Harpold & Bill Rodgers
Edward Hadnott
Eric Koester
Eric Schoonover
Evan Frolov
Howard Schutter
James Heller
Janet Hadnott
Jeffrey Samuelson
Jim Hulihan
Joe Caron
Lannette Rangel
Lo Bise

Leslie Holden
Linda Eich
lunatune
Marcie Frolov
marge4tennis
Marsha C Bise
Matthew Spencer
Melinda Bise
Melinda Chen
Melissa Crouse
Michael Crabbs
Mimi Zhou
Mingda Li
Nancy & Steve Bise
Pauline Luong

Phiet The Truong
Pranali Chhatbar
Rebecca Conover
Ren Higgins
Saki Cake
Scott Parker
Shyam Bharadwaj
Stephanie Mack
Tosh Rayadhurgam
Trevor Scott Grandstaff
Wade Keusder
Wes Keusder
William Boys
William Eich
Xinting Yu

ACKNOWLEDGMENTS

In addition to the lovely backers, a whole bunch of people helped make this book possible by providing me sage advice and multifaceted support as well as by generally being great.

Here are a few of them.

THANKS TO:

Dr. Eric Koester and Brian Bies at New Degree Press for taking a chance on me.

Melody Delgado Lorbeer, Kristy Carter, and Michelle Felich for editing this story at literally any time of day (or night, my bad).

Lanssie Ma, Jessica Bishop, Olivia Lai Shelter, Shacy, Lamb, Pidge, Mal, and Tio Brown for making wonderful art of the characters and world!

Dr. Mingda Li for committing absurd amounts of time and resources to help fund the printing of this book through Facebook Ads and social media outreach.

Dr. Bethan Davies for sharing her amazing experiences with arctic and anta4rctic expeditions.

Dr. Xinting Yu for contributing her scientific expertise on Titan and providing time and insight when we repeatedly bumped up against the edge of human knowledge.

Evan Frolov and Dr. Scott Parker for the countless hours we've spent exploring writing, often around a genuine fireplace.

My family for supporting me throughout the many, many years I tinkered with and talked about writing.

Finally, special thanks to the beta readers who really made this story shine.

MY BETA READERS:

Kayla Gray who took time away from her own novel to help with mine.

Pauline Luong who, in addition to beta reading, also contributed a ton of social media help.

Bryne Hadnott for doing practically all of the above and more. I couldn't ask for a better partner.

"NOTES FROM THE AUTHOR"

I began writing Titanborn at a particularly difficult stage in my life. I'd landed my dream job, was on the way to a career in science, and found it to be just the worst. I was racked with anxiety, struggled with my co-workers, was convinced that it was entirely my fault that I felt miserable. Here was step one in my career and I'd believed I'd permanently screwed it up. To cope, I started writing at night.

Meera shared a lot of the same fears, made a lot of the same mistakes, and blamed herself for the loss—maybe even the death—of a close friend. In other ways, her story was wholly different from mine. Meera was designed genetically and mechanically before her birth to fulfill a role on Titan. She was created to be something in a very literal sense. Despite this, she too realized what I learned while I wrote this story: it's never too late to change and your life is not set in stone.

Your future, my future, and her future are all determined by choices made every day, not just those made in our pasts. In her journey to save her friend's life, Meera will discover that many of those choices are her own to make.

For more book news and videos of me falling over:
IG: @bernanigan
TW: @BrianSchutter

www.ingramcontent.com/pod-product-compliance
Lightning Source LLC
LaVergne TN
LVHW011800060526
838200LV00053B/3637